PLAINVILLE, U.S.A.

PLAINVILLE, U.S.A.

James West [psend.]

[Withers, Carl]

New York: Columbia University Press

Published in Great Britain, Canada, India, and Pakistan
by the Oxford University Press
London, Toronto, Bombay, and Karachi

MANUFACTURED IN THE UNITED STATES OF AMERICA

To Ralph Linton

Introduction

IN this book I have attempted to describe from the viewpoint of an anthropologist, but with a minimum of anthropological language, certain phases in the life of a small contemporary American rural community. The materials on which it is based were collected between June, 1939, and August, 1940, and during July and August, 1941, as part of a larger research project on acculturation, financed by the Social Science Research Council of Columbia University, and directed by Professor Ralph Linton, Chairman of the Department of Anthropology of the same institution. The present study was undertaken to attempt to learn specifically and in detail how one relatively isolated and still "backward" American farming community reacts to the constant stream of traits and influences pouring into it from cities and from more "modern" farming communities.

I spent May and June, 1939, in search of a community which would meet certain requirements judged optimal for the investigation. For reasons unnecessary to relate, the selection was limited to the general region of the southern Midwest. Within this area the search was for a town with not over 1,000 inhabitants, which was still a lively trading and social center for farmers living within its trade area. To simplify my research task I sought a community which had the fewest possible economic and social factors which might complicate the problem under scrutiny. This means, economically, that no town was considered if its inhabitants drew any important portion of their income from mines, factories, summer resorts, or any other industrial or urbanizing activity that would confuse the economics of a traditional farming community. It means, socially, that the presence of any foreign-language-speaking group in or near a town, or of Negroes, or of any large non-Protestant or "atypical" religious congregation eliminated the town from consideration. A further requirement was that the community selected should be as "level" as possible socially and economically. It should have no recognized "aristocracy" or other well-defined social "classes," and I hoped to find a community where people were all living as nearly as possible on the same social and financial plane.

I visited for a few hours or a few days each about thirty towns, which, from regional hearsay, population figures, and their position on a road map, seemed likely to suit the requirements. Some were "river towns," some were "prairie towns," some were "hill towns." One or another of the factors mentioned above quickly removed many of these towns from consideration. Most frequently, however, the eliminating factor was a *highway:* during the last twenty years highways have siphoned off so much trade and social activity from small towns to larger towns that the majority of small-town people who were interviewed felt their own towns to be already dead or fast dying as business and social centers for the communities which they serve.

Plainville was discovered by accident. On a flinty detour through Woodland County my car broke down. Repairs at the Ford garage in Plainville took two days, and these days convinced me that Plainville was the town I had been looking for. The town contained only about sixty-five homes and a dozen stores and was therefore smaller than I had intended to select, but people bragged of its remarkable survival as a small town. They said, "This is *one* town that the highways haven't killed." They said, "People still fill this town up every Saturday." To questions intended to discover the absence or presence of rigid social stratifications people responded, "We're all just one plain old class of common average working people here. You don't find no very rich people here, and no very poor people, like you find lots of places." My first visit to Plainville fell in the middle of a week, but a continuous mild bustle of public activity was going on, of farmers marketing eggs and cream, women buying groceries, children playing and shouting in the street or eating ice-cream cones, youths enjoying cokes

and talk at the lunch counters, men—especially old men—
loafing on the sidewalk, in stores, or under the two large shade
trees in the "Square." People talked sociably to me about
crops, business, and the community, as I waited for my car.
The hotelkeeper, kept indoors by age, illness, and the extreme
hot weather, entertained me for hours with delightful stories
of happenings in the community during the seventy years
covered by his memory. People did not yet know that I was
a social scientist.

Two objections briefly delayed my decision to remain in
Plainville. A transcontinental highway was under construction through the county which touched the edge of Plainville.
It would not be finished in time to alter the social and marketing patterns of the community during my contemplated stay,
but a few highway workers lodged in town promised some
disruption of ordinary town life. The worst obstacle was the
problem of finding suitable living quarters. The hotel offered
poor opportunities for interviews, and for sanitary reasons it
seemed uninhabitable for longer than a few days. No other
living quarters were vacant except a few single rooms, none
of which seemed suitable to live and work in. Finally the
county agent, who lived in Plainville although his office was
at the county seat six miles away, offered me temporary quarters in his house. I lived there until November, 1939, when
I moved into a furnished apartment in a business building
on the town square formerly occupied by the undertaker.
This provided ideal convenience and excellent privacy for
interviews for nearly six months. In April, 1940, I rented part
of a house, where I lived during the rest of my stay.

It took about two months to establish satisfactory research
contact with community members. The first reaction of the
community to "being studied" was one of suspicion, great
constraint, and even resentment, which no amount of verbal
explanation of what I was doing and why I was doing it was
able to allay. I was suspected of being a detective or "federal
man" in disguise. My residence with the county agent, who
was popular with county leaders, helped "vouch" for me,

though ambivalently; the fact that he was a "government man" suggested to some people that I might have been sent into the county to "investigate the WPA" or to collect information about "all the old crimes."

My first paid informant helped to extend gradually the range of those who were not fearful or suspicious of me. He was a native-born young man, thirty-three years old, who had given up rural school teaching for farming. He lived in town with a relative, going out daily to his rented farm at the edge of town. We spent the midsummer afternoons during six weeks in conversation under a shade tree in the county agent's yard. Passers-by gradually got accustomed to the fact that I sometimes worked with a notebook. My best early stroke toward lessening hostility to my work was to print, some weeks after my arrival, a column-long news item (at space rates) in the county weekly, describing in detail my research intentions and thanking the people for their wholehearted cooperation to date. Numerous tensions slackened immediately, and a few people began to seek me out to show me "old" objects and documents and to ask just what I was "trying to find out."

Final widespread acceptance of my role as investigator-resident of Plainville came slowly, however, and only after I had gained the cooperation of one particular man. He was a "politician," forty-three years old, divorced from his wife and "batching it," a disabled veteran and small "pensioner" of the first World War, a voracious reader but able to write only slowly, personally very ambitious but passionately interested in community reform. He had great ability in manipulating rumor and opinion, and his local knowledge and social insights were astounding. For example, once after inquiring into the techniques by which I worked, he elaborated a plan for studying a community which corresponded very closely with the well-known "genealogical method." This man became convinced of the value of my work in October, 1939. Thenceforth, without pay ("You ain't *got* enough money to *hire* me!") he vouched for my "safety" as a repository of confidences and arranged numerous interviewing situations for me. Through the same techniques he employed in any "political" manipulation, he set rumor to working *for* me, rather than against me, and I finally came to be considered a full-fledged community member, welcome in men's loafing centers, in church, and in many homes, able to talk confidentially with numerous people in situations of my own devising, and free to record any private conversations I wanted to record, in the presence of informants, without arousing any apparent embarrassment. People often said, "People wouldn't talk to you when you come here, but now they've *adopted* you everybody will talk to you." Of great aid toward this "adoption" were the facts that I drove a two-year old car, "knew how to loaf and joke" on the street, wore "old clothes" and otherwise imitated the average level of everyday life, and already knew how to speak accurately whatever dialect level of the language was being spoken at any moment.

During the first two months, I idled a good many hours daily on the street and in stores, talking with whoever would talk, and listening as sociably as possible to public conversations. I studied maps and statistical records of the region and county. I drove over the county—alone or with the county agent and the Plainville vocational agriculture teacher—to meet people and familiarize myself with the landscape. Later I jotted down observations and what I could remember of all conversations, no matter how trivial. My first paid informant dictated for my notebooks a description, house by house, of the town and of such farm homes as came up in our conversation. For every inhabitant, young and old, he described their occupations, earnings, property, religion, kinship affiliations, interests, tastes, and "personality," as he understood or saw all these matters. All this, together with a large body of digressive material, amounted to a rather full revelation of his life and the life of Plainville, as he saw it.

As field materials accumulated, they began to alter and to expand the original scope of the problem set for investigation. My first efforts were divided between recording data related to "acculturation" and collecting enough background material on local history, religion, education, economics, social organization, and attitudes to render this data intelligible. As the outlines of Plainville life began to be revealed, my interest was drawn to two new problems which above all others seemed important.

The first was somewhat surprising, in view of the fact that Plainville had been selected as a community lacking "social classes," a point on which all early informants agreed. I had not been there long, however, before I realized that I was dealing with a discrimination system of enormous complexity. Friends began to warn and instruct me about whom I should or should not visit and be seen with, if I wanted to gain correct information and maintain the respect of "worth-while" people. Judgments of neighbor on neighbor, and all evaluations of individuals, appeared to be repeating patterns of great uniformity, despite the wariness with which they were phrased. I decided to find out whether or not this system of discrimination took a form which should be described under the label of rigid social classes.

Second, I came to feel that Plainvillers, in some ways slightly and in some ways considerably, differed from all other Americans I had known, and I became interested in the local problem of "socialization"—in how a newborn Plainville boy or girl baby comes gradually (in the honored phrase) to "pull the skin of the local culture" over him or her, and becomes the adult male or female Plainviller. I decided to study the local educational system, especially in its non-school aspects.

My interest in the original field problem was channeled into a direction I had not anticipated. I found Plainville, Woodland County, and the entire surrounding region to be in an agony of social and economic reorientation as a result of the activities of recently established governmental agencies.

The first full-time county agent had been working eighteen months in the county; a part-time agent had served since 1927. The county agent's headquarters were the AAA office at the county seat. Offices of the FSA and Social Security (administering Direct Relief, NYA, OAA, ADC, and WPA) were also operating. Work of the District Health Office was beginning to reach Woodland County. Most of the community's "talk" about itself as a changing community seemed to hinge—approvingly, resentfully, or speculatively—on these new agencies. The governmental efforts to supplant "traditional" farming methods with "rational" and "scientific" agriculture offered a dynamic situation for a typical case study of rural America's most important problem in applied anthropology and "acculturation."

These three problems were considered "fundamental" to the research during nearly a year, though at no time did I lose interest in recording whatever came along. I continued daily to make the rounds of several notable loafing centers, and visited several friends daily in their homes, to collect a continuous record of gossip, news, and current discussion. I went to church bazaars, basket dinners, and funerals; to basketball games, pie suppers, and other school entertainments; to picnics, public sales, Saturday afternoon "drawings," and to many other public events. I made a point of being seen and being considered "sociable and friendly" everywhere. I ate many meals and occasionally "stayed all night" on farms. I conducted for a few days the classes of a high school teacher who was sick. During my last few months in Plainville I participated actively in several "reform" projects which were afoot; I favored the projects themselves and participation admitted me to the secret caucuses where social action was initiated and planned.

Most afternoons and many evenings were spent in arranged or impromptu "notebook interviews" behind closed doors, in either my own home or informants' homes. I sometimes directed and sometimes permitted the informant to direct these interviews, which I recorded as nearly as possible verbatim. Formal interviews were held with more than fifty people, totaling from two hours to several hundred hours each. I met and talked at least briefly with about half the adults who "traded" mainly at Plainville, as well as many other people from the rest of the county.

Rather long "life histories" (30,000 to 75,000 words each) were taken from eight adult persons, ranging in age from 26 to 75. Three of these were women, though interviews with Plainville women were difficult to arrange. Two high school boys and two high school girls were hired (at ten cents per hour—300 words counting as an hour's work) to record their "autobiographies," 15,000 to 50,000 words in length, under the general assignment of "I Remember . . ."

Some local scrapbooks, collections of letters, and other private documents were put at my disposal.

The records in the county Court House and of the local offices of the AAA, FSA, and Social Security were opened partly or wholly to me. The most useful locally printed materials were the county weekly (on file since 1885 in the newspaper office), collections of other brief-lived local newspapers, and, for background and genealogies, a book-length *History of Woodland County,* published in 1907. For even an isolated community like Plainville there exists so vast a body of relevant printed or other documentary material that no one could read it all in a lifetime. For a year I kept lengthy scrapbooks of clippings from the two favorite daily papers which came into Plainville, especially from columns in each which presented folkloristic accounts of life in small towns in the state. Certain data from the Sixteenth National Census of 1940 became available in published form before my analysis of Plainville was completed.

The scope and form of this book were determined by the three problems already described, though I have tried to include enough additional facts to suggest what life is like to people who are born in Plainville and who live out their life-span there.

The method followed in presenting this material is designed to be factual and "inferential." I have chosen to let the facts speak mainly for themselves with a minimum of discussion beyond inferences regarding the scientific directions in which I believe their interpretation should lie.

Native quotations and stereotypes have been employed extensively in the presentation, for several reasons: first, I happen to like all the native varieties of English to be found here; second, language is the only aspect of native behavior which could be transmitted directly to the pages of a book; and third, wherever it is used, it seemed to me more accurate, more economical, more directly revealing, and therefore more useful as an instrument of scientific description than standard English would have been.

All place names and personal names, including my own, have been withheld or altered. This has been done out of no desire of mine for secrecy, but because every serious informant requested, and was promised, the protection of complete anonymity.

To the Social Science Research Council of Columbia University I am indebted for generous financial support during the year 1939–1940, and the summer of 1941, when the materials were collected in the field. I am also indebted to this body for additional funds which made publication possible.

To Professor Ralph Linton I owe a very great debt of gratitude. He suggested the original research project, arranged the circumstances by which it was undertaken, and sympathetically directed the field work. He also counseled and aided me in many ways connected with organizing and interpreting my field materials.

To Professor Ruth Benedict I am indebted for funds which enabled me during 1941 to write the first draft of this book, and for much valuable aid toward understanding the material collected.

To Dr. Gene Weltfish and to Professors Kimball Young, Robert K. Merton, and Conrad M. Arensberg I owe grateful thanks for reading my manuscript before its final revision and for suggesting numerous ways in which to correct, improve, and enrich it. My debt on this score to Professor Arensberg is particularly great. I am additionally indebted to Professors Young, Merton, and Arensberg for recommending the publication of this book under its present auspices. To Miss Elizabeth J. Sherwood of Columbia University Press I wish to express my thanks and appreciation for her valuable editorial assistance in preparing the manuscript for press. I wish also to thank Miss Eugenia Wallace for the excellent index.

Even greater than these obligations is my debt to the men, women, and children of Plainville, whom I cannot mention by name, but whose hospitality and personal warmth made Plainville my "home" for over a year, and to whose trustful cooperation is due whatever factual merit this book may possess.

Contents

1 Plainville

PLAINVILLE is a small town in the central part of the United States of America. The town is here called Plainville because it rests near the edge of a little prairie, once deep with bluestem but now given over to croplands and pastures, in a locality prevailingly hilly and timbered, rather than flat.

The Plainville Prairie is about eighteen miles long and four or five miles wide, and like other smaller prairies in the region it is hemmed in irregularly on both sides by timbered or brush-covered strings of hills that run generally north and south. These hills are too small to be called "mountains." The "real hills," or mountains, are southward, nearly a hundred miles. North and south traffic in the region follows the prairies, but the traveler who comes to Plainville over the new "hard road," a transcontinental highway which touches, or just misses, the town, drives over a road resembling a roller coaster. He climbs low ridge after ridge, and crosses a series of narrow prairies, roughly parallel with each other. The lonely prairie farms all lie plainly in sight. The farm houses are spaced a quarter mile or half mile apart, each with its shade trees, outbuildings, and rectangular fields and pastures where crops grow and livestock graze. Straight dirt roads mark off most of the section lines. Few houses are seen in the hills, though they are numerous. Trees and scrub growth hide all but those nearest the road, and enough of these were built after the hard road came through to deceive the mind into thinking that a development of hill homesteads is just beginning. Any road or trail leading off the main highway will wind rockily past the small grain and hay fields, the timbered pastures, and the clearings in which are set the poorer houses and barns of the hills, and to the bottom farms beside the streams.

Both geographically and culturally, Plainville is in the region which has been labeled the North-South Border,[1] a long belt extending from eastern Kentucky past the Ozark country, and lying everywhere just north of the mountains.

This means that Plainville stands between one of the well-known areas of American "hillbilly" culture and the richer farming plains of the Midwest. Plainville is marginal to both areas. The culture of the Plainville region is a composite, in origins and history, in the everyday attitudes of the people, and in technology, of two ways of life—the way of the "hill people" or mountain people further south, and the way of the Midwestern prairie farmer.

As a town Plainville depends wholly upon the produce and trade from about 200 farms, some of them "prairie farms" and some of them "hill farms." These cluster about the town in all directions. Plainville farmers, like all other American farmers—but unlike most European farmers, who live in a central village and go out to till the surrounding land—dwell on their farmlands in the country. Those who live in Plainville are the merchants; the retired or partially retired old: elderly couples and widows and widowers; a number of odd-jobbers and others who work for wages; and a handful of professional people, including an old but active doctor. For farmers, Plainville is their main local trading center and a social center too.

Plainville is near the geographical center of Woodland County, which covers an area of slightly over 400 square miles. Its population density is between sixteen and seventeen persons per square mile. The 6,500 people of Woodland County all live in or about one or another of the several trading centers of the county.

The present [2] population of Plainville is 275. That of the county seat, Discovery, five miles east, is 250. Discovery is one of the oldest towns in the county; its site was surveyed and

[1] See A. R. Mangus, *Rural Regions of the United States*, Washington, Works Projects Administration, Division of Research, 1940.

[2] The "present time" of this book unless otherwise indicated is 1939-40, when field work was done.

platted almost a hundred years ago and it lies on the Apple River, which loops through the central hill section of the county to join a still larger river about 100 miles north.

Stanton, eleven miles west, has 450 inhabitants. There are several other lesser towns with populations ranging downward from 200 to almost nothing. Some of them have only a country store, with perhaps a church, and a handful of small dwellings. For all these small towns a long local history is remembered, and each, in its landscape, is felt by Woodland County people to have a unique color and "personality." Each is a marketing and gathering center, especially on Saturday afternoon, and a focus of community loyalty for the people there and for farmers in its trade area.

People from an area about twenty miles long (north and south) and eight miles wide view Plainville as their main trading center, though most of them also rather frequently visit Stanton and Discovery. Stanton is the only town in the county with a dentist; it also has a lumber yard, the largest general store in the county, and a hardware store which stocks larger farm implements. The county seat, Discovery, is an important center for all Woodland County people. Eleven banks were once scattered among the towns; the only bank left is at Discovery. All legal and "courthouse" business must be transacted there. All of the recently established federal agencies have their offices there.

But Plainvillers also "go outside" nowadays. They go to "X," a county seat of 1,000 inhabitants, situated thirty miles north of Plainville, on the gravel road which runs through Woodland County. They go still more often to "Y," another county seat about the same distance south, likewise "on the gravel." The population of "Y" is 2,600. At both "X" and "Y" there are modern movies, chain stores, and larger stocks of merchandise of all kinds than in any of the home towns. For really important purchases, entertainment, or medical care, Plainvillers often travel to Largetown, a regional metropolis of 60,000 people, in the hills seventy miles south; or even to Metropolis itself, an important Midwestern city with a population of nearly half a million. Metropolis is northward, 135 miles. Regional traffic beyond the county runs mainly north or south, along the older roads which served before the "hard road" came through. The hard road or highway is therefore more useful to "outsiders" who pass swiftly through Woodland County than to the natives themselves. For a few of them it serves locally as a farm-to-market road, and it leads outward to join the highway to Metropolis. Most travel westward, especially to California, now also starts over this road, which symbolizes dramatically the decline in isolation which began with the widespread use of the automobile. Once Plainvillers knew little of the outside world, but most of them now have cars, and many "have been out and seen things."

EARLY SETTLEMENT

The white settlement of Woodland County was part of the main westward migration of a century ago. The sparse Indian population of the region was moved further west by governmental decree about 1825. The first wave of white settlers began to occupy the newly opened lands during the 1830's. The very first white men known to have entered the county were a Frenchman, a German, and an Englishman, trappers and fur traders with the Indians. The settlers themselves came mostly from the hills of Kentucky and Tennessee, with a sprinkling from the Pennsylvania mountains and a few others from Virginia, West Virginia, New York, and elsewhere. These were the pioneers, and most of their fathers had been pioneers in the lands which these men left for Woodland County.[3] Others of like origin followed them and by 1870 most of the bottom land and timbered land providing natural springs had been either "preempted," at a dollar or so an acre, or, after 1862, "homesteaded." Later, when it was discovered how to plow up the prairie bluestem, another wave of immigration occurred, and the prairie third of the county

---

[3] A very few Southern immigrants brought their slaves. However, no Negroes live now in Woodland County.

became homesteads. The town of Plainville was founded at about this time. Many Germans settled on the Plainville prairie, but before many years most of them moved on to better lands.

The last names borne by most present day Plainvillers are English or Scotch-Irish in origin, except for two interesting and prolific "clans," the Stauffers and the Ballous, part of whom live in the Plainville trade area. The ancestors of both families came early to Woodland County. The Stauffers were Pennsylvania Dutch, and are now Baptists and Republicans. The Ballous are an originally French Huguenot family; in Pennsylvania they became typical mountaineer frontiersmen and were converted to the Dunkard or Brethren faith, which most of them still follow. Many households of Stauffers and Ballous now live in the hill region north of Plainville. The Ballous are especially numerous in a nearly continuous area which reaches far northward toward the county seat "X" of the adjoining county. They are often referred to as the "Ballou nation." Both Stauffers and Ballous are noted for their "hillbilly ways."

About a dozen Swedish families settled in the county on the smaller but rather fertile prairie lying between the towns "A" and "B." They are considered exceptionally good "farmers and citizens," and the name "Swede" is still applied to all who bear Swedish names. The Swedes have intermarried widely with the Woodlanders, however, and nothing but the names, and the "broken English" of a few of the oldest men, distinguishes them from their neighbors. None of their "younger generation" learns Swedish or has any sentimental attachment to Sweden.

During the period of fresh land and large families, typical of the frontier, the population of Woodland County grew swiftly, reaching a peak of 10,000 in 1900. It has since declined gradually by 35 percent through migrations westward and to the cities, but especially to one region in the Sacramento Valley in California, where several hundred Woodland County people now live. The only important increase in population since 1900 came during the 1930's, when the great depression brought many migrants home, where they could at least be sure of a place to sleep and eat. Most of the houses left vacant by the decrease in population, perhaps 5 to 10 percent of all the houses in the county, were shacks and log cabins in the hills and woods. They are now used as corn cribs or livestock shelters or are tumbling into ruin and are seldom seen by the traveler who keeps to the main automobile roads.

Not all who came to the county in the early days stayed, nor has immigration wholly ceased. To many of the pioneers, here as elsewhere, the frontier was pleasant only so long as it was a frontier. As soon as large wild game became scarce, and farms, schools, churches, and towns were developed, they moved on to other frontiers. New settlers still come in, a dozen or two a year in the whole county. They include farmers from further south seeking better land, farmers from the north seeking cheaper land, men from Metropolis who want to retire from city life to "an easier, more independent life," and merchants hoping to make a small-town living from a small investment. Those who stay become in remarkably short time "just like everybody else here," in speech, dress, mannerisms, attitudes, and general way of life. Most of those who are unable to adjust to the community's mores soon sell out and move away.

NATURAL RESOURCES

The only excellent farmlands are the river bottoms, which range in size from 500 to 600 acres in wide bends of the river down to small bottom patches of only a few acres each. A man who "owns a big bottom field" is considered "well-off." Even years of careless farming practices have not depleted these alluvial deposits, which are also replenished by irregular overflows and by erosion from the uplands.

The next best land is the prairie, which farmers say used to produce "fifty bushels of corn an acre." Its present productivity averages: corn, 19 bushels per acre; wheat, 17 bushels;

oats, 12 bushels. The frost-free growing season falls normally between April 20 and October 20, and this is the season of maximal rainfall. It is also the season of maximal heat and evaporation, and therefore of "drouth." Occasional "bad drouths" sometimes cut production enormously, especially of corn and "summer gardens." Most farmers believe that their land no longer produces "big crops" because "it don't rain here like it used to."

Rainfall has averaged 40.3 inches a year at Plainville during the ten years since records have been kept. The average for the last thirty-eight years in the adjoining county north is 43.9 inches; in the next county west, 38 inches; in the next county south, 43.2 inches. These precipitations are heavier than those in the rich cornlands of Iowa and Illinois, but the thinner soil here dries out more easily and it contains fewer plant nutrients.

The climate is otherwise "temperate continental." Extreme temperatures during the last eight years in an adjoining county (no records having been kept in Woodland County) are +115° F. and –29° F., with July and January averages of 79.4° F. and 32° F., respectively, during the same period. Most summers bring thirty or more consecutive days when the thermometer rises above 100°; during one month of the winter of 1939–1940 the temperature, rather exceptionally, dropped nightly below –10°.

Agricultural scientists say that there has been a 52 percent erosion of the prairie topsoil, originally only about eight inches deep. Most of its lime has also been leached away.

The poorest land, over half of the land of the county, is thin, rocky hill land. Much of this hill land is waste brushwood and scrub timber. Much of it is farmed or serves as poor pasture. The smallest farms, as well as the poorest farmers, the "hillbillies," the "families that raise the most children" and have the poorest "improvements," are generally to be found on these shallow hillsides.

The timber of the region is poor, consisting chiefly of scrub oak, black oak, poor hickory, and occasional cedar. Buck bushes, persimmon trees, and scrub oaks quickly cover any land which has been exhausted by a few years of grain farming. "Sprouting persimmons" is the work remembered with the greatest distaste by many men who spent their boyhood on a hill farm. The fine hardwood black walnuts which once grew in the bottoms were cleared away early, and either burned for riddance or split into rails for fences or hewn into logs for the first buildings. A few of the early log buildings are still extant. Most of the houses lived in today were built later, however, and mainly of native lumber. Several old men still alive made their living during many years by running sawmills, and few trees large enough for lumber are now left. In the early days there was an abundance of game—deer, wild turkey, prairie chickens, and many furbearing animals. There are still fish in the creeks and the river; skunks, muskrats, raccoons, and possums to trap or hunt for furs; quail, squirrels, and rabbits in profusion; and great quantities of wild fruits, such as blackberries, gooseberries, plums, grapes, persimmons, and pawpaws. There are also chiggers, ticks, scorpions, and mosquitoes.

TECHNOLOGY

For any discussion of present-day agricultural technology of Plainville reference must be made to the technology of the early settlers. The tools, animals, and techniques which the early settlers brought to Woodland County were those that people took to new frontiers anywhere in America a hundred years ago. They brought horses, cows, sheep, hogs, and chickens; wagons, plows, guns, hoes, axes, and the art of home-smithing. They brought simple furniture and textiles, and techniques for grinding cereals, tanning hides, and weaving; garden seeds and pits of tame fruits; and grain for seeding corn, wheat, oats, and other cereals. All of these (except corn and perhaps tanning methods) were European in origin; but the pioneer's way of life had been "Indianized" on the earlier frontiers: with his ax he girdled and burned trees for a corn patch—then he lived off the wild game and fruits until his first cereal crop came in. He often wore clothing made of furs and deerskin. The first settlers only gradually became farmers, and even today some Plainvillers live more from the natural products of river, timber, and "patch farming" than from conventional field farming and livestock raising.

Most pioneer farmers were worse farmers by far than their contemporary European "cousins," who had not for a thousand years known a real land surplus. In occupying step by step the "limitless" American land frontier, men lost much of their traditional heed for, and skill in, soil protection through crop rotation, erosion control, and utilization of manure. This new carelessness itself became "traditional" and is both the chief cause of the widespread appalling exhaustion of American farm lands and the greatest obstacle to governmental efforts to introduce scientific farming methods.

It is impossible to list all the hoes, rakes, plows, harrows, cultivators, tractors, mowers, threshers, cream separators, and other tools now in use on Plainville farms. About fifty pages of such articles can be seen—priced and pictured—in any Sears Roebuck catalogue. Almost every common American farm tool or implement that is powered by hand, horse, steam, or gas can be found somewhere among Plainville farms, and a similar development, though less extensive, has taken place in household technology. The introduction of certain implements, machines, and other conveniences is well remembered and is often mentioned in Plainville conversation.

About 1870, kerosene lamps began to replace candles and grease ladles for home lighting, and metal stoves began to supplant fireplaces for cooking and warmth. These contrivances made great changes in indoor life. Cookstoves altered the patterns of women's work more than any other single invention except sewing machines, which came into widespread use about 1900. The Mason fruit jar, kerosene cooking stoves, cream separators, and linoleums were other important innovations in the woman's domain.

The first great innovations in outdoor work and technology

were the steel-beamed plow and the single-row cultivator. In the early 1870's these implements made prairie farming possible, and, with the later binder, increased greatly the acreage which one man and his team could farm. Later, the tractor somewhat impractically widened the scope of a single operator still further. The social and economic implications, for Plainville, of all these technological advances will be discussed in another place.

The automobile, introduced about 1912 and in wide use by 1920, while it is used for marketing farm products, is thought of as more a social convenience than a useful farm "implement," as are telephones (introduced about 1900), and radios (introduced about 1920).

Several facts are important about all of these innovations. First, nearly all tools and machines now in use are manufactured; few are homemade. Even blacksmiths, who a generation or two ago took over as specialists the formerly widespread arts of horseshoeing and the farm forge, now spend more time at welding broken car parts and tractor parts than at their earlier trade. There are no local wagon builders or coffin makers any more. No one makes ax handles or wagon tongues, few do their own shoe cobbling, few repair any broken tool or implement beyond "just fixin' her up with bailin' wire and lettin' 'er go." Spinning and weaving have also disappeared among women, but women are replacing the vanishing techniques with new ones, for example, pressure canning, in which they take pride equal to that taken in earlier handicrafts.

Second, some of the modern machines are nonfunctional. Tractors, for example, can be profitably used on only a few of the prairie farms, yet in 1940 as many as 145 tractors were owned on the 1,300-plus farms of the county. Some of these are found on hill farms "with no more farm land than a man and a mule could farm."

Third, almost all types of modern agricultural technology coexist with practices dating from the first settlement and before. One farmer still "cradles" his grain patches, and until recently "frailed" (flailed) out the wheat. Others harvest with combines. The "average farmer" harvests wheat with a binder, shocks and stacks the bundles, and then awaits the rounds of the gasoline-powered thresher.

It is the same with the magical aspects of the early technology. Side by side with efforts to understand and follow the advice of agricultural experts (as received from the county agent, the vocational agriculture teacher, agricultural bulletins, farm periodicals, and so forth) many magical practices still exist for planting crops, castrating livestock, weaning, gardening, girdling trees. Most of these relate to the "light" or "dark" of the moon or to signs of the zodiac. The average farmer thinks, "There's something in them signs, all right," and a diminishing few heed them carefully in practice. Sanctions are in general much stronger for "doing things the old way" rather than the "new way," and there is widespread criticism of the government's effort to instruct people how a better living can be made out of their mediocre land. The acreage payments, however, as well as the organizational skill of local "government men," are accomplishing very great cultural and economic changes in Woodland County.

COMMUNICATIONS

The earliest communications were by water and overland trail. The Apple River was too shallow for navigation but freight and passengers were able to come by water as far as "X" (thirty miles north), from which a federal military road extended southwest through Woodland County until the Civil War. The town "E" (see map) was an important stage route station on this road. In the late 1890's a railroad from Metropolis to Largetown came through Stanton, and a profitable stage line soon connected Stanton with Plainville, Discovery, and "A," carrying passengers, freight, and mail. Farmers had previously had to drive their livestock sixty-five or seventy-five miles to railroad towns for marketing or shipping. After the railroad came Stantonites felt that a great period of growth and prosperity lay ahead. They considered the other towns, "off the railroad," as comically backward. Stanton at that time boasted "a commodious and convenient

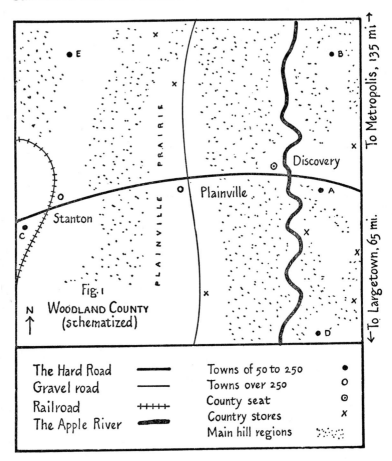

Fig. 1
WOODLAND COUNTY
(schematized)
N ↑

To Metropolis, 135 mi. ↑

←To Largetown, 65 mi.

The Hard Road	———	Towns of 50 to 250	•
Gravel road	———	Towns over 250	o
Railroad	++++	County seat	⊙
The Apple River	⬛⬛⬛	Country stores	x
		Main hill regions	

College," whose students sometimes laughed at Plainville visitors for "coming to town to see the train come in." The college is now only a memory, and the railroad has become obsolete for both passenger travel and freight. Yet other towns, Plainville especially, still call Stanton a "stuck-up town," and Stantonites feel rather ashamed of belonging to "so backwoods a county."

Highways are today the most important means of communication within the county and beyond it. Most towns once had a hotel and livery stable to accommodate "drummers," but a salesman can now visit every local town in a day in his car. Most people travel, even to California, by car or bus. Trucks carry most of Plainville's produce and livestock to large market centers and deliver to Plainville most of the merchandise sold there.

A network of local roads—often impassable in muddy weather—also connects the individual farm in Woodland County with neighboring farms, with its own trading center, and with all the other towns in the county. Nearly every man knows almost every other man in the whole county, though the acquaintanceship of women and children is less wide. There are also footpath shortcuts through pasture, field, and woods, between the farms of "neighbors" and from farm to rural school. Adult visits between farms beyond short walking distance apart are now made in car; travel by buggy or wagon and by horseback has nearly vanished. Twenty years ago scores of teams and saddle horses were tied to the hitch racks in Plainville on Saturday afternoon. Today on "trading days" not more than five or six farm wagons and perhaps one or two shabby buggies stand among the line of cars. The Square was formerly surrounded by hitch racks for the convenience of farmers. For heavy short-distance hauling, however, the gasoline truck has not replaced the "big wagon." Woodland County farmers own 1,000 cars but only about 100 farm trucks. Eggs, cream, and poultry are taken to local markets in cars, and provisions, up to a few sacks of feed, are brought home in the same way, but wood, grain, and small livestock are usually hauled short local distances by team and wagon.

Electricity is rather uncertainly supplied to Plainville by a a high line which serves a number of small towns. During electrical storms or after bad snowstorms and sleets the service is sometimes suspended for several hours. Two thirds of the houses in town "have lights." The rest, like nearly all the farm houses, are lighted by kerosene lamps. For forty years there have been telephones, rural mail delivery, and a way to "phone out" telegrams. About one third of the farmers are on party phone lines. The Plainville mail route, which extends beyond the trade area, serves about 200 mail boxes, accommodating 286 families; the mail carrier "picks up 75 to 100 envelope pieces" a day, including mail orders, insurance premiums paid by check, and business and personal letters.

Newsprint is another important form of communication. The county weekly, the *Discovery Beacon,* circulates one thousand copies, two thirds of them within the county, the rest forming an important link between natives and those who have "gone outside." News items, relating legal proceedings, visits and trips, sickness and death, church news, and other social doings are arranged by towns and neighborhoods. Obituary write-ups are long, and a remarkable quantity of verse, some of it original, is printed to commemorate the death anniversaries of kin, especially of mothers and small children. Subscribers generally read first the items from their own community, not only to add to their knowledge of neighborhood events, but to examine the extent of reporting of what they have already heard on the party line, over fences, in town, and from school children. An increasing volume of the *Beacon's* front page is now devoted to news propaganda releases by the various local offices of government agencies.

A number of newspapers also come in from outside. Ten or twelve copies of the *Metropolis Sun* come daily to Plainville; three subscribers take a famous liberal daily. The favorite daily paper, however, is the *Largetown Bee.* A Plainville girl has the agency for this paper, which arrives by bread truck each morning at about eight o'clock; she delivers about fifty copies among the seventy-five homes and the stores. The *Bee* is a very conservative and region-conscious organ and is an important medium of resistance to the "New Deal," including the AAA's efforts toward better diet, soil conservation practices, and other reforms. Only fifteen to twenty dailies go out on the mail route to farmers, most of whom subscribe to one or both of two weekly farm newspapers. Most of the farmers also take a number of monthly magazines costing from twenty-five to fifty cents a year. They take the *State Farmer* and other farm magazines, homemaker magazines, and story magazines. Periodicals are sold to farmers by agents,[4] who comb the countryside in cars with "premium offers" which may include magazine combinations, maps, fountain pens, or farm burglary protection service. When farmwives, whom they ordinarily canvass, lack ready cash, payment is taken in eggs, chickens, and other farm produce. Many farmers receive the *Country Gentleman* and *Pictorial Review,* because a man reared in the county sells them. He returns to canvass his home county every two or three years.

The Plainville liquor dealer recently installed a magazine stand from which his profit is about a dollar a day. Most of his magazine customers are town people. He sells ten to twenty copies a week each of *Life, Colliers, Liberty,* and the *Saturday Evening Post,* and a number of detective story, Western and movie, "dream romance," and confessional magazines. The purchasers of the magazines listed by name are mostly adult men of the better class. Men and youths purchase the detective and Western "books" (as magazines are generally called). Younger married women and older girls buy the others. A few boys of the high school age purchase comic "books" also, and the druggist has a number of "loafers and lookers" among youths and smaller boys, who scan all the comic and picture magazines from cover to cover, without buying. The dealer often saves unsold magazines for his friends after he has returned the outside covers to the wholesaler for credit. Magazines, especially story magazines and comics, are often passed around from reader to reader until they are "read out and worn out."

The first radio, a crystal set, was brought to Plainville about 1920 by a migrant from Metropolis, but radios are now con-

---

4 These agents selling farm magazines often give false "expert" advice about farming, treating sick poultry, etc. The county agent, complaining of one, said, "Why will the farmers believe what *he* says and not believe me?" A townsman replied, "You ain't sellin' 'em no paper, but then you ain't takin' no money away from 'em either. Somethin' for nothin'. People here don't *believe* that!"

sidered almost a necessity. Over half the townspeople and nearly half the farmers own them. The mail carrier's family owns five radios—one in each of his two cars, one in the boy's room, one in the girls' room, and a large "family" radio. Most of the town sets are operated electrically, but nearly all the country sets are battery-run. A few crystal sets are still in service. The programs favored by adults are livestock and produce markets, hillbilly music, religious hours, presidential speeches, "big election" news, and war news. Radio weather forecasts are closely followed; they have almost entirely replaced interest in the predictions of local "prognosticators." It is frequent to hear men ask, "Have you heard the radio? What's the news? What's the market like? What's the weather gonna be?" For famous prize fights men gather in the stores to listen, and they often form betting pools to add to their interest. Big league baseball games interest a good many men and youths, and one preacher is said to have stopped a sermon early on Sunday to hurry home to his radio to hear a decisive game. Jazz music and swing interest only a few of the young. Adults often say, "I can't stand that *jerkin'*." Commercial announcements bore the majority of listeners, who often lower the radio volume to avoid hearing them. Many people said, "It's a game with me never to hear the name of what them fellers is tryin' to sell!" Few small children are "radio-minded" in the way that many or most small city children are. This is perhaps partly due to the adult feeling that children should not waste radio tubes and batteries, which cost money, and that many programs are "worldly" and not very good for children. Indeed, as a "machine," the radio is much more of a device for men to "fool with" than for women; farm women seldom turn the radio on for entertainment while they work. Radios are considered to be "great comforts" and valuable "company" for men and women who are "too old to work or visit much."

Thus most Plainvillers are potentially linked, by roadways, cars, a rural mail route, the press, mail-order catalogues, telephones and telegraph, and the radio, not only with every neighborhood and town in their own region, but with all corners of the known world. Their reception, understanding, and interpretation of traits and news from "outside," however, are limited and colored by the local environment. As a single striking example: several farmers and merchants were squatting on their heels or sitting on bins and sacks in the Produce House on a June day in 1940, listening to an American news reporter broadcast a description of the events he was witnessing from outside a railway carriage in the forest of Compiègne. The solemnity of this hour was visible in all the faces of the listeners. A man commented with wonder on the fact that the radio could bring events to people "even here," and "right when they're happening." Others observed that the war could not end before America's strength was added to that of England. A middle-aged man agreed to this and then said, "One thing I cain't understand—you read of England and France and Germany all a-fightin'. What I want to know is when *Europe's* gonna get into this war. It's over close to them other countries, ain't it?"

With respect to several of the traits mentioned above and certain others, it is interesting to know how average Plainvillers reacted to them when they were first introduced. The first cars were resented as ostentatious, as impractical, as extravagant, as immoral "for people to own and run," as dangerous to people who drove them and to people and beasts obliged to meet them on the roads, as "just a passing fad," and as a threat to the value of horses and the market for grain sold as horse feed. The first telephones were considered impossible, but they were not opposed on moral grounds. Telephone lines and the phones themselves were long feared rather intensely as lightning conductors, endangering the lives of persons during thunderstorms. Some still fear them. Surprisingly enough, few people seem ever to have condemned radios as sinful or dangerous in any way to the community. Preachers did not attack radios or radio listening, though from their pulpits they condemn "dance music" as severely as cardplaying or beer drinking. Only rarely are people heard to protest that the young hear jazz music and beer advertising over the air. It was not believed possible when the rural mail route was established that the government could "pay out money to carry the mail to farmers everywhere," but the service was gladly accepted.

For a generation, many hard feelings and a long dispute between town and country centered on the mail-order catalogue. The farmers were glad to receive the catalogues and to order from them. The old-style merchants forecast the "doom and ruination of this country" if the farmers persisted in "sending their money away to the cities." It used to be a mark of defiance against the "home merchant" for a farmer to say, "I'll order it!" The big catalogues now lie on the counter in most stores, for all to consult. Both merchants and farmers "order" many items which local stores no longer carry in stock.

OCCUPATIONS

Plainvillers are in a sense aware of the whole range of American occupations. They contribute steadily in each generation about half their children to the outside world. These surplus children migrate west, north, south, and less frequently east, but there are few states without inhabitants born in Plainville. Most Plainville people "take at least one long trip," perhaps to visit children who have moved away. Young men take work trips outside, often with no clear idea of whether they are "moving away" or only "seeing the world." The majority of Plainville males make at least one trip to California. Ex-Plainvillers write letters home, they come home on visits, and they sometimes return home to live, either through preference or because of failure to make their way elsewhere. The press, the radio, catalogues, and hearsay inform Plainvillers further about the rest of the world. Through all these means they have heard at least the names of most American occupations. They subscribe in the main to the American credo of vertical mobility and believe that a man (though hardly a woman) can become anything he wants to, "if he'll just work at it." Actually opportunities are very limited for them, even if they go away.

Opportunities at home are quite limited indeed. A WPA survey taken in 1935 showed that 1,949 men and 177 women (aside from housewives) were earning a living in Woodland County. Of the men listed, 1,234 were farmers—owners or tenants; there were also 39 women farmers. Two men and one woman were farm managers. Farm laborers numbered 339 men and 5 women: 174 of these earned wages; 165 were unpaid (they were "grown" sons or others who worked for their board). One person worked at mining (coal or lead. There are some veins of poor coal and pockets of lead in the county; many people have dreamt of getting rich from rediscovering a legendary silver mine). Seven were blacksmiths, one was in the leather trade (a harness maker or mender), two worked in a saw-planing mill. Nine were in printing and newspaper work (the *Discovery Beacon*). Workers at independent hand trades, including "seamstresses and tailors," numbered 13 men and 3 women (the shoe cobblers must belong here; there is no tailor). One was engaged in "clay, glass, and stone work"; 3 worked in bakeries; 2 in auto repair shops (this seems inaccurate, since in Plainville alone there were 4 auto repairmen, in as many shops, in 1939.) Twelve men were in greasing services (filling stations). Ten men and 5 women were in the postal service. One man was employed with the railway, and 2 men and 3 women with the telephone and telegraph services. Twenty-one men were engaged in other communications and transportation work (mostly truck and school bus drivers). Banking and brokerage occupied 9 men and 3 women. Six men handled real estate and insurance. Seven ran car agencies and filling stations. Wholesale and retail businesses, excluding cars, engaged 91 men and 8 women. Three were in other trade industries, and 15 men and 2 women were in public services not elsewhere listed (probably including county officers). Two people were employed in recreation. Fifty-three men and 55 women were listed in other professional and semi-professional services (mostly school teachers). Eight men and 14 women ran hotels, restaurants, and boardinghouses. Ten men and 37 women performed such services as laundering, cleaning, and pressing; 35 men and 2 women were engaged in unspecified occupations (the men must include the carpenters and all kinds of "odd-jobbers" who live in each town).

Since the Plainville area covers about one sixth of the county, this listing divided by six is fairly representative of occupations around Plainville, despite some inaccuracies and some shifting in stress from the local point of view. It omits, for example, Plainville's leading "dog man," Homer Bland. Homer, like certain other dog-trainers, the rest of whom, however, live in the country rather than in town, breeds, raises, trains, and sells dogs—bird dogs and fox and 'possum hounds. He also boards and trains dogs for others, including a few clients in Largetown and Metropolis, who also pay him, during quail season, as a "guide" and fellow huntsman who is able to make arrangements with local farm owners for shooting quail on their land. Dog training is an occupation respected and admired by many dog enthusiasts, but many other people consider it almost, or even quite, dishonorable.

There also live in and about Plainville a number of part-time "traders," and several full-time "traders." "Trading" serves in this community three very important functions: (1) It is an important form of barter through which people exchange livestock and other possessions outside the regular commercial system except for cash "boot." (2) It is a sociable male pastime. (3) It provides the most approved channel for male aggression against other males ("nobody ever heard of a woman trader"). (4) It provides for some males a full release, and for nearly all males an occasional release, from the community's sanctions for hard work—the approved "making it the hard way." Many merchants and farmers "trade on the side."

The point of trading is of course "profit," but it is also to "get the best of" or to "outwit" one's "trading partner" (opponent). The ritual of trading is both long and complicated. Most trades involve lengthy verbal sparring and bantering; disparagement of the partner's goods, and "brags" regarding one's own goods; numerous offers, refusals, and counteroffers; and (often) recountings of "famous" local trades. A man is admired for trading victories, and even for deception of his trading partner, if he has only concealed or evaded reference to flaws in articles offered. Deception must follow rigid rules. To lie directly is to "cheat."

A trade may take an hour or a day, or may be protracted over several sessions. The preliminary session of a trade between a merchant and a farmer, for a child's pony, lasted an afternoon and was joined by many spectators and commentators. Toward the end of the afternoon, the merchant's business partner told of a local trader who rode his horse to town one Saturday afternoon, traded it off, made nine subsequent trades, and then rode home on his original horse, without making or losing a cent. "Now that's what I call *tradin'*," he said.

The "old time trader" was primarily a "horsetrader." A trader in land and crops (either harvested or still in the field) was usually called a "speculator." Traders now trade anything —pigs, calves, crops, tools, cars, car parts, odds and ends accumulated at farm auctions. One trader, speaking of cars, said, "if the gub'ment just didn't make you license them things to run 'em, there'd be more car-traders now than there ever was horse-traders." I asked a country preacher if he "traded much." He said, "Oh, yes. If I hadn't be'n called to preach, I'd 'a' be'n a trader." Trading is included in many a "commercial" transaction. The Plainsville Ford dealer said, "I never just sell a car. I have to take in another car, and generally a cow or some pigs or chickens or corn or something. They want to trade." Shopping is also called "trading," and much of the trading ritual is often jokingly inserted into marketing a case of eggs or buying a sack of flour.

The listing of customary occupations further omits, or fails to separate from "farmers," men whose main living comes from wood chopping and the sale of wood, or from hunting, fishing, and trapping. Nor does it list people on WPA.

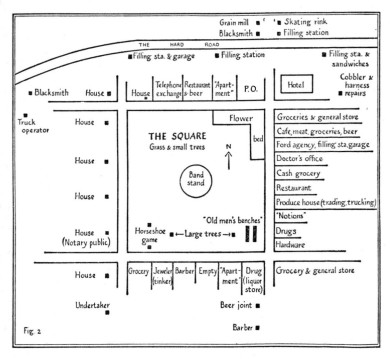

Fig. 2

The "business houses" in Plainville in August, 1940, are shown in Figure 2. Of these 32 businesses, 9 are run by the heirs or descendants of "old-time Plainville business people." Ten belong to "newcomers" (people who came to Plainville within the last ten or twenty years to "start up a business"), and 13 are owned by ex-farmers or the sons of near-by farmers. Only six business or professional men are considered to run "really paying propositions." They are the undertaker, the doctor, the Produce House, and the owners of the Ford agency and garage, one grocery and general store, and the liquor store. The undertaker buries perhaps a hundred people a year at an average charge per funeral of about $135. The doctor collects probably $300 a month. The liquor dealer's gross profits are

about $150 a month; his rent is $6 monthly, and he hires no
help. He bought the business in 1939 for $550, paying $150
down and the rest at $50 monthly. He calls the store a "drug
store"—the drugs date from about 1900 and are transferred
from one dealer to another as a "$1,500 drug inventory," neces-
sary for securing a license to sell liquor. The owner of the
cash grocery told me that he sold $15,000 worth of merchan-
dise in 1939 and would sell $10,000 worth in 1940, at a profit
of "less than 10 percent." His rent is $12 monthly; he and his
family, like several other business families, live in the back
of the store. No estimate can be ventured regarding other business income in Plainville, because merchants guard the facts
jealously. Most stores, however, "just get along." The average
Woodland County retail business reported to the 16th census
gross sales of $5,300 in 1939, and hired one third of one em-
ployee. The "average" employee was paid $366 per year.
Stores, like farms, are run by families.

These facts and figures suggest the answer to the question,
What can a young man do? The local opportunities are not
many. A farm boy can set up farming as owner or renter. His
"start" is financed by parental gifts, loans, or inheritance, by
savings from work (especially from a long work trip outside),
or by a bank loan or private loan secured by his parents or his
wife's parents. Or he can begin his farming operations through
some sort of easy partnership or tenancy arrangement with
one of these parents. These are all frequent roads to farming.
A "poor man's start" costs no more than $300, which is a large
enough sum to provide a poor team, odds and ends of second-
hand furniture and farm tools, a dozen or two hens, perhaps
a cow, and "a little money to run on until something starts
coming in." A man can "start up good" on $1,000. A boy from
the "hunter-trapper class" of timber dwellers can continue
into manhood the traditional life of his family by any combination of subsistence and cash activities he wishes to undertake, including patch farming, hunting for food, trapping,
wood chopping, and odd jobbing at timber or farm work. He
can buy a small timber tract for $25–$100, build a shack on it

for less than $100, and "marry, settle down, and start raising a bunch of children and dogs."

There is nothing to prevent a town boy from becoming a farmer in one of the ways mentioned above except his ignorance of farming and his traditional distaste and partial contempt for farm life. Few town boys become farmers; the movement is rather in the opposite direction. A farm boy can enter local business on very small capital. One started a hardware store in 1936 with "not over $300 worth of stock and that mostly bought on his father's good name." By 1940 he owned a stock "worth over $1,000 and all paid for," and had built a pretty and modern cottage, which he "almost owned." He and his tubercular wife lived in the rear of his store until 1940. Many of course who start up in business fail, and several of the local businesses change hands frequently.

A town boy can aspire to a job as clerk or paid helper in his father's store or another store; he can start a new business [5] on earned or borrowed money, or on parental gifts. He can become an odd-jobber or a truck or bus driver—these opportunities are equally available to the farm lad. Or he, like the farm boy, can "go away."

The outside world absorbs about half of all who are born in and around Plainville. At eighteen or so "the average boy begins to want to see the world." He often wants also to "sow some wild oats" in fields beyond the critical view of his neighbors. Kin, friendship, and economic factors generally determine what part of the world he decides to see first. He may travel to kin in California [6] who write that "there is plenty of work around here," or a group of young men may together "make the Kansas harvest" or the "Iowa corn-shucking" season. Youths going forth to see the world formerly traveled by train, "on the cushions" if they could pay their fares, but "on

[5] One of the commonest new business ventures in this whole area, for farmers and townsmen alike, is the filling station. Families seem to be able to "escape hard work" and keep from starving on incredibly small sales of gas, oil, and (often) sandwiches.

[6] "A boy's education ain't considered finished around here till he's been to Californy."

the rods" if they lacked money. Now they generally band together and travel cheaply in a "jalopy." They very seldom "hitchhike." A young man may hear from kin or former neighbors of jobs in Largetown or Metropolis; many Woodland County people live and work in both cities. At any rate, he goes away, gets a job, and stays away or returns home. If he comes home, he often stays only a short time before setting forth again. While emigration from his home community seems to him to unfold almost limitless occupational possibilities, most of the men who emigrate become day laborers on farms or ranches or in cities. The training they have received at home and in school neither prepares them for social contacts nor equips them with the economic insight which might lead to occupations beyond unskilled labor.

The ramification of Plainville kin bonds into the Sacramento Valley, Metropolis, Largetown, and other regions is very extensive and offers many interesting possibilities for studying the structure of American society, including urban society. A Plainviller arriving in the Sacramento Valley finds a complete replica of his social situation (kin, neighbors, intimacies, security system) back home. As a visitor and news bearer from home he is warmly received in the homes of kinfolks or old neighbors. He need spend no money for food or shelter until he finds a job.

Emigration opportunities on the "new land" pattern began to slacken about forty years ago when good homestead land further west grew scarce. The industrial expansion of the next thirty years absorbed many, especially as farm and ranch hands, miners, rough carpenters, and unskilled machine operators. During the 1930's opportunities "outside" became very few and poor, and there was an increase in the local population.[7]

Half the Plainville boys, and more than half the girls, now

[7] After 1941, of course, there began to be more jobs than people to take them, at home and outside. Woodland County also contributed (up to September 3, 1942) 187 men (and 2 women) to the armed services, despite an apparently rather high rate of rejection on physical grounds. Of the 189, fifty-nine enlisted; of these, thirty-two were under registration age.

go to high school. So much education might be expected to suggest further training outside as a road to professional life, but the high school hardly accomplishes so much. Most high school teachers carefully avoid stimulating their pupils in any way which might arouse criticism among the more religious, watchful, or meddlesome members of the community.

A few farm boys do acquire from their excellent vocational agriculture teacher a vision of becoming soil chemists, county agents, vocational education teachers, or scientific farmers. For even these few, however, family poverty, the poverty of the local earth, and parental hostility to "higher education" usually blast the dream. Only four or five students from Plainville were attending college during the regular school year 1939–40. One girl was studying at a normal school. The son of the supervisor of the WPA sewing room in Plainville was at a small Baptist junior college at "Y." Another boy was an "NYA student" at a normal school. A farm boy with unusually poor and prolific parents was successfully working his way through the State College of Agriculture. He left home in September, 1939, with only fifty dollars which his father had borrowed for him, and quickly secured an excellent student's job, which enabled him to live and to send some money home to help clothe younger brothers. The vocational agriculture teacher attributed the ambition of this lad to his excessive poverty and the social scorn which he felt directed toward his family. "He felt too awkward to play basket ball in high school so he studied."

An interesting fact is that of the above four youngsters only one, the girl, came from a thoroughly "respected" family. When a youth of "excellent family" was offered a scholarship and a job which would enable him to enter college in Metropolis in the fall of 1940, some people thought it would be "fine" for him to go, but the emotions of many were greatly disturbed. Several people said of him, "Well, he's goin' to hell for sure now." The high school principal and his wife (a teacher) said that he was "too dumb" for college work and predicted that he would soon "learn to dance and drink." The superintendent said, non-committally, "College may be bad for him, but it might be all right." He made honor grades in his college studies.

Until recent years, school teaching offered the readiest stepping stones to professional or business life, at home or outside. The three lawyers in Discovery all started life as rural school teachers. The elder tells how he "used to hide (his) Blackstone in a hollow log in the timber, and read a chapter each trip to and from the school house, so the parents wouldn't find out and complain." The younger is now a member of the State Senate. A number of people made first payments on their farms with savings from teaching. Most of the ex-Woodland County people who reached success beyond the county taught one-roomers at home for "a start." Twenty years ago a young person could become a teacher after completing the eighth grade and passing the county teacher's examination. Teachers who lived at home could usually save most of their salaries, then $25 or $30 a month; board and room away from home cost only $5–$8 a month. A teacher could soon accumulate "a start," or enough money for further education. Teachers now earn from $60 to $100 a month, during eight or nine months of the year, but all expenses are higher, and the certification requirements for new teachers have stiffened so much over the years that a considerable investment must be made in normal school or college training before it is possible to become a teacher. This training is usually begun and continued at summer sessions of normal schools or at the small Baptist Junior College at "Y." It is possible for a student to graduate from any one of these colleges without once encountering a social or religious idea much different from the ideas familiar to him at home.

Some of the "non-ag" boys (that is, boys from town or farm who do not take the vocational agriculture courses) say they would like to "take a business course somewhere," or "study some line of machinery," or "take up aviation," but almost none do.

For girls there are very few occupational opportunities.

Plainville society is—ostensibly at least—dominated by men. Plainville men are considered to have the ultimate say-so in all important decisions, even regarding the handling or disciplining of children if a "final authority" is required. The morals of boys and men are less restricted than the morals of girls and women, and men have much greater mobility than women within the community. With regard to migration, women say, "A boy (man) can git up and *go*. Nobody criticizes him and nobody *stops* him." It is not surprising therefore that more occupations are open to men than to women, although Plainville girls have heard that "women are supposed to be the equals of men nowadays."

Teaching remains the leading "professional" occupation open to girls. Slightly over half the county's hundred teachers are girls and women. Teaching is honorable, especially for women; it is only ambiguously honorable for men, who might reasonably be expected to do something "harder," more "active," less "lazy," less "like women's work." Teaching enhances the respect a girl enjoys in the eyes of the community, unless she keeps on teaching until she begins to grow "old-maidish."

There are also a few office jobs for women in the county, most of them at the county seat. These are considered "good." It is "all right" for a girl to "clerk" in a store, though there are not many opportunities for her to do so. "Working out" (housework) is considered undignified. It is not thought good for a girl to train herself for secretarial or office work in a large city. A few girls do get jobs "outside," in factories and offices, or as waitresses, housemaids, and hotel maids, but with much difficulty because their families (and in a sense the whole community) must know much about the job in advance before feeling that their daughters will be "safe." Parents of a girl doing housework for a city family sometimes boast about how "rich" the family is and how well they "treat" the girl, so that people at home will not think of her as simply "working out." When a girl becomes a "hasher" (waitress) or hotel maid in Largetown or elsewhere, as some lower-class girls do, she is generally assumed to have become a prostitute also.

More girls than boys are sent away for teacher's training; a few go to business schools and "beauty colleges." Only as wives can women migrate as freely as men.

It is curious, in view of their destiny, that almost all Plainville high school girls say they want above all things to become beauty operators, stenographers, or teachers (fewer). Few express a desire to become the wives of small-town men, still fewer to be farmers' wives. Rural studies everywhere show that more girls than boys leave the farm and small towns; the same may be true for Plainville and Woodland County, but my impression and the impression of Plainvillers is otherwise. Girls certainly feel that it is very hard for them to migrate.

This section on possible occupations cannot be left without mention of WPA, and even direct relief, as ways of livelihood. The average monthly case load of persons receiving general relief in the county during 1937 was 90. It was less in 1939 and 1940, but had been much higher in previous years, and applicants had greatly exceeded recipients. Sixty or 70 men in the county, 10 or 15 of them Plainvillers, were earning WPA money during 1940, mainly at road work. Twelve or 14 women of the county also gathered daily in the Plainville WPA Sewing Room to "milk their needles," as one of them phrased it. An elderly woman who reported the phrase remarked, "To milk the gub'ment and us taxpayers, she ort to say." About 200 people in 1937 drew old age "pensions" (OAA) averaging about $12 each per month. In 1938 an average of 15 families with two to eight children each drew Aid for Dependent Children. Some young people drew NYA checks. Many disabled veterans of the first World War and the Spanish American War received checks. Two Civil War pensioners were still alive. "I don't *think* we've got any Revolutionary soldiers drawin' money, but you might scratch one of 'em up way back in the timber somewheres," said an informant who was critical of "all this gub'ment spendin'." One Plainville woman, the relict, with many children—including several sets of twins—of a man who succeeded in committing suicide with a chopping ax, had drawn ADC for six or eight children, was sending one son (already mentioned) to Teacher's College on NYA, and was herself working at the Sewing Room in 1940. "And every day she roams up and down the street cussin' Roosevelt and the New Deal," said the produce dealer, a Democrat in a Republican county. No recipients of government money, except those on WPA and NYA were considered to be in any manner "earning their living," and a great stigma was attached to being "one o' them WP-ers!" This stigma was lessening, however, and most people thought that government funds, for relief and paid work, would flow permanently into the community. "That gub'ment money has *ruined* half the people, but they cain't *stop* it."

Charity was apparently once fairly well handled through neighbors, lodges, and churches. Except for the activities of one church among its congregation—the Plainville church that is lowest in prestige—charity is now left almost entirely to government agencies, all of which (including the AAA) are utilized nearly to the fullest, and "cussed" constantly for "ruining this country," for "making people unwilling to work and ruining people's characters," for "meddling with business" and with "the way farmers know how to do things," etc. etc. The produce dealer said, "If this New Deal had just been put in by Republicans instead of Democrats, everybody here would have liked it." Actually, the New Deal did disrupt many "values" in a "traditional" community like Plainville. For example, it disrupted the entire value system of a subsistence economy. A man who left a farm for WPA began to draw $34 each month in cash, which was usually more cash than he had ever handled in his life. It was more than most of his still "independent" neighbors had ever taken in. If he moved to town, he sold his milk cow and hogs, and either stopped gardening or raised only a small garden. He began to spend more money for gasoline and repairs for his car, now a daily necessity. His main food began to come from the grocery stores. His children needed a nickel or dime a day apiece for ice-cream cones and candy bars, as they "roamed the streets." He did not understand why with so much money coming in he was now "poorer than ever," and his neighbors wondered why he could not "save money." Even the poorest Plainville farmers handle some money, and therefore most of them think that they live from money. Their real living is the meat and garden products which they produce and consume without attributing to it a cash "value."

HOUSES

Plainville people live in "log houses," in "native lumber houses," or in "frame houses." A small log house is sometimes called a "cabin." A small or run-down native lumber house is often called a "shack." This type of dwelling is walled with unplaned oak boards set upright; cracks between the boards are lathed against the weather. Frame buildings are weatherboarded, and they are the commonest type of dwelling in town and on the prairie. There are only three "completely modern homes" in the Plainville area. The undertaker's house, the doctor's house, and the produce dealer's house all have bathrooms, flush toilets, and hot running water. Houses are built one story, one and a half stories, or two stories high.

Not many log houses are left from earlier days, and they are held in scorn as contemporary dwellings. A number of them are in complete decay and abandoned; others have been weatherboarded to hide the logs; others now form part of the structure of larger and later frame houses.

The smallest houses are generally the oldest ones, or the very new ones. The oldest ones, the cabins or shacks have two or three small rooms with low ceilings and sometimes an attic between ridgepole and eaves into which boys, in the days of large families, were crowded for sleeping. The newest houses are generally built in a perfect square, 24–28 feet on a side, and divided into four extremely small rooms, in a style which both imitates bungalows and attains the tight compression in which city-dwellers live. They are usually constructed of cheap or second-hand frame materials, covered with commercial rolled roofing and inexpensive surface board, of-

ten imitating bricks painted white. Such a house often costs
no more than $200–$300 to build, including whatever construction work the owner hires done. A neat cottage rents for
$8 to $12 a month. One Plainville man recently built four
cheap houses on lots which he owned. He takes in $30 a
month from them. With this income, and with savings from
his $24 a month veteran's disability check, he plans to build
other houses to rent. He says, "There has always been a short-
age of houses in Plainville."

The largest houses, the one or two-story houses containing
seven or eight large rooms, were built in towns and over the
countryside (mostly on the prairie) during two periods in the
past: (1) thirty to fifty years ago, when local sawmills provided
cheaply all materials except weatherboarding, floors, and
doors and windows; and (2) the period of first World War prosperity. One two-story, red-brick, seven-room house, on a farm
one mile from Plainville was formerly the show place, or
"mansion" of the community. It was built by a Plainville
banker some thirty years ago, "at no regard for expense," and
is said to have cost $3,000. The farm is now rented and the
house is falling into disrepair. One farmer built his house
of untrimmed stones. His neighbors consider it ugly, and "too
damp" for comfortable living.

The "average" private dwelling is perhaps a frame house of
four or five rooms, built in a square, an L, a T, or a double-T,
with or without a porch, but without running water or any
other "modern convenience," except that the majority of
houses in town have electric lights.[8] It is heated in winter by
a stove; it is really heated by two stoves, the kitchen stove, or
kitchen range, and the living-room "heater." The common

---

[8] And probably an electric radio and an iron; perhaps also a curler, or
toaster, or some other electrical gadget. It seems odd that there are as many
electric ranges (three) in Plainville as there are modern bathrooms. No one
owning a range has also a bathroom. A trait from outside may "take" or "not
take." Many people would like to have a range; few want a bathroom. No one
wishes (aloud, at any rate) that the town had a water tower. Nearly all have,
or want, a radio. Telephones, once popular, are declining in number and use,
and most of the lines are in poor repair. The car, once considered "impractical
for here," increases in popularity, despite its exorbitant cost in maintenance.

fuel for these stoves is wood, which sells, chopped, sawn, split, and delivered, at $1.50–$2.00 a rank (a half cord). Ten or twenty ranks of wood a year are required for the average household. The majority of farmers "get up" their own wood.

Windows and doors are generally screened in summer against flies. Screens are thought of as primarily conducive to comfort rather than to cleanliness or sanitation. All adults remember "when you couldn't take a nap or eat, for the flies," and "people without screens" are looked down on.

Water is brought into the house in buckets from a well in the yard, from which it is pumped up, or drawn up hand over hand with a rope and bucket, or else by a bucket and pulley. Many people living back in the hills and timber still get their water from springs. The "water bucket" is set on a table in the kitchen, and water is taken from it for washing or drinking, with a common tin or enameled dipper or (older) gourd. A washpan sits near the water bucket, and a family towel, made of flour sacks, huck, or Turkish toweling (in order of ascending distinction) hangs on a near-by nail. Most people consider an interest in individual drinking vessels (except at meals) or in individual towels to be rather comically "squeamish" or insulting to the others who use the objects.

Each house is set absolutely square with the four directions. Any other orientation would be unthinkable. People jokingly label any other orientation for a house or barn as "anti-Godlin'."

In front of each house is a "front yard," where there are usually shade trees and flowers. Roses, lilacs, hollyhocks, cosmos, and smaller flowers are often grown in symmetrical flower beds bordered with stones, tin cans, bottles, bricks, or old rubber tires, or made of discarded wheels of corn planters, wagons, and other farm implements. The shade trees of prairie homes were planted, and are most frequently maples. In yards of hill homes the shade is usually from native oaks left standing when the house site was cleared. Behind the house is a "back yard." The whole yard is usually fenced off as one large space with the house near the center. Well-trodden paths lead from the front door of the house to the front gate, and from the back door to the well, the smokehouse, the barn, and other outbuildings. Short paths, especially "front paths," are occasionally graveled or laid with stone.

The garden is either behind or to one side of the yard, and the chicken house is generally behind the house, sometimes in a special "chicken yard," which contains not only the main shelter, with its straw-lined nests for laying-hens, and the night roosts, but a dozen or two coops used in spring as individual shelters for mother hens and their flocks.

On the farms the barn and other "outbuildings" (sheds, hog houses, cow barn, and so forth) are collected closely or loosely together at some distance behind the house, the garden, and the area for chickens. Enclosures around these farm buildings are called "lots," and are fenced off with staves or rails (rare nowadays, even in the timber), barbed wire, or woven wire. All these farm buildings and the lot-fences, and wherever possible the fences surrounding pasture and field, are also set sheer with the cardinal directions.

In moving from the woman's domain of house, garden, and poultry yard to the man's domain of "outbuildings," "lots," livestock, and farm implements, one often feels that he is moving from neatness to disorder, from management to mismanagement, from the family's realm of real "living" and subsistence to its sometimes fruitless efforts to deal with money. One does not feel this of course about the house and garden of a slatternly housewife or the barns and fields of a "good farmer."

One of the rooms of the average four- or five-room house is a living room. It is called "living room," or "front room," or "sitting room." "Parlors" are a thing of the past. Another room is the kitchen, where all cooking and most eating are done. Few families have a "dining room," and those who do generally eat in the kitchen, at least when alone. If the kitchen is big enough, many families "live" there mainly, too. The other rooms are bedrooms, often one for the parents (or for the parents and the "baby," who is the youngest child and may be as old as seven or eight years), the other or others for the children. Large families often have an extra bed or cot in the living room. Almost all beds are double beds. Parents generally dislike having children "above school age" sleeping in the same room with them. Another point in sleeping arrangements is to separate the children by sex, preferably in separate rooms, but at least in separate beds. No "harm" is felt, however, in putting a small boy to sleep with an older sister. Where there are lots of children a bedroom may have two beds, in each of which from two to four children may sleep. Even when there is no question of space, children generally sleep together, brothers with brothers and sisters with sisters. I have heard grown people regret not having had "a brother (or sister) to sleep with" when they were children.

There is the same range, from "old style" to "modern" in furniture as in housing, though no one, I think, any longer cooks on an open fire, which, with "borrowing fire," "taller candles," and homespun, every one over sixty remembers tenderly and wonderingly, in view of "all the changes that's gone on sence them days." The living room is ordinarily carpeted with a rag carpet (oldest), Brussels rug, or linoleum (newest).[9] Other rooms may or may not be carpeted or linoleumed; the wife wants a linoleum for her kitchen if she has none. Completely bare floors are considered appropriate only for kitchens or for poor backwoods families.

The living-room stove, or "heater," is the center of the family's leisure in winter: the best chairs are set around it, the two best ones, rockers or overstuffed, generally restricted to parental use when the parents are present. There may be a davenport. The walls are papered, in floral patterns from Montgomery Ward or the drug or hardware store. They are further decorated with family "enlargements" (especially of children or of the dead), pretty advertising calendars, perhaps a magazine cover or two, and a few other mementoes (picture

---

[9] The weaving of rag rugs and carpets, to which the old looms were put when "boughten" cloth supplanted homespun, has about ceased. Linoleum has been accepted as very practical, cleanly, cheerful, and pretty.

cards or Valentines; a whip, a paper hat, or a colored feather won or bought at a picnic). All these things are attached to the walls with nails and string. There is also a shelf for a clock which strikes the hours, and beside the clock stand the bottles of pills (for physic) and other medicines. On other nails in the kitchen are a large-lettered Cardui calendar, forecasting the daily weather for the year (the forecasts are no longer considered anything but a joke), and several farmer's almanacs. Almanacs were formerly very useful in planning work according to moon phases and zodiacal signs and are still brought home annually as gifts from the merchants who sell patent medicines, to be hung in their traditional place.

The walls of other rooms are decorated unimportantly, if at all, except for wallpaper and perhaps some photographs and colored pictures that once hung in the living room, though the bed quilts, especially if old, may be intricately and beautifully quilted. The beds themselves may be slat-bottomed or have coiled springs. Most commonly they have cheap, non-coiled springs, and thin, purchased mattresses. Few corn-husk mattresses ("shuck ticks") are left, and featherbeds, while numerous, are beginning to lose popularity. Perhaps ten percent of the beds are infested with bedbugs, though it is not hard to find somebody willing to accuse many more housewives than that of "having bugs." All material possessions, of course, indoors and out, like manners, morals, and speech usages, are set in a pattern of social discriminations, infinite in number.

Lacking bathrooms, people bathe infrequently. The stated ideal of cleanliness is "a bath once a week." Many women bathe weekly, if no more than a sponge bath, and most of them keep their babies and small children fairly clean; but among men no particular value is attached to cleanliness. Many men are said to go through the whole winter without a bath. Women consider most men to be "dirty as animals," this criticism applying not only to their "dread of washwater" but to their use of pipes, chewing tobacco, and cigarettes, their spitting, and so forth. In summer, most boys swim in the river, but home bathing is generally done in the kitchen (in winter) or smokehouse (in summer). Baths are taken in the large galvanized iron tub used for washing or rinsing clothes, with water heated on the cookstove. Children are often bathed in series in the same water, the larger ones or the girls before the smaller ones and the boys.

There are few closets. Instead, clothing is packed into dressers, bureaus, or boxes, or hung on nails or hangers, on one wall of each bedroom, and often curtained from sight with paper, chintz, or cretonne. Work hats and everyday coats and sweaters are hung on nails in the kitchen or living room.

The staple groceries (flour, sugar, coffee, spices) are stored in the "kitchen cabinet" or the cupboard (older, and called a "safe"). In winter the potatoes are in the cellar, or are "holed in" outside the house in a straw-lined pit. Meat is hung from rafters in the smokehouse for protection against mice and rats. Very few houses have basements. Home-canned foods are on shelves in the kitchen or in the pantry (if there is one) or under the nearest bed, or in the cellar. A woman prides herself on having from 100 to 400 jars (quarts or half gallons) of "stuff put up." A woman considered improvident, or a woman who "has no jars" or who is "too poor to buy lids, rubbers, and sugar," has to feed her family mainly "out of the safe," from "store goods," or from what her boys and husband "bring in out of the timber."

CLOTHING

A first and week-day impression of Plainville people's clothing is, like a first social impression of the whole community, one of great uniformity. So many men and boys are dressed for ordinary wear in blue denim bibbed overalls that one almost fails to notice the many wash pants, union-alls, occasional slack suits, and cheap wool trousers (or wool trousers worn out "for best" and now descended to everyday use) which are also worn. Overalls are the standard male uniform. Little boys barely able to walk wear overalls which imitate in every detail of pocket, cut, and shape, the overalls their fathers wear. Men wear for everyday also: in summer, a plain blue or tan cotton shirt, a straw or old felt hat or a cotton "mechanic's" cap; coarse work shoes; sometimes ten-cent blue-mixed or brown-mixed cotton socks; ordinarily no underclothing. For sleeping, they remove everything except the shirt. In winter, the same, except socks always; plus long, heavy-ribbed cotton union suits, and a coat sweater, blue denim coat or an old dress coat, or some combination of these. Men wear overcoats only for dress or in the coldest weather. For sleeping, they strip to the union suit. Few wear pajamas, fewer wear a nightshirt. For everyday work, or idle wear, "just any old thing is good enough for a man."

The everyday dress of women and girls is more varied, but the "average" is a cheap, ready-made print ($.98 to $1.98), not very colorful, or a home-made cotton dress in summer; also low shoes with moderately lifted heels; rayon or lisle flesh-colored stockings, or black cotton ones. This is the way a woman looks when she "tidies up" to "go downtown a minute" or to greet a stranger at the door. At her work she is "wearing out some old dress" or shoes or stockings. A few women "have no dress that they could wear anywhere." Old-fashioned women wear sunbonnets at their outdoor summer work to prevent tanning.

It is different on Saturday afternoon, when country people come to town and town people go downtown. Women "dress up" for Saturday afternoon. Some of the men dress up too: men are supposed at least to "clean up and wear fresh clothes," even if these are overalls. Farmers and their sons almost never dress up for week-day business trips to town. Both girls and lads "of the sparking age" ordinarily wear their best clothes on Saturday afternoon, though lads sometimes affect the station and indifference of fully adult males by wearing their overalls to town even on Saturday afternoon. A youth's best summer wear is usually a slack suit or two; his best winter wear is a wool suit.

People dress up in their best for picnics, "home-comings,"

or "reunions," which occur annually at each trading center and are widely attended both by residents and by ex-natives, who time their visits home to coincide with their community's picnic. People also dress up for church, though this varies with each church. In the Christian Church, everyone dresses; the majority dress for Methodist services; Baptists value dressing up less, especially during revivals; the Holiness faith, while officially stressing cleanliness, places moral insistence upon the utmost plainness in dress. Holiness women must wear long-sleeved and long-skirted dresses without ornament or jewelry. They must use no make-up, and must not bob their hair. Holiness men of good faith will "stop wanting to wear a necktie," at the same time when they cease desiring to swear, drink, quarrel, or think evil thoughts.

The peak of ostentation in dress is seen at funerals. This might be expected, since more people gather for funerals than for any other formal rituals except the annual high school commencement exercises, and funerals are even more solemn than graduation for the spectators. People who otherwise "never darken a church door" "show their respect to the dead" and to the bereaved families by "attending the services for the dead."

The majority of men and grown boys "own a suit." A youth's suit lasts two or three years. A man's suit lasts many years, because it is worn only rarely. One comfortably-off old man bought his "last suit" for his wife's funeral twenty years ago, "and it is still good." While I was in Plainville, he wore it three times—to funerals. Many of the men look in their suits much as men look in suits anywhere, though few can tie a necktie passably. Many look awkward and uncomfortable —like the city conception of "hicks." They neither look awkward nor feel uncomfortable in their work clothes.

The average woman, however, when dressed up, is practically indistinguishable from women anywhere. Her clothes are cheaper than city women's clothes, but they are neatly cut and sewn, or selected ready-made, according to current fashions. She "studies the catalogue," examines the advertisements and "home pages" in whatever newspapers and magazines she takes or can borrow, discusses styles with her friends, and "tries to look as well as other women look." It is often surprising to see what a clever mother turns out for her daughter, with only a needle, some yards of cheap cloth, and a catalogue picture to go by. Some women, of course, are "frumps" or "dowdies" or "old-fashioned" or "too poor or tired from having to take care of all them children" to care. Some, on the other hand, have $100–$300 fur coats, smart shoes, and all the other belongings of well-dressed women. Most of them use make-up with reasonable skill, and many patronize the beauty shops at Stanton, Discovery, "Y," or Largetown.

The difference in appearance between Plainville men and women is very striking. Women wear more "modern" clothes than men wear, and they are more "progressive" than men in many other ways. They read the "home pages" and poultry pages of farm magazines with interest and willingness to believe. They began to acquire "scientific attitudes" toward poultry-raising when men still thought that "the only way to learn farming is out there between the low handles." The county agent said, "If we had just the women to deal with, our program would go over fast. They want to learn and to *do*. The men won't even listen."

THE ECONOMY: SUBSISTENCE AND MONEY

Introductory.—Nearly every Plainviller is in two separate and simultaneous economic systems, a "money economy" and a "subsistence economy." For reasons which I hope to make clear, the average farmer is deceived into feeling that he operates more in the "money system" than he actually does. Most town people, too—even the most prosperous—are oriented to the patterns of local farm life, and spend no money for much of their subsistence. The doctor and the produce man both raise large gardens and keep hogs and cows; for a quart of milk daily, a high school boy feeds and milks the doctor's cow and does other chores. A widow drawing Old Age Assistance of twelve dollars a month—for "food, clothing, and medicine," if she owns her home, lives well according to Plainville standards as long as she is able to tend a few hens and work her garden. One spinster of fifty-nine lives from her garden and six dollars monthly rent for half her house; she "wants for nothing necessary." The majority of farmers raise most of what they eat. Some raise practically everything except flour, sugar, and coffee. Others, more prosperous or less "saving," buy many luxuries.

The most recent census figures cast some interesting lights on the economy of Plainville farmers. Of 1,300-plus farms in Woodland County reporting on the "value of farm products sold, traded, or used" during 1939, over one fifth reported farm incomes "under $250." The average for this group was $145 per family, over 60 percent of which was the value placed by farmers on products produced and used at home. The next poorest group, totaling 230 families, reported an average income from farming of $320; almost half of this was the value they placed on home-produced and home-consumed products. The figures for all the groups are listed in Table 1.

TABLE 1

APPROXIMATE VALUE OF WOODLAND COUNTY FARM PRODUCTS, 1939

Income Group	Farms Reporting	Total Value of Products	Farms Reporting Value of Products Used	Value of Products Used
UNDER $250	298	$43,000	265	$26,500
250– 399	230	74,000	226	36,000
400– 599	262	131,000	256	50,000
600– 999	302	234,000	301	70,000
1,000–1,499	128	155,000	127	35,000
1,500–2,499	64	117,000	64	18,000
2,500–3,999	24	73,000	23	7,500
4,000–5,999	6	30,000	6	1,000
6,000–9,999	5	37,000	5	1,300
10,000 & OVER [a]				

a For less than 3 farms no figures published.

Such figures are illuminating but deceptive. They omit augmentations to income from frequent or occasional wage-jobs and the sale and consumption of most natural products —game, furs, fish, and wild fruits. They also omit such cash-outgo items as payments of interest and principal on personal debts and mortgages on land, livestock, and machinery. Furthermore, for what they are intended to reveal they are very inaccurate. Many farmers are unwilling or unable to supply much of the information which census takers request. They overvalue a farm, if it is mortgaged, to enhance in their own eyes their equity in it. They "know how many hogs and calves they sold, and what they brought, from a way back," but most farmers scratch their heads in dismay when asked how many eggs or how much cream was sold during a year. When asked to put a value on the eggs, milk, potatoes, vegetables, and fruit they ate, they have very poor notions of the quantity or money value of what was consumed at home. The wife can tell the ages of children and the grades they reached in school when the husband calls her in to help supply information to the census taker; but while she knows that "what we raise is our living," she is unable to help out much with actual figures. The published figures, especially in the lower categories, reflect the differences in values, attitudes, and bookkeeping habits between urban people who think in terms of money (for example, Census Bureau officials) and people who live mainly from what they raise or gather, but who ordinarily think they think in terms of money.

Another important point regarding the figures given is that despite the great statistical gaps in income stated above, and the gaps in expenditures thereby suggested, Plainville (and all of Woodland County) society and culture "appears" and "is" much more level and uniform than such figures suggest. There is real poverty, with suffering, in Plainville, and there is real wealth, with sufficiency. There are also "social classes." There are wide variations in food, housing, education, techniques, religious and magical beliefs and disbeliefs, attitudes and values. Yet the "wheat-cradler" mentioned previously

actually "lives" much more as the farmer-with-a-combine lives
than might be supposed. An observer who has seen a farmer's
land, improvements, and machinery; who has counted his
livestock; and who knows his general situation as owner or
tenant, and as debtor, can estimate with fair accuracy whether
he falls within certain ranges of the above income listings
(under $600, between $600 and $1,500, and over $1,500).
From the food that goes on tables, however, except in a few
extreme cases, it would be hazardous to classify the "worth"
of farming families.

Subsistence—Farmers think of their "living" mainly as
"what we eat," and food is considered plentiful in Plainville.
People frequently say, "No one here ever needs to go hungry."
Lack of *quantity* in food is considered shameful. In fact, the
greatest obstacle to dietary reform lies in the fact that "if you
tell these people they aren't getting the right food, they get
mad. They think you're saying they don't have *enough* food."
Three meals a day are formally eaten—breakfast, dinner, and
supper besides much "piecing" between meals. The typical
"good meal" consists of meat (or eggs, especially for breakfast),
potatoes, and skillet gravy; vegetables in season or home-
canned; bread and butter; pie or cake; often fruit; milk, if they
have it; and jam or jelly. Often, the more prosperous or the
more "old fashioned" the family, the more sweets they have on
the table; sometimes pie and cake and glasses of jam, jelly, preserves, syrup, honey, and molasses. A "feast" merely adds
variety to the items of a "good meal."

The staple meat is "hog-meat," which is home butchered
and cured in early winter. A family consumes from three to
six large hogs a year. The "best" meats are fried or boiled ham,
fried chicken, or game (squirrel, quail, or fish). Rabbits, ex-
ceedingly plentiful and hunted with guns or dogs, or caught in
box traps baited with corn or apples, are the easiest game meat
to get, but rabbit is coming to be less eaten and less valued,
since "rabbit fever" became known. 'Possum meat is scorned
by most people except some hill families who "run hounds."
The few who will eat woodchuck or muskrat are held in great

ridicule. "Shoulder" is also well valued, but "side meat" is "ordinary." Beef, without much regard for urban discriminations concerning "cuts," is considered good eating, though little beef is butchered. A grown steer is too large and valuable an animal to kill without refrigeration facilities or traditional curing techniques for its preservation. Mutton and lamb are occasionally butchered by a few farmers who keep sheep. There are a number of herds of goats in the country, used to clear out the underbrush in timbered pastures, but goat meat, while very cheap and actually indistinguishable from lamb or mutton, is considered "strong" and is almost never eaten.

Meals of "the poorest families" are often limited to "fat-side," potatoes, and bread; rabbit or fish (if there are boys to hunt and fish) often substitutes for the "fat-side," which costs money at the grocery. It is curious that catfish is relished as a delicacy, as deer would be if there were any deer left, and yet is spoken of as typical "backwoods fare" because it is frequently eaten by people who live near the creeks and river. Another odd fact is that the backwoods people are often *said* to "live on just corn meal and molasses." These two food items, staples for everybody in the early days, were almost completely supplanted by white flour and commercial syrups, to the great detriment of local diet.

Good eating is very highly valued, but not in terms of the market money value of the food, since it is home produced. A can of pineapple, or a half-dozen bananas, or a loaf of "baker's bread" has a money value in the eating, but not a loaf of ordinary home-made "light bread," nor even a ham, though the actual sales value of the ham is understood well enough, and many people have sold hams.

People are often apologetic about food, about even a "company meal." A host frequently says to a guest, "Well, here it is! You ought to stand it once, if we can stand it all the time." The meal is set on the table in platters and bowls, and passed around or asked for, with little ritual after the father has said grace. Grace is omitted in many families. Bread is passed first, and is followed by vegetables and meat. A single guest, or the "head guest," is served first, regardless of sex, and the dishes move around the table from the first recipient. As head guest, a preacher takes precedence over any one else. A woman takes precedence over her husband—unless he is much older than she is.

Meals are generally eaten rather fast. Men, women, and nowadays even children talk freely together at the table, though children were once supposed to "eat it and keep still," unless spoken to. Another earlier hardship for children was the custom of feeding smaller children at the second table, in large families or when the company was large. When the children finally got to the table, their hunger stimulated by waiting, they often found the choice foods and choice portions of food already gone. Older people sometimes say, "I was nearly grown before I knowed chicken *had* any other pieces except wings and necks."

The main vegetable is potatoes. A farmer may raise and store from twenty to fifty bushels of these, as a "winter's supply." All other vegetable foods are raised in gardens, their variety and quantity varying with the gardener's initiative, taste, and skill, with insect pests, and with the lateness of the summer drought. Other vegetables commonly grown are lettuce, radishes, cucumbers, tomatoes, onions, turnips, beets, cabbage, green peas and beans, pumpkin and squash, and sweet corn. Young field corn is also eaten. Some vegetables are canned for winter—a growing quantity nowadays under the stimulus of the AAA's Home Economics clubs.

Most farms have a few fruit trees, but orchards do not thrive about Plainville. A small total quantity of fruit is eaten, aside from wild blackberries. Peaches, apples, cherries, plums, pears, strawberries, and wild blackberries are valued highly, however—raw "between meals," stewed fresh in season (except strawberries) or canned for dessert, and especially as jams, jellies, or "sweet preserves." The government's effort is to keep fruits and jellies out of a farm woman's available "fruit jars," and to get them filled each summer with vegetables. The experts consider Plainville diet, as well as sanitation, to be poor, pointing out the high, but unmeasured, incidence of rickets and tuberculosis among the children.

Butchering hogs and curing meat are the work of men and large boys. Men kill the animals, and scald, scrape, clean, cut up, and trim the carcasses. Women and girls generally cut the fat into thin strips for rendering into lard, and they grind the lean trim into sausage, which they season and pack into long cloth bags or intestines for storage. The father in a household cures the meat, often nowadays by applying commercial "liquid smoke," which is gradually replacing the traditional method of actually smoking hams, shoulders, and "side-meat." With team and plows, men "break" their wives' gardens in the spring. Women, girls, small boys and old men usually plant them, hoe and weed them, and gather the produce. Tame fruits are gathered by either sex, though men are apter to help with apples or pears than with peaches, plums, or cherries. Women and children pick most of the wild blackberries, a thorny task coinciding with the worst chigger season. Men "don't mind" gathering wild or tame grapes, but wild strawberries, valued for shortcakes, are mostly gathered by children. All preparation, cooking, serving, or canning of food is woman's work, as is generally the whole care of the chickens or other poultry, and the handling of all dairy products after the men have brought in the milk from the barn.

Many interesting changes have occurred in the rural division of labor here, as the acceptance of new inventions has impinged on traditional practices. For example, the cream separator, a "heavy" machine, is usually operated by boys or men, relieving women of many duties connected with care of milk, which had formerly to be cooled in shallow pans and skimmed by hand. Women are thought to have "no head" for machinery, and most tasks involving machines are appropriated by men. Sewing machines and washing machines are exceptions; the vacuum cleaner will be another exception if it is ever effectively introduced in Plainville. Field work is practically prohibited to women, though their grandmothers and mothers often hoed and pitched hay beside the men.

Plainville girls are learning to drive cars, but most of their mothers felt that they neither could nor should learn this skill.

On most Plainville farms, the income from eggs, poultry, and cream (earlier butter) belongs to the women; with it they pay for all "boughten food," plain clothing, and other frequent small expenses of "running the home"—which is the woman's domain. These products pay for a family's normal "living." Until a few years ago women traded out directly the value of farm produce at a grocery store or general store. The system of exchanging home products for other necessities has changed slightly, however, since the Produce House came to Plainville. At prices identical by preagreement with those paid by grocers the Produce House buys for cash. With cash a woman feels free to shop around for her purchases. Since the Produce House is primarily a "man's place," husbands now sell much of the produce, either turning the money over to their wives or paying for the latters' purchases. Thus men are beginning to transgress into the women's economic world, and people are beginning to think of their subsistence in terms of money. While actual money—$1 to $10 or $12 weekly, the average is perhaps $5—does change hands between farmer and merchant, all such transactions are only a slight step removed from the earlier days when "women span and wove," and when almost every item consumed on a farm was produced there.

Another development which confuses the subsistence economy and the money economy still further is the new tendency for a few farmers to "specialize" in egg production or cream production as a main source of cash income. This involves a completely new orientation of traditional economic relationships between men and their wives. Most men prefer "outdoors work" to "piddling with chickens." They are less hostile to cream production because it is only an extension of their customary work with larger livestock. What keeps many out of the latter field is their resistance to scientific breeding and feeding.

Money—On Plainville farms the real "money economy" begins with the work of men. Men "tend to" the big livestock: hogs, cattle, horses, mules, sheep; and the field crops: corn, wheat, oats, and hay. Men own the animals and the crops. The man ordinarily also owns the land he tills though deeds are often jointly in the names of husband and wife, or else he rents it as a male responsibility. He is responsible for mortgage and other debts, and for large expenditures. He pays for a car or tractor, farm implements, an "operation" or other doctor's bills, men's and large boys' suits, overcoats and shoes, and often the more costly items of women's clothing. Either the man or the woman (from her cream and egg savings) may buy a washing machine, a cream separator, household furniture, or children's or women's clothing. The man usually handles the bank account, when there is one. He pays the taxes and the fire, hail, and tornado insurance. He seldom has life insurance.

He decides what to plant and where to plant it and whether the crops are to be sold as grain or hay, or fed to sell as livestock or livestock products. From his hogs he supplies the family's meat for butchering. From his grain the wife's poultry is fed. From his cows he furnishes to his wife the dairy products eaten in the household or sold for its benefit, but the live increase in pigs and calves is his. Women are "not supposed to know" or to be able to learn much about crops and livestock, just as men are supposed to be "awkward and dirty" about household techniques. A widowed farm wife is expected to "sell out" unless she has large sons or can hire a hand to "do and manage the outdoors" for her. She is expected to fail, if she "climbs on a plow" or starts "working with a team." A farmer left wifeless is considered only half a farmer. People express special pity for father and children when a widower farms and keeps house for motherless children. His house, his cooking, and his children are expected to be "dirty." If he does all his tasks well, however, he is admired for being "both a father and a mother." A farm is a man-wife enterprise, and no farm can be "run right" if either partner is lacking.

Once or twice a year or oftener the man receives, if fortunate, a rather sizable sum ($50 to several hundred dollars) from the sale of crops or surplus livestock. What he does with this cash depends much on how his farming operations are financed. Some of it, of course, goes for certain expenditures already mentioned.

An "owner-operator" who is out of debt on his farm and livestock and whose family lives mainly "from the farm" (that is, directly from its products) can add something to his capital in good years. With this capital he can buy more land, livestock, or luxuries, or he can lend it out at interest. Owner-operators and "part-owners" (who own a farm but rent additional land) total 64 percent of Woodland County farmers; the rate of tenancy is much greater on the prairie farms than on the poorer hill farms.

The first obligation of a farm owner whose land is mortgaged, however, is his interest payments. About half of the "owner-operated" farms are mortgaged, for about half of their value, and more prairie farms than hill farms are mortgaged. The fact that customary local interest rates are from 6 to 8 percent suggests the heavy burden involved in this form of "tenancy," which gives, however, the pleasant feeling of "ownership," and of progress in the realm of "money." Not only land, but livestock herds and farm machinery are also "owned" under mortgages, and there is an additional structure of personal debts—loans made on a man's "character," or guaranteed by his friends or kinsmen. Payment of debts is a man's first financial and moral obligation.

A tenant farmer's primary financial obligation each year is his rent, which he pays in cash or in crops. About half the tenants are cash renters; the rest pay as "shares" one third or two fifths of what they raise. Cash rent works in favor of the tenant in good crop years; in poor years it works against him.

A farmer's prestige as "manager" and "money-maker" depends on his skill and luck in accumulating land, livestock, and savings. This is not his only prestige, nor even the most important factor in his prestige, but what he has in money and the important local symbols of wealth "place" him and his family in the local and national money economy. Beneath this superstructure of "money economy," and altered by it for better or worse, goes on the subsistence activity of the family, guided and manipulated by the wife. The husband, however, is called the "provider."

The external legal system imposed on these traditional patterns alters their forms somewhat, yet the way I have described them is considered "the way things are" or "the way they rightly ought to be." A man who tills his wife's inherited farm is considered to be somewhat less the man for his wife's ownership; a man's status as a man is somewhat lowered by his wife's "doing field work," or owning livestock (except as a pet, or just an animal "to claim"), or in any way meddling, except as a wifely and private adviser, with "a man's business."

What might be called the financial "fantasy" wish of most Plainvillers, including farmers, is to be rich. Only two farmers are rich, however, and no one believes that "getting rich" on a Plainville farm is much more practicable than to become President or a famous movie star. The common real hope—at least until dispelled by years of bad luck, poor management, and struggling with debts—is to be "independent." To a farmer independence means "owing your own farm and some good stock, being out of debt, and having money in the bank." From three to four hundred dollars is considered a tidy sum to have laid by. It is, or rather was until recent years, a common ambition to accumulate $5,000, lend it out at 8 percent, and retire to town when old, to "live on interest." Another widespread ambition and frequent achievement until recent years was for a man to climb what the literature of rural life calls "the agricultural ladder." The successive rungs of this ladder are usually labeled, from the bottom upward, "hired man," "tenant," "owner, with mortgage," and "owner, mortgage-free."

On April, 1940, the average age of all Woodland County owner-operators of farms was over 56.1 years. They had operated the farms they lived on for an average of eighteen years.

The average age of all farm tenants was 40.3 years; four years was their average period of tenancy without moving to a new farm. Farmers marry and start farming very young, often at twenty or twenty-two. The mortgage burden of "owners" has already been mentioned. These facts and figures suggest what reasonable hope a young man has of climbing the agricultural ladder. Confidence in the practicability of the "old time farmers' " hopes is under considerable strain at present. The depression years deeply ingrained among farmers the unwelcome notion that the only "independence" they are apt to know when old is the state's Old Age Assistance.

A whole new form of rural social reorganization and security seems to be implied in the government's present agricultural program. Woodland County received a county agent in January, 1938. A part-time agent had served since 1927. A few of the main resulting changes are: (1) a huge decline in the acreages of soil-depleting crops (corn, wheat); a huge increase in acreage of *lespedeza* (a low-grade clover); a resulting shift from grain sales to livestock, and a growing interest in purebred stock. (2) The beginnings of "program planning" (of crops, gardens, livestock, poultry, soil conservation, diet improvement, sanitation, home economics, etc.) by organized local groups, including farmers' committees, Home Economics clubs, and 4-H clubs. The reaction to these changes is still turbulent. An older system of farming methods, social aims, and personal security is breaking down. The new changes are too recent to have supplanted old sanctions with new sanctions.

Plainville merchants, professional men, teachers, store clerks and other wage earners, war and old-age "pensioners," and even some odd-jobbers obviously operate more according to the American money system than do the majority of farmers. A few additional data will illustrate how completely the town is permeated by the interests of the countryside: (1) The doctor not only gardens and keeps a cow and chickens in town but he still owns and operates, with a hired tenant, his "old home place," at probably no gain other than a sentimental one.

(2) John Blade, the produce dealer, is prosperous, having accumulated stock, trucks, and working capital worth at least $10,000 since settling in Plainville eleven years ago. He operates competently in the "money economy," speculating cannily in grain, feed, livestock, and eggs. He is a keen student and judge of market trends. His bookkeeping system is complete and efficient. Yet he draws out of his business only $40 a month; with $10 of this he makes a payment on his modern bungalow. His family of three lives well on the balance, because his "real living" comes from a garden and livestock. (3) At least half the vegetables and fruit served at the hotel are raised by the hotelkeeper and his wife, both over seventy years old. (4) The undertaker, the vocational agriculture teacher, and the county agent all raise big gardens. Town people physically able to work who buy all or most of what they eat are condemned as lazy and extravagant.

Most businessmen, like farmers, keep no record, or no accurate record, of their transactions. "They work and their wives work, and they try not to pay out any more than they take in." They felt great distress in 1939 when state officers descended upon them for an accounting of sales taxes which they had seldom troubled to collect. Merchants and their customers greatly resented "the bother of all them mills and pennies." One grocer who "kept enough books" to enable the officers to estimate his sales tax complained bitterly that a rival completely without records had to pay nothing. Most merchants angrily condemned the new necessity for record-keeping as an infringement on their rights to their traditional business methods. Independence, to a Plainville wage earner, means "having a good job." The average regular job pays $30 to $50 monthly. To most Plainvillers, $50 a month means "good money," and $100 a month means "great big money." To a merchant, profits, above interest on debts, of $80 to $150 a month provide a good living; money or real capital of from $5,000 to $10,000, plus such earnings, would be "independence."

Town people frequently invest accumulated capital in land.

which they call "the safest investment there is." Sometime they say, "Land is the only thing that has any *real* value." The mail carrier now owns several farms. The undertaker owns a large and well-equipped "ranch." John Blade "aims to retire" at thirty-five to a "good farm with lots of good stock on it." The idea of land ownership is very attractive, though no re- tired merchant now lives on land, and no landowner, I think, makes reasonable interest on land farmed by a tenant or hired man. In earlier days, of course, the "natural increase" in the sale value of land brought profits here, as elsewhere, to all who owned it.

2 Social Structure: General

In spite of the many channels of communications now connecting Plainville with the outside world, the entire community—of town and surrounding neighborhoods—impresses a city dweller as both "isolated" and "backward." For all the encroachment of machines and of ideas from larger towns and cities, Plainville lags far behind "modernity," and the tempo of change seems less swift than in more prosperous farming communities. Even speech and physical motions seem slower to ear and eye than customary language and body movements. To a city person, also, despite all the cultural variety which close observation reveals, the whole community, casually viewed, appears remarkably uniform.

Plainvillers sense and frequently express their own similar feelings that they live in isolation, that their community is "behind the times," and that their culture is uniform and dull. Young people often say "There's nothin' to *do,* away off back here *away* from ever'place!" Old people sometimes say ruefully, "When we was children, we didn't know there was any better country than this anywhere . . . Some of us didn't know there *was* any place else." All now know that the world is very large and that their part of it is small, poor, and humble. More than once people were heard to say, "Everybody here has an infer'ity complex about theirselves (or the country)." The remark illustrates how even very modern city ideas trickle in—not always to the encouragement of local self-esteem. People often apologize for "poverty," "this poor country," personal "ignorance," "poor education," not knowing "how to act," and especially bad grammar—"I don't know how to talk right." "Inferior" English has been selected as a primary and almost universal trait for apology because the school teacher, the press, and the radio have all cooperated to arouse self-consciousness concerning dialect forms, phrases, and phonetics. All but the "most backwoodsy" speakers frequently ridicule and parody the stratum or strata of speech beneath or older than their own, and at the same time feel uncertain about their own usages.

In compensation, natives brag about the very factors that contribute most to their comparatively low status: cheap soil, the low cost of living, the intense churchly stress on morals, the resistance to "law," to education, to agricultural and dietary reform. "Where else can you buy a good farm so cheap? Where can you live on less money (or work)? Where else are people as good and as old-fashioned? Where can you be so free from meddlers?" Next to "independence" the most highly prized local trait is perhaps "sociability." People say, "I guess we're all just ignorant hillbillies, but I bet you never found friendlier people anywhere, did you?" They are indeed both sociable and hospitable toward people they know and trust. A visitor is always invited to "stay for dinner" or to "stay all night." Invitations for a meal are generally meant, though most people would be surprised if a visitor accepted an invitation to sleep without exceptional cause, for example, unusual intimacy, or a sudden and severe storm rendering travel difficult.

Toward "strangers" or "outsiders" (sometimes called "foreigners"), however, constraint or even real hostility is frequently felt. People "want to know your business" before showing friendliness. A newcomer, especially, is feared or suspected, until acceptable reasons are given for his appearance in the community. Purchase of a farm or store is understandable, but a well-dressed stranger is often feared as a "government man" or a "detective." Reassurance regarding newcomers usually develops slowly. The surest way for them to gain social acceptance is to be friendly but not "forward," to be interested without "nosiness" in local doings, to refrain for a while from criticism of local people and from unfavorable comparisons of Plainville with other regions, and to imitate quietly the average level of native life. The commonly stated criteria for judging a newcomer are, "We want to know his business, how honest he is, and what his morals are." His ultimate full status, however, depends on the number and kinds of ties he and his family are able to establish in the formal social structure of the community. He never becomes a Plainviller as fully as one who was born there, but he finds a certain niche in community-membership—he becomes "one of us" as soon as he has lived there long enough to cease "belonging anywhere else." For Plainville is a community in the sense that all the people who live or trade there are labeled together under the name of their town. Wherever they go, they "came from Plainville." If they return they "come home to Plainville," if only on a visit from their "present home." In terms of social usages, sanctions, and status, they might just as well be called "Woodland County People" as Plainvillers; their county is indeed a larger community to which they belong or feel that they belong—or which they "came from," when they migrate. Most sentiments for county are identical with sentiments for trading center, but within the county, rivalries between the towns create special feelings of "community" for each. Plainvillers are Plainvillers, and not Stantonites or Discoveryites.

In yet larger senses, Plainvillers belong to a "region" of four or five neighboring counties, to "this quarter of the state," to "this state," to "this section of the United States," and to the nation. Yet only feeble sentiments attach to all of these larger areas, except the state and the nation. Identification with the state is felt during "big elections" but it is felt most keenly when traveling in other states—travelers look at car license plates and start conversations with "people from home." Identification with the nation mounts notably during wars and when past wars are remembered. None of these sentiments compares in intensity or complexity with the feeling for Woodland County and for Plainville. A still smaller geographical unit to which people are attached by residence and sentiment is the neighborhood.

The units of social organization are very numerous, however, including individual families, extended kin groups, members of a neighborhood, schools, church congregations, political parties, clubs and lodges, age grades and sex groups, and all the formal and informal cliques and associations into which people are joined for purposes of entertainment, work, livelihood, and worship. In the present section all these local forms of social organization will be described except churches, which are treated later.

THE FAMILY

The central unit of American home life and domestic obligations is the immediate family, which ordinarily includes only husband and wife, or parents and unmarried children who still live at home. The salient feature in the American kinship system, however, is the complex and yet tenuous quality of the loyalties, obligations, and privileges inherent in kinship bonds extending beyond the immediate family. In Plainville the immediate family is called, "my (his, her, your, their) family," or for stress "my *own* family." The greater kin group, including even "in-laws," is also called "family," but it is more often called "kinfolks," "connections," or "relatives." Confusing as the extended use of the word "family" may seem, there is never any difficulty in knowing which "family" is meant in Plainville verbal context.

As each individual born into Plainville society begins to talk and to "understand," the language begins transmitting to him a series of kinship terms. Through observation, "correction," direct instruction, and innuendo, he learns to feel the sentiments and practice the behavior considered appropriate toward each relative. His task is not easy, however, because there is a great gap between the way in which Plainville "kinfolks" actually treat each other and the way in which they are "supposed to act." The kinship terms themselves, and the obligations associated with them, are rooted in rural and city England, and in a day before either horizontal (geographical)

or vertical (social or economic) mobility became commonplace for individuals. For Plainville these terms are more
recently and specifically rooted in the American frontier.

The American pioneers raised large families, which repeatedly organized themselves into a "clan" system. A man
occupied frontier land, and his sons, when they married,
spread out over the surrounding countryside. As land became
scarce, clan members migrated to new frontiers and repeated
the same pattern. In any locality, extended families often
formed whole neighborhoods, political units, and entire
church congregations. Sometimes they "feuded" with rival
clans, or split in two and feuded with each other. Though land-
ownership was from the first individual, wide kin groups cooperated extensively in work, exchanged products of field,
stream, timber, and pasture, and often shared the care of
children and old people. In individual households the father's
control was more absolute than it is today and often developed into patriarchal control over many households of
sons, sons-in-law, and grandchildren. Parents, when old, simply
brought in a married "child" to run the "home place," or
moved into a child's household. Such a system, where no one's
living was felt in the least to depend on money, enforced en-
during respect for the old, whose care was distributed among
many people, and who were considered "wise," useful, and
entertaining. A grandmother, costing nothing to feed, could
usefully mend, knit, spin, and weave, or could "mind" and
entertain a child. An old man could "hoe a little," flail out
grain, skim a vat of boiling molasses. With his knife he could
whittle out an ax handle or a child's toy. Nowadays he can't
plow, pitch wheat to a thresher, or "wire up a Ford so she'll
run."

Half a dozen extended families living near Plainville still
maintain many features of "clan" organization. One is the
"Ballou nation," so big that it has broken up into smaller
groups with semi-patriarchal leaders, and there are several
other "big clans." All these are "hill families," however, and
they hardly set the style for Plainville social organization. The

term "clan" is applied to them in ridicule of their "backward" ways. Yet kinship behavior that was practicable when the "ideal" family was the extended family is still remembered and "taught" as ideal behavior.

Migration, machinery, money, have all weakened the functioning of kinship. Brothers sometimes lose complete track of each other: one goes away, fails or forgets to write, or "finds it hard to write," and people no longer know where he is. A man fails "to help out his own sister with even a cent, and her left alone with a houseful of children to raise." Mutual helpfulness was greater when it cost only work, rather than money. Formerly a brother would have taken care of a sister's crops, if only to avoid the ceremonial charity of a neighborhood "work bee," with its implied criticism of his own unbrotherly neglect. Aged parents and grandparents are considered neither very entertaining, nor useful, nor wise nowadays, even in Plainville. They are considered to be "cares." They are less welcome in their children's homes than they used to be. They are made to feel that they are "tedious," and that there is not enough "room" for them. To avoid becoming "burdens," they are beginning not "to mind asking for the pension." The decline in respect toward the old works out neatly: father and mother formally "teach respect" for grandparents, but laugh at their weaknesses, foibles, and "old-fashioned ways" before the children. The children turn the tables by applying the lesson a generation later against their parents, thus intensifying the conflict and lack of mutual interest between the generations. When Old Age Assistance became available for needy old people, the old began to enjoy a new "value" in the eyes of children, who sometimes vie with each other to "keep" the parent whose maintenance may bring in from ten to twenty dollars a month.

Yet many Plainville people still live "surrounded by kin," and all live surrounded by neighbors whose sharp eyes and tongues are persuasive goads to conscience when questions of familial "duty" arise. Some people completely outside the recognized "clans" can establish kinship with fully half the families in the community, and most people are "kin to" a dozen or more other Woodland County families. Most people also keep in touch with many emigrant kin (for example, in California), who are potentially useful for hospitality, as intermediaries in getting jobs, etc., when people take a trip or migrate. People are said to be growing "stingy" with kin where money is involved, but kin will "gladly help each other out or put each other up for awhile."

The firmest kinship bonds are between members of one's "own" or immediate family. The husband "owes his wife a good living;" he should "be true to her," and "kind to her;" he should not "meddle with the house." The wifely obligation is "to be a good helpmate." She should be a good cook, a clean housewife; "saving and not extravagant." [1] Her "average conception" of her "wifely duties" includes also the idea, I believe, that she should "yield to her husband (sexually) without minding it too much." She should be "a good and patient mother to her children" and a "comforter" to children and husband. She should not "nag" children or husband, especially the latter. She should "tend to her business" and "not meddle with the farm" or with "money matters." Husband and wife should "advise with" each other, however, when important decisions must be made in either's economic domain, or when problems arise concerning their children. If they fail to reach a common decision, then the wife should yield to her husband's judgment. All such consultations should occur beyond earshot of the children, and are frequently held in bed. Publicly, neither husband nor wife should "look with (sexual) interest at another person," nor should they ever demonstrate affection toward each other, by word or deed.

Parents are supposed to take care of their children until they are "educated," "grown," "married," or "able to make their own living." This "care" includes affection, feeding,

---

[1] "Saving and not extravagant" means: (1) She should cook mostly what they raise, and not waste anything ("not throw anything out"); (2) she should not "spend too much" (on foodstuffs, clothing, household knicknacks); (3) she should ask for as little of "his money" as possible and should make "her (cream and egg) money" extend as far as possible beyond table expenses.

clothing, medical attention through home remedies and by
doctors if necessary, and home discipline and teaching. Parents also owe their children an "education" the formal level
of which may be determined by the child's own interest or
ability, by a family's means, or by parental ideas about what
amount of formal education is either useful or harmless to
children. Through all this "support" and "loving care," a
"debt of gratitude" is built up in the growing child which he
must "pay off" as well as he can—he can never fully repay it
—through work at home and through "leading a good moral
life," both as a child and as an adult. A farm boy is supposed to
be "earning his way" when he begins to do full-time field work.
A girl "earns her way partly" by helping her mother, but a
girl who does not marry remains a "care" until she fully re-
places her mother in the tasks of house, garden, and poultry
yard.

The care and home-teaching of children are considered to
be mostly maternal, though the father teaches [2] the boys at
least as many things as the mother does. What children are particularly expected to learn from their parents at home are
morals, financial honesty, obedience, and work techniques.
The ideal child is docile, obedient, and willing to work, never
questioning the rightness of parental authority. While boys
are expected to develop from influences other than parental
a special aggressive and somewhat rebellious "male spirit,"
this spirit should not be displayed against parents. What children, while children, owe their parents is love, respect and
obedience. Grown children owe parents love, or at least respect, the gratitude already mentioned, and economic care in
case of need.

The obligations between siblings vary with sex and age.
Young brothers (or sisters) near the same age are presumably
leagued into especially tight bonds of love, intimacy, confidence, secrecy, and mutual support against aggression from

[2] Much of what is taught in the home, especially in regard to sex-typing, is
not considered taught material. "A boy just naturally acts different from a
girl." A child "just naturally knows a lot of things that you don't have to tell it."

other siblings, parents, or other (especially "bigger") children. They should willingly help each other with chores. Theoretically the bonds between a brother and a sister resemble those between two brothers or two sisters. So close and cooperative a brother-sister relationship is considered very odd, however, if it lasts much beyond school age. In regard to work, especially, a boy learns early to separate proper male work from "women's and girls' work," and becomes unwilling to help his sister with her tasks. She acquires no such prejudice against *his* work, and helps him oftener than he helps her. Yet "any boy will protect his sister," with his fists if necessary, against bad language, insult, or harsh teasing from another boy, unless he is with boys who are banded together for cruelty against girls. A boy must also protect a younger brother from ill-treatment by a larger boy. These dictates for protection of a sister or a younger brother are the strongest obligations of a sibling toward another sibling, and they are enforced mainly by influences beyond the home. Since the obligations for mutual aid within the home are completely subject to parental judgment and authority, they are felt by the children as arbitrary pronouncements from above, rather than as personal obligations. After marriage, real responsibility ceases, though a man will always "protect his sister's honor or reputation," and will usually "offer a home" to a needy unmarried sister. Brothers or sisters can also be called upon more freely than "strangers" for help in sickness or at any task where help is needed.

Grandparents and grandchildren treat each other "with the same affection" that exists between parents and children, but more familiarly. The same restrictions on obedience, respect, and mutual care theoretically obtain, but they are actually relaxed greatly. The child "does not really have to mind" its grandparent; he can be "sassy" with a grandparent, and such "sassiness" is considered very "cute" (charming and laughable) in a child. This joking relationship which tends to equate the old and the very young in a relationship of "childishness" and at the same time to ridicule the disciplinary system by which children are governed, is more frequently established by a child with a grandfather than with a grandmother. The grand-maternal dignity is better upheld. (In general, the frailties of old women are pitied more and ridiculed less than those of old men, whose fading minds and bodies often excite laughter, and whose fixed mannerisms become motifs of parody.) Grand-parents love grandchildren dearly and are proud of them. They often "spoil the child" with leniency, gifts, and candy. The grandparental home is always open to grandchildren, who visit there, not only with parents, but alone, to "spend a night" or stay a week or two. It is sometimes used as a threat of sympathetic refuge or as an actual refuge from stern parents. Parents with several children sometimes let one child live permanently with their grandparents, or send children in turn to "stay with" them.

Uncles and aunts have few fixed obligations to nieces and nephews beyond being the warm persons called Uncle This and Aunt That. Children feel little if any distinction between their blood uncles and aunts and the spouses of these. The spouses, however, are supposed to "feel but not show" warmer feelings toward their own "blood nieces and nephews." Uncles and aunts treat nieces and nephews affectionately and "give them a lot of nice things to eat" whenever the children visit them. Uncles and aunts would take an orphan nephew or niece into their home and care for it as an "own child," if its grandparents were dead or "too old to do for it." The orphan might instead go to live with a married sibling. Cousins [3] who

---

[3] The varying degrees of cousinship are not well known. A first cousin is spoken of as "a cousin" or a "first cousin;" a first cousin once removed is called "a second cousin" or "some kind of cousin;" and a second cousin is ordinarily called "a second cousin" or "maybe he's really my third cousin," etc. Anything beyond first cousin is sometimes called "a distant cousin" or "some kind of a cousin." The term "cousin" is almost never used now in direct address, though it was once quite common.

The kinship terms of address in frequent use and in order of frequency of their use are: (1) Mamma, Mom, Maw ("old-fashioned"), Mother ("new-fangled"); (2) Papa, Dad, Pop, Paw ("old-fashioned"), Father ("new-fangled"); (3) Bud (not very frequent); Brother (rare); (4) Sis (not very rare), Sister (rare); (5) Grandma; (6) Grandpa, Grand-dad, (the same terms are used for great-grandparents); (7) Uncle (plus his first name); if the seniority or dignity at-tributed to uncleship is lacking, the uncle is sometimes called merely by his

live near together enjoy very intimate relationships, closely resembling those between siblings. Children often feel that even very distant cousins are "close kin." When they grow up, these bonds disappear almost completely.

In short, most real obligations between relatives stop with the immediate family and with the parent-child relationship. The "own family" is the unit of obligation as it is the economic unit. At marriage one's "own family" changes. At marriage one also acquires a whole new and duplicate set of kin, the spouse's kin. These are called "my wife's (or husband's) family (or kinfolks)," or "my in-laws." Only if exceptionally warm sentiments develop are they called "my kinfolks." Between husband or wife and the new set of kin, warm sentiments are likely to develop only with the spouse's parents and unmarried siblings, or with married siblings who live very near. The new son-in-law or daughter-in-law usually begins to call parents-in-law by terms of parental address. These words for father and mother are at first considered very "hard to say" by most children-in-law, who ordinarily select a pair which they do not use in addressing their own parents. Whatever degree of warmth develops arises out of visits, mutual aid, and the tact of all persons concerned. A special new relationship is also set up between both sets of parents. If they approved the marriage, they now come to feel "almost like kin," and begin to visit "all day Sunday" just "like kinfolks."

The mother-in-law myth circulates here as elsewhere, but without much basis in fact. It is much like the stepmother myth. Stepchildren that were observed seemed to enjoy a relationship with stepmother about as warm as that between "own parents and children," yet a child with "only a step-mother" is considered unfortunate. People talk of "meddle-some" mothers-in-law, but father-in-law interference through the male spouse is more troublesome than mother-in-law med-

first name; (8) Aunt (plus her first name), or sometimes merely by first name as with uncle. Uncle, Aunt, Grandpa and Grandma are still sometimes attached as community-wide honorific or affectionate terms of address to certain old people who are respected, well-liked, or considered pleasantly old-fashioned. Formerly, "half the old people in the country was called uncle (etc)."

dling. Fathers sometimes attempt to continue to tell their married sons "just when and where to plant everything."

Most complaints against mothers-in-law refer to two real or mythical situations. Either the husband's mother attempts to tell the young wife how to run her household, or the husband contrasts her cooking and housekeeping with his mother's. Occasional complaints are also heard against the wife's mother: she criticizes her son-in-law's "house-manners": he drops ashes on the floor, comes in from the barn with dirty feet; or she feels that her daughter is mistreated and urges her to "stick up for her rights." The danger of "mother-in-law trouble" is confined to the first few months after marriage. Later trouble caused by in-laws is called "parent trouble," or "kinfolks trouble," or "in-law trouble." It is considered best for married children to move away from their parents—to another community or neighborhood, or at least to a separate farm or household. They frequently go to California.

Most parents feel "sad" about marriages though they "try to seem glad;" mothers feel sadder than fathers because women "have more tender feelings than men." Some pity is added to a mother's sadness when a "daughter is lost in marriage," and the mother contemplates the cycle of childbirth and "hard work," combined with the permanent role of secondary authority, that is in store for her daughter. The marriage of each child also symbolizes dramatically to both parents the depletion of their own immediate family, and their own prospective old age, loss of status, and loss of respect in the community. In pioneer days a new son-in-law or daughter-in-law was felt to be an "addition to the family."

Marriages are arranged only by the contracting individuals, though their families have a large veto power through supervision of the "company that young people (especially girls) keep." The "matchmaker" is not unknown, but is not taken very seriously. An older woman may introduce "two young people that ought to meet," and may suggest her intentions with approving nods, smiles, and words. More effective matchmaking is done by a younger person, usually an engaged girl, who arranges dates and transportation for a couple whom she would like to bring together.

People who marry should not be kin, or at least close kin. It is "not right" to marry a "close cousin" (that is, a first cousin or a first cousin once removed). Such marriages often occur, however, since nearly all the families in the county of "old-time stock" are related in some way, and frequently in numerous ways. Fears are often expressed that the offspring of cousins who marry will be mentally, morally, or physically deficient. The mother of three attractive children, who had married a kinsman bearing her maiden name, said, "I was certainly relieved when my children had only five fingers! One branch of my family has six fingers, you know." The "backwoods ways" of the Ballou Nation, the "drunkenness and chicken-thieving habits" of another large family, and the feebleminded sons in a third family were all pointed out as the results of inbreeding, but no one with six fingers was encountered or otherwise heard of.

Marriages are quite permanent. Only three or four divorces are applied for each half year in the circuit court. Other divorces are granted elsewhere, of course, but "the better class of people" are nearly as unwilling to solve family problems by divorce as by "wife beating" or the "rolling pin." Preachers seldom lose an opportunity in the pulpit to rail against divorces, which, with cocktails, dancing, card playing, red-light districts, ostentation of wealth, and sometimes "theaters" are condemned as "sins of the cities." People say, "Divorces are all right, I guess. They're legal, but I wouldn't want one for myself." Cases of violence between husbands and wives are celebrated in folklore—husbands and wives have fist fights and get into screaming wrangles, men beat or horsewhip their wives, women attack their husbands with frying pans, rolling pins or brooms—but such violence is extremely rare and seems to be confined or attributed entirely to people who on many other grounds do not enjoy the community's respect. Others say, "people that fight like that *like* to fight, or they wouldn't do it." No very high degree of sexual compatibility seems necessary to the placid continuation of the average marriage, which is an economic, a social, and a sexual union giving both spouses adult status, a home, a working partnership by which both earn a living, and an "own family," including children.

For all the looseness in family obligations beyond the immediate family, there is always an emotional lien on a blood relative. A place to sleep and a seat at the table can be expected from a kinsman anywhere, unless there is "bad blood" or "trouble" in the family. Grudges between branches of the same family usually are the result of (1) quarrels, recent or long ago, over an inheritance or other property, (2) a disapproved marriage, or (3) a change in relative rank. The family member who rose "got too big for his britches" and is condemned or disliked. In community schisms and hostilities kin groups tend to line up together.

The old people "count kin" accurately through many complexities of generation and intermarriage, using for the most part "descriptive," rather than "classificatory," terminology: "She's this much kin to me: her father's mother and my mother's mother was sisters." One high school youth who failed to indicate the meaning of the word "nephew" on an intelligence test explained later that he had always heard this kind of relative referred to as "my brother (sister) So-and-So's boy." Young people know less than their elders about kinship ramifications and are less interested in them. These facts may reflect the recent decrease in family solidarities, though they reflect mainly only a difference in interest and experience between the old and the young. The young, however, always "know who they're kin to."

The maintenance of kin solidarity (or even neighborly and friendly solidarity), is aided not only by hospitable acts or attitudes toward others, but also by acts that demonstrate the willingness to *receive* hospitality. People are criticized for not "eating a meal" with kin folks, or for not staying at the houses of kin, when traveling, just as they are criticized for unwillingness to entertain and feed their kin. People say, "It's about time we eat at John's, to show 'em we're still kin."

While kinship does not at present involve real money obligations, one important function of kinship lies in the realm of money. It is easier to borrow money on poor collateral or without collateral from kin who can spare the money than to borrow from "strangers." People say, "The first place a feller'd look, if he had to borry money, would naturally be his kinfolks." Kinsmen most likely to be asked for a loan are, in order, parents, grandparents, a favorite brother, or an uncle. Some married sons "break up their parents" through repeated unrepaid borrowings. Interest on such loans is ordinarily the same as "bank interest" (8 percent) or "gub'ment interest" (4½–6 percent), but there is less pressure for collection. Kinfolks would not be likely to charge interest on only $25 or $50 lent for a few months' living expenses. Some people say, however, that "the last people on earth you'd ask money from are your kinfolks." The community's axioms stress both the "loving" and "hard" qualities of kin. A young Plainville teacher who wanted further schooling and whose uncle was an "oil millionaire" outside, said he'd "work his fingers to the bone and do it the hard way," rather than lower his pride by "asking for it." This uncle once gave $25,000 toward building a church in Plainville.

Although the pioneer ideals of kinship obligations are broken as often as they are observed, they remain ideals, ready for restoration under certain conditions. When several members of a kin group become prosperous, the older patterns of mutual helpfulness are sometimes restored, but on a level *that makes money* for the kin group rather than guaranteeing its mere subsistence. The county Democratic machine, called by a local agricultural expert, also a Democrat, "the worst racket in this county," is an extended family. All are farmers, and the wealthiest and most progressive farmers in the county. They live in separate neighborhoods, and no one thinks of them as a "clan," but they work together solidly for profit and political control. The banking family is somewhat similarly organized, and its members have large power in the county Republican machine.

NEIGHBORHOODS

The word "neighborhood," like the word "family," means several different things to Plainville people; the same thing is true of related words like "neighbor," "to neighbor," "neighborly," etc. The meanings of all these words will be clear if I use Plainville terms in Plainville meanings. Town people speak of which "neighborhood" in town (that is, which section of the town—the "south part," the "east part," or the "west part") they live in and which one is best to live in (their own is generally best). They speak of what people they "neighbor with" (visit, exchange meals with, borrow [4] from, etc.), or "neighbor with most." They also speak of their "neighbors" as the people whose houses are nearest their own, whether or not they actually "neighbor back and forth" with them.

Even farm neighborhoods cannot be described in topographical terms only. Each farm family belongs to at least three separate "neighborhoods," only two of which have any remote likelihood of congruence, aside from all the other focal centers which the world may provide for their "neighboring" (such as Plainville on Saturday afternoon).

A farmer's "real close neighborhood" includes geographically his own house and farm, at the center, and the four to eight or ten adjoining or nearly adjoining households and farms. The occupants of these farms are his "near neighbors." They are within easy walking distance for himself, his wife,

[4] Exchanging meals and "borrowing sugar or flour" seem to be declining among town people. Town men seldom eat a meal at a neighbor's; club meeting and luncheons are becoming the favored social life of women. The old lament the passing of all-day visiting but not of borrowing. One old woman told me of her "last bad borrier." A younger woman kept borrowing a fruit jar full of flour and returning it not quite full of poorer flour. "So I fixed her. I kept that fruit jar just for her. When she brought it back with less flour than she took, I set it on the shelf for next time. Finally it didn't have no flour in it. But when she come to borry I handed it to her just the same and said, 'This is *your* flour.' So then she seen what I meant, and she ain't never been back."

and his children. These are the people whom he and his family supposedly neighbor with most. Each neighborhood of this type is unique; there are as many of them in America as there are farm houses.

Yet actually a man's "close neighborhood," functionally speaking, is more apt to resemble the following scheme:

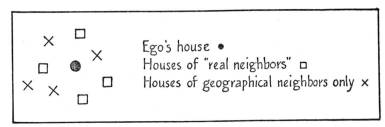

Ideally the occupants of these houses should be close, friendly, and cooperative neighbors, but feelings of difference in "class" or "morals" may make two separate, and what might be called "geographically simultaneous," neighborhoods out of the area. An old quarrel, rooted in a "line fence" (boundary) dispute, or in crop damage by livestock, or in a children's fight, may cause unfriendliness between neighbors; as may family alliances or misalliances; or a neighborhood division on a tax levy or an election; or a remembered quarrel over hiring a teacher, perhaps kin to one of the disaffected neighbors. The situation is rendered even more complex by the fact that social discriminations may result in very extraordinary neighboring situations: a man may "neighbor" with another man, when the wife of one "would not neighbor" or "could not neighbor" with the other wife. Their small children may play together freely, running in and out of both homes and fed between meals by both mothers, while the post-adolescent girls of the "better family" are unable to "speak friendly in town" to the big boys of the other family. Meanwhile, perhaps, the larger boys in both families can hunt and "run around" together, and even "stay all night" with each other. It is astounding how complex the ritual and taboos on human intercourse can become even in a small rural community where people like to say, "We're just one plain old average, everyday, working class of people here."

Each farm also lies in a larger neighborhood, a neighborhood which the farmer calls "my neighborhood," or "my big neighborhood." He considers himself and is described by others as "belonging to" or "living in" this neighborhood. A man can live near the edge of this neighborhood, or at its center, or he can live just between two such neighborhoods, which are clearly defined with little overlapping, by the limits of a rural school district, by some natural feature—a valley, a prairie, a barrier of hills, or a bend in the Apple River—by the arrangement of roads, even by a telephone line. A telephone line can set off families who want or need a telephone, who "own a share in the line," and who are willing to pay thirty-three and a third cents a month for switchboard service in Plainville, into a certain kind of neighborhood within a neighborhood. Women "neighbor" a good deal over the telephone. A telephone line can also form a new kind of neighborhood of phone-owners, which traverses two or more geographical neighborhoods. Church membership can do the same. The big neighborhoods are named, after a church or school house, a natural feature, a leading or old-time family, or a combination of these. Some names of neighborhoods are: Owl Roost, Greasy Flat, Pickett's Bend, Home Prairie, Wilson's Valley. I heard no other name for Owl Roost, but the proper (and infrequent) name for Greasy Flat is Pleasant Hill.

This arrangement and classification of people into named neighborhoods serves many useful functions, including provision of a method for giving directions, by which travelers or traders can find the houses where people live. Most neighborhoods serve also as convenient units for elementary schooling and school taxation. Some have a church.

The important function of neighborhoods is to provide "neighbors"—people to know more intimately than anyone else except "kinfolks;" [5] people to visit and be visited by, for

---

[5] Many "neighbors" are also "kinfolks," of course. Kinship adds great warmth to the neighborly relationship, especially among children.

a brief chat, "all day," or, frequently among children, all night; people with whom to exchange household commodities, tools, implements, and work. Women and children do much informal daily running along the roads and footpaths connecting the houses of neighbors. Children run over to a neighbor's to play, or are sent there to borrow or to "see how Miz Miller's all are." Sometimes the boys of a close neighborhood "spend their childhood together"—when they are not working they hunt, swim, and "run the timber" together. Children and women borrow, exchange, and pass on magazines, newspapers, and the few books owned in these neighborhoods. Women borrow and repay staple groceries or women's tools (knitting needles, a cooking pot, dishes for "a big dinner," even a pressure cooker). Women often "give" each other surplus garden vegetables and wild or tame fruit which "might spoil if not eaten now," or one takes or sends the other a "mess" of any particularly "nice" home-grown or native food. She might send, for example, wild honey, or fish—if her boys have had a lucky day in the timber—, or a panful of unusually early potatoes or peas. She would not ordinarily send cooked food or "boughten" food.

Men make fewer calls, unmotivated by an errand, to neighbors' houses than women make. They "visit" with each other more in town, in fields, and at barns. Men do much borrowing and lending, however. They lend each other an ax, a plow, a wheelbarrow, a cultivator, a mower, a hay rake, a wagon, a horse or mule, or a team. Modern and expensive machines like gasoline engines, cars, tractors, and binders, are seldom asked for or lent. If a man without a car needs one in an emergency, a neighbor who owns a car will take him wherever he has to go, at no cost ordinarily above the cost of gasoline, but expensive farm machinery is generally made available to neighbors only through rather highly paid work. Men lend ordinary work freely, however, or "lend a boy" to work for a neighbor. They often "give" work lasting less than a day. They would certainly "give" the short labor of helping a neighbor lift a broken pump shaft out of a well, or set up a chicken house or shed that the wind has blown over.

Much of the economic exchange between neighbors is informal and individual, but there is formal exchange, too. Neighborhood gangs of men operate together year after year for mutual help in harvesting and threshing, in butchering, and sometimes in sawing wood. Sawing gangs are rarer than the others. Harvesting and threshing require fifteen to twenty men and many teams and implements; the thresher is paid for with money, but all the rest of the work is done cooperatively. Butchering requires four or five helpers. Each man's harvesting, threshing, and butchering are done in a turn decided on in advance, and the whole task force shows up for each job.

There is a smaller womanly counterpart to each of these gangs. It requires a good deal of cooking to provide all the cakes, pies, and fried chicken that a "bunch of hungry harvesters can eat," and many wives make the rounds from farm to farm. "All the women come that can, but not enough to get in each other's way." At butchering, all the wives "try to come," for women have many tasks in the preparation of meat, lard, and sausage for storage. The social aspects of both harvesting and butchering are very important. These are almost ritualistically gay times, in spite of the hard work that is done. The quantity of food consumed at every household is enormous, though "harvest food" differs from what is eaten on butchering day. When hogs are killed, everybody gorges on fresh meat: on the hearts, livers, "melts," and so forth. All the visitors also receive meat—spareribs, sausage, and portions of the uneaten livers and hearts—to eat at home.

While all this borrowing, lending, and exchange of work tends to be phrased as "neighborly accommodation," careful mental record is kept on a tit-for-tat basis of all "accommodations" given and received. Tools should be returned in good condition. A little more sugar should be returned than was borrowed. A man unable to appear with his harvesting gang should hire a hand. Tasks performed, errands run, and favors received should be compensated by at least equal tasks, errands, and favors. So long as these exchanges follow each other both informally and rather frequently no strain is felt, but the receiver of a favor often feels a "heavy weight of obligation" if some time elapses before he can repay it. Scores are not supposed to be kept on such neighborly duties as visiting or sitting up with the sick, or sitting up with the dead. Before Plainville had an undertaker, a special duty of neighbors who "knew how" was to wash and dress a corpse for burial. All adults are expected to be willing to "help in sickness or in death" at any time they "are called upon" or "know that they are needed."

There is much backbiting and criticism and blaming of neighbors for sins of omission and commission against the ideal of neighborliness. A man returns tools dulled, or broken and unmended: a woman "borrows too often" or too often "returns less than she took." One woman, "and you always see her in the choir," would not lend a bedpan to her husband's mother, who was "lying at death's door." (Her husband's brother said, "All I thought of when I watched her singin' after that was just, 'Pot! pot!' ") An effort is made to judge people "on their average" for neighborliness, not on one dull ax or one skimpy repayment of flour. Yet people are in general thought to be much more "selfish and stingy and unneighborly" than they were in the old days: they don't want to "visit" or "help" or "borry" or "loan" as they once did. Many blame "the car" for the decline in neighborliness.

The car has indeed changed neighborhood life, as it has contributed to many other cultural changes in Plainville. Faster and more frequent travel has lessened isolation and solidarity for families, neighborhoods, and the entire community. It has altered the patterns of visiting, entertainment, courtship, and mutual help. The car is a primary contributor to the general fact that values and stereotypes of the outside world are gradually replacing local values. Yet the current criticisms of declining neighborliness were frequent long before the car was introduced. In 1907, the native author of a history of the county wrote, "between 1840 and 1850 . . . the man who had a house to raise (or a log rolling) had to go ten to fifteen miles to invite his neighbors to help him. No neighbor ever charged anything . . . the pioneers here were much more clever ["accommodating"], open hearted . . . and much less selfish than we are now, and we are growing more selfish each year . . . Few people had things they would not loan, even half what they had or a little more than half . . . There was not many of that sort of stingy fellows in pioneer days, whose chins grow to a sharp point before . . . forty-five years old, but we have them with us now, and they are increasing in numbers."

"No neighbor ever charged anything!" The ideals of neighborliness, in 1940 as in 1907, and like the present-day ideal of kinship behavior, are rooted in early days of full economic subsistence. In 1907, "money" and the idea of money had already disrupted the real or mythical early functioning of neighborliness. All the changes which accompanied the introduction of the car disrupted it still further. But neighborliness, even according to the ideal, is still enormous about Plainville, and the more "backwoodsy" the neighborhood, the greater the amount of visiting, sitting up with the sick, borrowing and lending, and work exchange which still go on.

SCHOOLS

Until recent years a one-room schoolhouse stood near the center of every county neighborhood. Each schoolhouse was an important neighborhood center for socials, singing schools, literaries, debates, and often Sunday school and preaching. Old people still remember the early log schoolhouses, with their puncheon benches, writing tables, and floors, the slates that children "wrote and figgered on," and the old-time teachers. Oldsters tell how "splintery" the puncheon floors were for children without shoes, "until a big crowd'd come in and dance 'em down smooth." With the slates, they say, "you could write your problem down, spit on it, rub it out with your sleeve, and go right on to the next one. But these *tablets* cost money." The teachers they remember chiefly for their whips. "That *whup* was the main thing *to* school in them days." Many believe that earlier books and teachers were better than "what children gits now'days." Some consider logs, puncheons, slates, books, and old-time teachers a good riddance. As a matter of fact, children still get the whip, in some country schools, despite the present state law against corporal punishment; commoner punishments left over from early days are "standing in the corner," "toeing the mark," and standing with nose pressed against the center of a ring drawn on the blackboard.

Before 1900, many farm children, boys especially, never started to school. Many boys who did start attended a total of only seven or eight months, scattered over several years—about a hundred older adults in the county are listed as "totally illiterate." The county schools used to run a short term in mid-winter, when farm work was lightest, and a shorter term between planting and harvest, so that children who went to school would lose as little time as possible from farm work.

Frame structure and weatherboarding replaced logs in schoolhouse construction about the same time they became popular in dwellings, but the one-room country schools remained symbols of neighborhood solidarity until the days of automobiles. Consolidation of schools began about 1920. Of the fifty country schools left in the county, only eight are in the Plainville trade area—and these eight are "in the hills." The prairie schools and most of the hill schools were voted one by one into the Plainville consolidation after much neighborhood "friction and fraction." The original consolidation with the town school of several rural schools split the community into two sectors so angry that after twenty years not all the wounds have healed. Many people still mourn the loss of their neighborhood school and "blame consolidation" for destroying old-time neighborhood life. Many, however, commend consolidation for "bringing the community up to date," raising the level of education, dispelling the earlier geographical isolation in which farm children lived, and leveling town and country social differences. "Country people used to be scared when they came to town—the children especially. And the town people used to laugh at 'em, but now you can't hardly tell no difference."

Buses now bring children in daily from a wide area to the Plainville school, and other buses serve the consolidated schools in other towns in the county.

At first the Plainville Consolidated School offered eight grades and two high school years of study. The high school course now covers four years. The two additional years were installed about 1922, by a method which forestalled opposition: the superintendent simply "offered the complete course, as if it was a state requirement," and when it was approved by the state inspector, the *fait accompli* was accepted by the school board and the community. The same superintendent put a piano into the school by a similar technique of ordering the piano on approval, letting the children and parents get accustomed to the idea of its being there, and then letting them decide whether to keep it or return it. "He didn't last long here, but he *built* the schools."

Eighty-five percent of the children in Woodland county are enrolled in school, and fully half of those eligible now go to high school. Children who "don't go to high school" belong mostly to several large backwoods extended families or "clans," who "don't feel the need of education," or to certain families who consider so much education "harmful" or "sinful."

The Plainville school runs nine months a year. Most other Woodland County schools run eight months, from late August or early September until April. Attendance is still poor, however. The average child misses, through truancy, sickness, bad roads and weather, parental indifference, or labor at home, 25 percent of his 160 or 180 school days. This heavy proportion of absence means that the majority of children attend school faithfully, but a minority go with great irregularity. None of the children of one large family living in the hills near Plainville were in school in 1939-40. Their father was brought into court by the county superintendent of schools. The father pleaded that the children had unsuitable clothing for school, because clothing he had ordered by mail several months before had failed to arrive. Upon his promise to try to trace the order, the complaint was dismissed, and his children remained out of school.

Educational aims are theoretically established by the State Department of Education. Each teacher is "required to follow the state course of study." Most teachers consider the state syllabus as "all right for city kids, I guess, but not practical for *here*." Deviations from it are great, especially in the rural schools. A rural school teacher "teaches as much as she can," or "as much as the parents will stand for." One country school teacher said, "I begin with the Sears Roebuck catalogue, and try to show them how many things there are to *own* and *want,* and try to get them to read in that way." Another said, "I try mainly to teach them to be clean, but they don't even want to drink out of separate cups." All children learn to read, write, and figure—after a fashion; some learn to do all these things proficiently; some are graduated from high school unable to read newsprint with facility. Few teachers dare to "fail a child" from promotion.

Town schools attempt somewhat more to imitate city-made and city-oriented educational programs. The Plainville high school program for 1939–40, arranged according to teachers, is given in Table 2.

This looks like a program in which modern social, business, and vocational studies have replaced old-time "solid" subjects, for example, Latin and geometry. The high school is less "modern" than it seems, however. The teachers in charge of commercial and social subjects have not been trained to teach in a way that might make these studies useful or functional to Plainville youngsters. The commercial teacher learned his subjects in a summer school, just after he received his appointment. For that matter, bookkeeping and typing are relatively useless techniques in Plainville and a teacher who attempted to present them as aids to migration cityward would not be

TABLE 2

PLAINVILLE HIGH SCHOOL PROGRAM FOR 1939–40

40 Min-utes	Superintendent	Principal	Music and English Teacher	Teacher of Vocational Agriculture	Domestic Science Teacher
1	STUDY HALL	BOOK-	FUNDAMENTALS OF MUSIC	AGRICULTURE	ENGLISH I
2	ALGEBRA	KEEPING	STUDY HALL	II	SPEECH
3	ARITHMETIC	TYPEWRITING	THEORY AND HARMONY	STUDY HALL	ENGLISH II
4	GIRLS' PHYSICAL EDUCATION	BOYS' PHYSICAL EDUCATION	GLEE CLUB	CONFERENCES	STUDY HALL
5	STUDY	AMERICAN	ENGLISH	AGRICULTURE	SEWING
6	HALL	HISTORY	III	I	
7	SUPERVISION	STUDY HALL	ORCHESTRA	AGRICULTURE	CITIZENSHIP
8	GEOGRAPHY	TYPEWRITING	[GRADE MUSIC]	III	

tolerated long. The domestic science teacher lacks vocational training. The class hours in citizenship and American history are often "just spent in hashing over the last (basket) ball game, or the next one." Only music and vocational agriculture are well taught. Vocational agriculture is the only subject in the high school curriculum which in content and instructional method is completely appropriate functionally to the needs of the community—and it is the only subject which a large portion of the community opposes and ridicules.

Beyond their "regular course of study" Plainville high
school children engage in a good many extracurricular activities. There is a gymnasium, and boys' and girls' basketball
games are very popular. Contests with neighboring high
schools are held almost weekly during part of the year. Some
patrons oppose basketball on moral grounds, but the games
are well attended. The vocational agriculture teacher once
complained, "People remember all the ball players from the
1931 winning team, but they don't even know about the
prizes my boys take every year." His vocational agriculture
students have made remarkable records in regional and state-
wide contests in livestock and poultry judging. Annual "music
contests," oratorical contests, and debates are also held between Plainville and neighboring rivals. The "orations" and
debates are bought "ready-made" by the schools and are
memorized, including rebuttals, by the contestants. Parents
and other patrons turn out to "root for the home team." In
addition to the contests, various social events are undertaken:
a "program" in which selected pupils entertain the rest with
reciting, music, and dialogue; a carefully supervised class
picnic or trip; a senior play; an occasional Valentine box or
Christmas box. The vocational agriculture boys annually initiate new boys into their chapter of the Future Farmers of
America, and this ceremony is followed by a Fathers and Sons
banquet. No "parties," however, are given for or by high
school youngsters, and occasional suggestions that "young girls
and boys" need or might enjoy parties arouse unfavorable
comment by a large sector of the community.

The most common adult phrasings in Plainville of the aims
of formal schooling are (1) "to learn children readin', writin',
and 'rithmetic and maybe a little joggerfy"; (2) "to give our
children the same kind of education and the same chance that
children have anywhere"; (3) "to keep children out of the way
and out of trouble until they get old enough to know how to
act"; and (4) "to keep children from growing up as wild and
ignorant as the animals." The frank aim of the Plainville
school superintendent, like that of most neighboring school

administrators, is "to give my patrons exactly the kind of a
school that they want."

The main social function of Woodland County schools is
to gather the children together from their mothers at age
six, into various types of age, sex, and play groups—the separate, special, secret, and complex "world of children" in
which they live until they leave school. They leave school
"upon completing the eighth grade," when they finish high
school, or when they "get big enough to be ashamed to go to
school any longer."

For Plainville adults the high school represents a new focus
of community life and ritual. Those who sanction and attend
the basketball games, plays, debates, and musical contests
think of them as symbols of community "modernity"—as
events which prove that Plainville either is, or is trying to be,
especially in educational matters, "just as up-to-date as other
communities." The ritualistic expression of the new role of
consolidated schools reaches its height with the annual high
school commencement. At commencement the Christian
Church auditorium fills with school children and with parents
of present and past high school children. Those who are about
to graduate are seated on the platform facing the audience.
In token of the honor about to befall them, they are "scrubbed
and shined," and dressed up better than ever before in their
lives. Those whose families "can possibly afford it" wear new
suits or new dresses. The audience watches and listens with
great solemnity to all the graduating exercises, which include
speeches by the student salutatorian and valedictorian, a commencement sermon delivered by a preacher invited from
Largetown or elsewhere, and finally the presentation of di-
plomas. The graduating class is felt to have passed successfully
through a very important rite.

LODGES AND CLUBS

Recent culture changes in Plainville are especially great in
the shift of interest away from old-style lodges to newer kinds

of clubs and cliques. The lodges were for men, but the newer organizations mainly involve only women. Until a few years ago every formally approved male joined one or more of the well-known lodges—Odd Fellows, Woodmen, and Masons. In the 1880's Masonic halls were built in all the larger Woodland County towns. The most attractive features in these lodges seem to have been male solidarity, mutual help, "exclusiveness," the horseplay and practical joking of initiations and meetings, insurance and burial benefits, and—especially among the Masons—the solemnity of the rituals, including the public ceremonials for burying the dead. Progress upward through the "degrees" of Masonry once brought cherished esteem, and membership in the brotherhood formerly "established" a man both at home and wherever he might travel. ("A man that knew the Masonic handshake used to could cash a check anywheres.")

Today these lodges are all dying in function. The Woodmen and Oddfellows seem to have declined mainly because of increasing dues and assessments to pay the insurance policies of the dead. It was easy to handle death payments when the lodges were expanding rapidly with new and young entrants, but as members grew older their dues became greater than most could pay.

Why the interest in Masonry is declining is less clear. I suggest the following main reasons: (1) a general secularization of life: interest has declined in formal "theology," and in all other rituals; (2) the decline in community solidarity; (3) the decline in small town "business" (the older business leaders were relatively "rich"; as lodge leaders they were worth being "brothers" with); (4) acceptance of new forms of entertainment: movies, radio, and all "enjoyments" made possible by the car.

Young men are no longer anxious to join. Some of them laugh at "people who like to join things and belong to things." The rituals are carried on mainly by the old, and perhaps, as one of them furtively complained, "in garbled form. They no longer want to say things right." The Eastern Star, women's auxiliary of the Masons, is also composed mainly of older women. Outside organizers were apparently "able to get join-ers (and initiation fees) for anything," in the old days, "if they just came in with a smooth way and a handshake for every-body, and that word 'brother.' " One of the latest, and shortest-lived, of these organizational forays into local pocketbooks was the coming of the K.K.K. in the middle twenties. "Half the people joined and paid up and burnt a few fiery crosses, and had some Klan-buryin's, but it soon died down," said an in-formant.[6]

The old lodges are dying out and nothing has replaced them yet for the men. The towns are too poor to support Rotary, Kiwanis, or Lions clubs; the businessmen sometimes try to organize for mutual cooperation and profit, but out of mutual jealousy they never stick together long.

A newly formed Progressive Club, composed of Plainville merchants and a few other men, met weekly in the Produce House for a while in 1940. They pledged contributions to finance a weekly concert in the bandstand by a group of radio musicians from the nearest broadcasting station. This brought a crowd to town each Thursday evening, until some merchants stopped contributing "their dollar." They said, "These farm-ers have only got so much money to spend, and they don't spend any more by coming to town oftener." When the con-certs stopped, the club fell apart. The other effort of the club also failed. It was to increase public light bulbs in town from one, maintained privately by one merchant, to four, to be maintained cooperatively by all.

Some farmers and their wives are being gathered under the stimulus of the county agent into committees and clubs, de-signed to function for both entertainment and reform. A traveling emissary of the WPA attempted without success to

---

[6] He also said, "Course, here they didn't really have no niggers or Catholics to hate. About all we've got to hate is each other and the gub'ment." The same informant traveled to "Y" one night to see the burning of a fiery cross. He recognized, among the participants, the president of the Junior College. "The wind blowed his sheet off, and you'd ought to seen him grab it back over his face." An old woman who had attended a Klan funeral said, "The men come dressed in sheets, but I knowed 'em all (including her husband) by their *feet*."

introduce various entertainment programs and "community activities" into Plainville and other Woodland County towns. The Plainville school superintendent gave her a cold shoulder. Others thought it wrong (and ridiculous) for "tax money to be spent just for fun." A WPA library was founded in Plainville in 1940, with a paid librarian and donated books, in the face of angry opposition. Other towns in the county quickly followed suit. ("They was jealous of our liberry so naturally they had to start one too.") A rural sociologist from the State Agriculture College spent a futile [7] evening in 1940 teaching traditional English morris dances and folk games to a group of twenty gathered into a schoolroom.

The most stable and active of the new organizations formed under outside stimulus are Home Economics clubs, to which over ten percent of the eligible women already belong. In some of these clubs, social or religious activities [8] predominate over the activities for which the clubs were founded; others carry on their reform programs energetically. About ten percent of the farm children have also been induced to join 4-H clubs sponsored by adult local leaders. The 4-H clubs, however, are less successful than the Home Economics clubs. The children lose interest in their "projects"; parents ridicule these as useless, time-wasting, or even immoral. One 4-H club was criticized because the children "laughed together." The 4-H clubs disband nearly as rapidly as they are formed. One reason why they fail may lie in the silly names adults give to them: Fancy Stitchers, Priscilla Pals, Stitch and Chatter, Cook and

[7] Futile (1) because totally foreign to the concepts as well as to the felt and real needs of Plainville; (2) because nobody who really needs to be persuaded to participate in community life came or would dream of coming, and (3) because the whole attempt, from the point of view of applied sociology, looks backward and not forward. It smacks of the idea of recreating a contented peasantry on thirteenth-century lines, dancing merrily, not even on a green, but on a schoolhouse floor. The word "game," by the way, was substituted for "dance" in these festivities, in order not to arouse the antagonism of the many people who consider dancing sinful.

[8] The Plainville Boosters Club, according to the vocational agriculture teacher, "meets only to exchange lunches and boost." In others, the county agent said, "They pray more than they do the things I tell them to. But we are patient with them—they gradually begin to study sewing and canning and diet and sanitation."

Chatter, Stitch and Tie, Rope Rangers, Jolly Workers, Pleasant Workers, Sunshine Workers, Hustlers, Busy Bees, Sunbeams. It would not be easy for a child to bear up under the certain kidding of older children and adults who learned that he or she was a Jolly Worker or a Dainty Stitcher. Of the two clubs which in 1939 completed their projects with the greatest profits, one was called the "Future Farmers" and the other was unnamed. Boy Scout troops are occasionally organized, but they never last long; urban interests in knot-tying, hiking, camping, and woodcraft appeal little to Woodland County boys.

REPUBLICANS AND DEMOCRATS

Both men and women belong to political parties; about two-thirds of them are normally Republicans. The rest are Democrats, except for a handful of Socialists—a hangover from the Populist movement and considered eccentric and laughable, but rather "atheistic." Women, however, though they generally "vote along with" their husbands, also in general express distrust of all politics and politicians and consider that "the whole mess is crooked." Only a few women take a lively interest in elections; they are usually the wives of established politicians whose influence and activity prove useful to their husbands. Politics is an essentially male preoccupation. Men are emotionally, even religiously, Republicans or Democrats. A college-educated young teacher named an old man who happened to symbolize illiteracy and comical ignorance in Plainville and said, "I'd rather see *him* in the White House than any Democrat."

"Changes in politics" occur—they were numerous in 1932—but a change of party breeds suspicion regarding a man's stability of character. Republicans who voted for Roosevelt in 1932 are still labeled "renegades," even if they returned to the fold in 1936, as most did. A man is born into his political party just as he is born into probable future membership in the church of his parents. Men, like women, all recognize the crooked aspects of politics, but when their party is in power they tend to ignore its misdeeds, locally and nationally, and to gloat over the discomfiture of the rival political moiety much as they enjoy the fallen position of a trading partner.

The party out of power accuses, often justifiably, the party in power of incessant sinning: vote buying, and favoritism and graft in securing and filling all the small local contracts for county roads, building repairs, and supplies for schools and the country court house. The total direct profit to the "ins" from all these sources cannot be large. Votes can cost indirectly, "anything from a dish of ice cream, or nothing, to five dollars—but five dollars should bring in all a man's kinfolks, too!" said one politician. As for contracts, the whispering campaign against one candidate for reelection was that he had paid nine cents a roll for toilet paper (used in the wooden outhouse on the courthouse lawn) purchasable at six cents a roll in any grocery. Patronage is small because there are few jobs to distribute. The best ones, in 1939–40, were WPA foremanships and the AAA jobs of "signing up farmers." Important spoils are indirect, as the following example—apocryphal or true, but common gossip—will illustrate. The wife of the Democratic boss of the county was elected president of the school board of her town. (Any office for women is very rare.) She initiated a bond issue to build a new schoolhouse; the bond issue carried because of her husband's power over his neighbors, many of whom owe mortgages and other money to him. She turned the building contract to Democratic contractors, who charged too much, built shoddily—"they used green beams and didn't even trim off all the leaves!"—and "kicked back" to her a part of their contract money.

The simple division of men and their wives into two major political parties represents only the surface of political organization in Woodland County. Republicans win all the local offices. The important local campaigns are therefore the primaries, and most Republican competition is with other Republicans. In and around Plainville alone there are several rival and "semi-permanent" Republican cliques, all interconnected for bargaining power with each other and with other Republican cliques over the county, and also, for state-wide elections, with cliques beyond the county. The main Republican cliques also preserve connection with the Democratic cliques.

The Democratic, or minority party, wields tremendous power, not only when its party is "in" nationally, giving it control of the limited patronage, but at all times. The Democratic "machine" consists of several related and influential families, including the wealthiest farmer near Plainville. These families throw great weight in the elections of Republican county officers.

Other groupings are more important than party in local elections. These include rivalrous "natural divisions" of the county into north, south, east, and west; towns; neighborhoods; separate church affiliations; the "church class" vs. the "whiskey element"; "progressive" vs. "unprogressive"; "rich" vs. "poor"; and "timber" vs. "prairie." Those who back a winning candidate must tactfully arouse in several quarters interests and prejudices that are not always mutually harmonious.

The heads of cliques are the "politicians," who for money, past favors, "love of party," and the gratification of controlling people and manipulating events attempt to accomplish the election of "their candidates." How all this works is too complicated to tell in detail, but it involves skillfully "lining up" —and "keepin' 'em lined up even between elections"—the most influential neighborhood leaders, the most respected members of large kin groups, preachers, church deacons, and so forth, all of whom can sway votes. This means direct and indirect bribes, contributions to churches, compliments to women, admiration of babies, head pattings and ice-cream cones for children, the lending of tools and dispensing of "trade information" to men, pressure on debtors, subtle threats of disclosing moral or financial "secrets," and the circulation of gossip, rumors, and outright lies along "the grapevine."

One politician whom we shall call Bob extended "complete confidence," during the county primary of 1940, regarding his political machinations. They were bewildering enough, and remarkably successful. Each day for a month he mentioned what rumors he intended to "start on the grapevine," regarding "his" candidates and those he was opposing. These "rumors" were extremely varied, and covered many matters not directly related to the work at hand. Some of them were only gossip stories set in motion again out of the distant past. For each rumor an innocent ear was generally chosen, and the politician was able to predict with fair accuracy whose ear it would next reach (and in how garbled a form, and why garbled) and what its effect would be. He knew enough of people's daily habits to know whom they were likely to meet and talk with in the course of a day. He also discussed very intelligently individual motives for retelling or not retelling a rumor—such motives were related to kin and friendship loyalties, past "favors," "trades," cheatings, hatreds. In short he exploited all the remembrances and sentiments of men and women living their lives out in a face-to-face community. He checked results by the speed and channels through which rumors came back to him. This man received small payments from a few candidates (he would not divulge the sums), and he hoped to build up gradually enough political strength for himself to win (in "about 1946") the best-paying county office. He had a good deal of contempt for the lack of shrewdness in people by which he was able to gull and manipulate them. He said he had never before divulged his "teck'nick," not even to his "own brother."

One typical item in his campaign manipulations was the following: An enemy, *A*—— was working against Bob's candidate for assessor. *A*—— normally controlled from ten to twelve votes, including that of an elderly widow whom he partially supported. On the afternoon before the primaries Bob walked past the widow's house, on a real errand to buy eggs (the errand would "check" if questioned), at an hour when he knew she would be sitting on her porch. He "spoke friendly" in passing and allowed the widow to start a conversation. She invited him into the shade, but he had no time to stop because of his errand. When she asked, "How's the election going tomorrow, Bob?" he said he didn't know, because he'd lost interest. He led her to believe he was "hurt" because his "man for assessor" was double-crossing him by opposing "the only man runnin' for office that's really worth electin'." Here Bob named one of the candidates for sheriff. Bob said he had promised to back the first man only to gain his support for the second. Now Bob said he was going to turn his own and every other vote he could against the man who had betrayed him. Couldn't he maybe persuade her to go downtown tomorrow and vote against him too? "That kind of story is dynamite," said Bob later, "because if you do it just an hour too soon it goes farther than you want it to. But I knowed it was workin' when I come back with my eggs because she wasn't settin' on the porch any longer. She'd trotted over to tell *A*——'s wife." *A*——'s wife told *A*——, who "voted his friends" *for* the would-be assessor Bob had reviled. The trick worked doubly because Bob had secretly been backing another candidate for sheriff than the one he had mentioned as his favorite. *A*—— voted his friends against Bob there too, as he thought, but he actually voted for Bob's candidate. "I know he did," said Bob, "because I had a poll watcher look especially to see how all them people voted."

The "big" local politicians follow similar techniques, but they have other weapons more powerful than rumor. The leading Democrat in the county lives near Plainville. People owe him many mortgages and promissory notes. ("He has a stack of paper that high!") His recommendation is frequently decisive concerning applicants for relief, WPA work, and so forth. He could expect no man to change his *party* any more than he could expect him to change his church, but he decides how many people vote on bond issues and in other elections, including Republican primaries. The fact that any politician can learn from a poll watcher how people vote makes a farce of the "secret" ballot but it prevents ballot-stuffing and certain other widespread voting abuses. The "surprise" aspect in elections comes from the fact that some people "don't owe nobody *nothin'*," in money or favors, and thus form a considerable body of independent voters. Another surprise is for a politician to keep a number of voters away from the polls until just before sundown, and turn early defeat into late victory.[9]

As might be expected in a county where "everybody knows everybody else," the leading ideal qualities that candidates and their backers try to establish in the eyes of voters are the personal honesty and the unimpeachable morals of the candidate and his whole family, his universal friendliness, his need for the job, and his competence to perform it as proved by previous competence in business or farming. To prove his friendliness, a candidate attempts to visit the house of every voter during a campaign; voters whose houses cannot be reached by car he visits on horseback or afoot. He also appears frequently in church, at picnics, and at as many towns as possible on Saturday afternoon, to "smile, nod, say hello, and give everybody the glad hand." A candidate's election enemies or long-time enemies try to puncture his reputation wherever they can. The opponents of a Baptist preacher (and good farmer) attacked his sect affiliation among members of other churches and his "fanaticism" among the non-religious. In neighborhoods distant from his own they told what a "poor farmer" he was. They attacked the morals of his married children now living elsewhere. To Baptists they said, "A good preacher should preach, but not get mixed up in politics, 'cause politics will ruin him and all the good he can do, *both.*" To all voters they mentioned his lack of need for the job. Opponents of a rival candidate attacked him as a careless debtor and "one of the worst and *laziest* farmers in this country." They revived or invented, and scattered widely, the following story about him: One spring the "cuckleburrs" got so

---

[9] For an excellent treatment of political techniques in an urban setting, see D. H. Kurzman, *Methods of Controlling Votes in Philadelphia* (Philadelphia, 1935).

big in his corn field that you couldn't see the young corn. A passing neighbor mistook them for flourishing young sweet potato plants, stopped, walked up to the porch where the candidate was rocking when he should have been weeding his corn, and tried to buy some for transplanting.

During the weeks before an election, and especially on election eve and election day itself, male feeling runs extremely high. Most women find this amusing and ridiculous. "Why do the men get so excited over nothin' when they know it's all lies?" Until recently anger frequently broke out into fist fights and sometimes knife fights. Nowadays open quarrels are infrequent. When the elections are over, "most fellers soon forget all about 'em and start speakin' agin just like always," and the politicians whose candidates lose try to figure out, for use next time, "just what went haywire with their schemes."

LAW AND ORDER

The form of government is ostensibly the same as that anywhere else in the United States. No discussion of state and national government is necessary here, further than what has been stated or implied concerning Relief, WPA, and the agricultural program.

The county government includes the usual county officers, a sheriff and his deputy or deputies, the prosecuting attorney, the county clerk, the tax assessor, the recorder of deeds, the rural school superintendent, and a three-member county court. It is interesting that the outside government functionaries with offices at Discovery—the county agent, the FSA executive, and the secretary-director of Social Security—have begun to outrank the local officials in social importance. The duties of the county officers are varied, but have mostly to do with maintaining the formal structure of the property system, with taxation, and with the preservation of law and order. Only the sheriff and the prosecuting attorney have much to do with actual law enforcement or with punishment for crimes or misdemeanors. The sheriff or a deputy sheriff arrests a lawbreaker on sight or formal complaint. Misdemeanors are settled by local officials, who may release, fine, or jail. In criminal cases the accused is jailed or "bailed out," until the next term of circuit court, when the action against him is prosecuted in the name of the state, by the prosecuting attorney. The circuit court is a traveling court, covering seven or eight counties, and with one presiding judge, who sits at Discovery two or three days every six months to hear Woodland County cases. All criminal charges against individuals are tried before him, as well as civil actions between individuals (for example, damage suits, property-partition suits, foreclosures, divorce cases; and condemnation proceedings originating with the state.) The circuit court's time is about evenly divided between criminal and civil cases.

The sheriff "delivers to the court" any defendant against whom criminal charges are made, and the prosecuting attorney theoretically attempts to secure a conviction. The cases with advance docketing that were tried during two recent sessions of the circuit court are listed. A few are duplicates, having been carried over from one session to the next.

Driving while intoxicated	23
Petty or grand larceny	17 [a]
Common assault	8
Burglary	6
Disturbing the peace	6
Reckless driving	4
Driving without a license	3
Selling liquor on Sunday	3
Possession or display of a deadly weapon	3
Forgery	3
Leaving the scene of an accident	2
Violating the compulsory school attendance law	2

One each: rape, maintaining a public nuisance, passing a bogus check, obtaining money under false pretenses, stealing an automobile, creating an affray, assault with intent to kill, failure to provide for wife and children, wife desertion, and malicious killing of a dog

[a] About evenly divided.

Before the days of automobiles the "catch-all" charge for punishing local people of chronically undesirable conduct was "disturbing the peace." When youths and men of the "rougher element" came to town on Saturday night or to picnics they were watched until they got drunk and started to "holler or fight." Then they were thrown into jail and fined. Nowadays they are arrested when they start up their cars. Convictions for "driving when intoxicated" are easy to obtain and punishments are severe. Many "foreigners" speeding through the county have been flagged down and arrested; those with "any smell of liquor on their breaths" receive extremely severe punishments.

An even greater number of cases reaching court concern stealing—petty larceny, grand larceny, burglary. Whatever the charge, most of the stealing is petty thievery: chicken stealing from hen houses, stealing meat from cellar or smoke house, stealing corn or other grain from barns. Sometimes canned stuff is stolen. Livestock is rarely stolen. Mail-order packages are occasionally stolen from mailboxes, which are often a quarter or half mile from the house.

Much more stealing occurs than ever reaches the court dockets but much more stealing is "imagined" than really occurs: (1) The elderly widow who continues to run her late husband's Notions Store in Plainville hears footsteps outside her house at night; the neighbor's dog barks loudly, then stops suddenly as he "recognizes somebody"; she misses arm loads of wood off her woodpile "nearly every morning." "I know who it is, but I wouldn't want to disgrace his family by naming him." (2) A man kept missing corn out of his crib. So he had one of the children bring home a piece of chalk from school. He leveled the corn down "flat," and then "drawed a chalk-mark round the crib," level with the corn. "You know I never *could* see where that corn went down any, but I kept right on missin' it." (3) A farm woman said of her nearest neighbors, "Their children stole some of our turkey eggs and tried to poison our young turkeys. They watched our traps to get the rabbits out first. They took water out of our pond at night and even stole our apple customers."

One type of stealing is interesting in that it is at least partially approved. "A boy that ain't never stole watermelons out of a patch, to *eat,* or apples off a tree, ain't much of a boy."

Twenty years ago, circuit court sessions each lasted for a week or two. People filled the town and camped outside it in their wagons. "It was just like a big picnic or a camp meeting." Today's shorter sessions reflect perhaps a slight change in entertainment patterns, but they more importantly reflect both fewer and shorter "court trials." Less violence occurs now in the county, where violence was rife until lately. No murder (except the unsolved ax-killing of a socially unimportant hermit) has occurred for nearly ten years: yet fifteen or twenty men were slain within the memory of living men. Fist fights are becoming few, and "cuttings" almost unknown, though most grown men remember when "you couldn't vote or go to a picnic or sometimes even wind up a meetin' (revival) without somebody gittin' into a scrap and maybe git cut half to pieces." Few "land disputes" occur now, because boundaries and landrights are well established, and livestock have been fenced up [10] for a long time. Likewise the compounding of cases out of court and their partial "compounding" [11] in connection with formal legal procedure has lessened the number of cases brought to court and shortened the time which each requires for settlement.

These trends are well illustrated by a court case (in 1939) already mentioned as an "assault with intent to kill." Hobart Proudy shot his distant cousin, Mort Proudy, "in the seat of his britches" with a double-barreled shotgun. "He give him both barrels." The occasion of the shooting was this: Hobart's only convenient access to the public road was by a lane through

10 The "fence laws" split the community into two angry factions: the "crop people," who wanted fence laws, and the "stock people," who wanted free range.

11 The word "compounding" as used in this book must be understood in a sense different from its American legal sense. The word here means "settlement by agreement."

Mort's timber. Trouble had long been brewing between the two men, and Mort suddenly forbade use of this lane, to which Hobart claimed a "right of way" as his nearest route to a regular road. This matter might have been settled by a civil action in Circuit Court, but it was not. On a Sunday when Hobart had invited many kin to a family reunion and big dinner to honor his aged mother on her birthday, he discovered that Mort was cutting and piling brush in the wood-lane to prevent passage. Taking his shotgun, he walked into the woods where Mort was working and ordered him to remove all the brush from the lane. Mort started to run for cover instead, and Hobart pulled the two triggers.

In the old days both men would have been armed since both were Proudys and "high-blooded," and "were expecting trouble." [12] One of them would likely have been killed. Indeed it was offered as court evidence that Hobart could hardly have "intended to kill" Mort or he would have killed him—since Hobart "won't shoot a squirrel down out of a tree, anywhere except in the eye."

The most interesting aspect of the case, however, lies in the "compounding" which led to its disposal in court. The prosecuting attorney, William Siler, represented the state on charges filed by Mort, while Hobart's defense was handled by a Discovery lawyer named Jim Morningstar, who later explained the arrangements that had been made. Siler and Morningstar agreed before the trial that Hobart ought to get "a bad scare" but not actually be imprisoned for his crime. Presumably neither Mort nor Hobart was a full party to this agreement, which would represent much less punishment than Mort wanted to see his enemy receive. Siler was to "talk to" the circuit judge ahead of the trial and arrange for a suspended

[12] In the earlier days, however, a Proudy would have been expecting trouble with, and armed against, the Hixes, rather than another Proudy. Half a dozen killings occurred about 1900 between the Proudy and Hix families in a long feud originating in "woman trouble" (and before that in a dispute about land settlement). The dispute finally quieted down (but not without leaving scars that still break open in the community) after the killings, short penitentiary sentences served by some of the Hix men, and the emigration of several others of the generation which "felt the worst blood."

sentence in return for a "plea of guilty" by Hobart. At the trial Hobart quietly pleaded guilty, and Morningstar offered no defense except a general plea for leniency. Mort, however, vigorously expressed his hope that the judge would remove "so bad a neighbor" from the community, and Siler requested a conviction. The Judge sentenced Hobart to two years at hard labor in the penitentiary.

Both Hobart and Morningstar were stunned by this decision and as soon as court was adjourned Morningstar began looking for the prosecuting attorney to ask why the agreement had not been carried out. After a sleepless night, Morningstar found Siler early in the morning. Siler explained that he had not spoken to the judge as he had promised because his conscience had hurt him about their agreement. He promised to do so if possible yet, however, and he did. To Mort's great dissatisfaction the judge permitted a rehearing of the case on the second day of court. He now suspended the sentence, put Hobart on strict parole, and directed him not to go hunting or shooting for at least two years. He also advised him to "stay out of the timber" entirely for the period of his parole. Most people approved the suspended sentence, but were rather amused at the "ignorance" of the judge's advice, since Hobart *"lives* in the timber" and lives a good deal off wild game.[13]

Perhaps the majority of cases are compounded, either partially or fully, before their legal settlement in court. Some are initiated by legal mechanism and then "settled out of court." A few are played out with full panoply (and expense) of rival

[13] The next development in Hobart's life may be of interest. About two months after the trial, Hobart found his fine young mare dead in the pasture. She had been shot. At first he suspected Mort of killing her for revenge. He later decided, however, that a neighboring brother-in-law, who likes neither Hobart nor Mort, had probably killed her. The motive, as explained by Hobart to a grocer (and old neighbor), to whom he went for advice, was as follows: The brother-in-law figured that if he killed the mare, Hobart would think Mort killed her and would kill Mort. The "law" would then "hang" Hobart (already under suspended sentence) or at least send him up for life. Thus the brother-in-law would be "shut of" both enemies. Hobart decided to fall into no such trap. The "horse murder" had not been solved in 1941, nor had any further open trouble broken out between Hobart and either of the other men. People said however, "That trouble ain't ended yet. That Mort and Hobart are tellin' their *boys* all about it, and they'll finally shoot it out."

teams of attorneys, changes of venue, and appeals. Such a case, which scandalized the community of Plainville with its obscenity and rocked it with old and new divisions and hatreds, began its court history early in 1939, and had not been settled two years later. This was a suit by a Plainville garage keeper against the undertaker, for large damages for an alleged adulterous relationship between the undertaker and the garage keeper's wife. People lined up about evenly in sympathy for the two contestants, and the atmosphere was electric with spiteful talk for many months, though most people said, "Nobody will make any money out of that trial and it may break both men up." The testimony was said to be so spicy that "several old women that hadn't been out of Plainville for years went down to the courtroom in Discovery and set there for two days so's not to miss a word." The most suggestive disclosures were those of a Plainville odd-jobber, whom the garage owner hired to bore two augur holes at eye's height in the garage-office walls in order to spy upon the owner's wife and the undertaker. About one important "sex scandal" reaches the courtroom during each generation. In fact, only two other current sex scandals involving "respectable people" were even gossiped about during a year in Plainville. The wife of a teacher contrasted Plainville in this regard with another small town she had lived in somewhat further south. "A good scandal broke out down there every week. The people here are either a lot better or a lot smarter."

One gets the feeling regarding court cases and "outside law" in general that "the law" is dreaded and even hated. Game laws, for instance, are hated intensely by many, and observed rigidly by few. Almost no one considers it wrong to "noodle" female catfish out of the river during spawning season, so long as the fish are eaten. Noodling is illegal. Quail and migrating ducks are shot without license and out of season. Many think game laws are "city laws" set up to preserve game for city sportsmen against use by its rightful owners, the country people. Few people now condemn the laws dealing with murder, but a generation ago many upheld "feud law." A retired preacher recounted tales of a dozen murders that had occurred within his memory. He and many other people knew the motives and details of each murder, but when officers came into the community to investigate, practically everybody questioned withheld all important information. Part of this unwillingness to cooperate came from fear of reprisals by kinsmen of the guilty, but part of it came from the feeling that men should be allowed to settle disputes in their own way. Some cases finally reached trial, but few men were convicted, and no convicted man spent over four years in the penitentiary. If a murder occurred today, people would still try to avoid telling what they knew about it. The completely sacred laws, in the sense that everybody believes in them as right, are the laws dealing with property, inheritance, and marriage.

Lawsuits are avoided as expensive and they are in no wise considered a safe or sure way to justice. "The people with the most money win the cases. . . . Only the lawyers make anything out of the law. . . . I don't think much of a man that hollers 'law.' " These and other criticisms are frequent. The law seems to be used more often as a threat than a reality, except for its minor but frequent punitive use against local "bad characters," in actions against drunken drivers, peace disturbers, petty larceners, and so forth. As a threat "the law's always there," and under it can be initiated the traditional procedures for settling trouble and punishing violators of the mores.

Most petty offenses are settled out of court, or are controlled before their occurrence. Henry Tally caught a neighbor and his boy stealing roasting ears out of his cornfield. They had gathered about two bushels. Henry, instead of "hollering law," made the thief promise to return later the equivalent of the gathered corn, ear for ear, out of ripe corn. A group of high school boys living on farms started raiding the chicken houses of their parents; they sold the chickens for spending money. A country storekeeper who bought some of the poultry became suspicious and reported his suspicions to a father, who accused his son of the theft. The boy confessed and implicated other boys. The boys were disciplined in various ways by their parents, who also for several reasons carefully hushed up the whole matter. They wanted to avoid the "family shame" which would result from gossip. They also feared the scandal of court action in case some enterprising and greedy neighbor might attempt to gain the $25 reward which he could collect (in case of conviction) by reporting the thefts to the Detective Protection Bureau of the *Farmer's Weekly*. Nearly every father subscribed to that newspaper and had its metal "protection signs" posted prominently at the entry to his farm. At least one of the fathers considered the whole matter as a lesson to himself, for "not knowin' that a boy has to spend somethin'."

LOAFING AND GOSSIP GROUPS

The main function of "law" in Plainville (and Woodland County) is to regularize the ownership, lending, transfer, and inheritance of important property. The role of actual legal organization among all other mechanisms which force Plainvillers to conform to their society's established patterns of behavior is really very slight. More important mechanisms, both preventive and punitive, for social control are gossip, ridicule, and in the widest sense of the term folklore. These function "individually," of course, but they also function "by groups," and it is necessary to describe the organizations which I shall call "loafing groups" and "gossip cells."

Every Plainville group, no matter what its primary function, is of course partly a gossip and loafing group too. The members of a church loaf and gossip together at the church door or around the stove, before and after church. A harvest gang is also a center of news dissemination, enjoyable discourse, and social criticism. The long hours that merchants spend in their stores are not like long hours in an office or at a factory assembly line, because the "assembly line" here is of intimates who gather to sit, spit,[14] smoke, chew, chat, and whittle together. Actual "business," except for Saturday afternoons, when most merchants do about half their total weekly business, and a few other "big days," takes really very little of a merchant's time.[15]

Each loafing group, while not rigidly organized, involves a central nucleus of membership, some communion of interest, and frequently an informal meeting place. The most visible loafing group in Plainville is that of the old men who "put in their time" at loafing. They are called the "Old Men," the "Club," the "Story Tellers," the "real loafers here," or sometimes the "Spit and Whittle (or Argue) Club." These names used by others (and sometimes in imitation by themselves) are arranged in descending order of respect, and suggest the pastimes (loafing and talking) and the social functionlessness of the old men. Their nucleus is about half a dozen men ranging in age from their late sixties to early eighties. The main "members" are three retired and respected farmers, an old-time "timber man" (wood chopper), an aged illiterate who is celebrated throughout the county for superstitions and malapropisms,[16] a drunken blacksmith, and a "lifetime loafer"—

14 Spitting is a notable male gesture in Plainville. Few males, standing, sitting, or squatting on their heels together for conversation anywhere outdoors or in a store, and whether or not they chew tobacco (a waning habit like whittling), fail to spit several times a minute. Boys take up this gesture young.

15 Hence his long hours (often from 7 A. M. to 10 P.M.) are more pleasurable than tiresome. In fact, the great distinctive characteristics of rural work, contrasted with most urban work, are these: (1) the great variety in rural tasks; (2) the individual control of speed with which they are performed; (3) the freedom of the worker's mind from "racket" (noise). overseers, and the tedium of strict, enforced, unsociable cooperation with other workers. Rural group work is, of course, highly social, but most rural work is done alone, or with a child "follering" (looking on). The solitary worker's mind is free to roam, dream, scheme. (4) The immediate, personally understood, and simple relationships between work and livelihood.

These characteristics of rural work apply particularly to farmers, but they also apply to small-town businessmen. It is perhaps significant that while many Plainvillers were heard to complain of distasteful individual *tasks*, of having to work "too hard," and of poor rewards for their work, no adult was heard to express general distaste for his work.

16 It was of him that a teacher said, "I'd rather see him in the White House than any Democrat." He typifies "ignorance" for the entire community. He believes in ghosts and many other "superstitions." He sometimes "pretends to

all leveled socially into the companionship of age. One of the retired farmers is the best carpenter in town, and he still works a few days from time to time when the job interests him or he likes the man who offers it. Another is Plainville's notary public; he charges 15¢ for each service. The former wood-chopper, who is harelipped, partially tongue-tied, and very full of conversation, and the illiterate both raise large gardens —the latter's is a model of expert gardening—but otherwise do nothing but draw their "pensions." The blacksmith still "makes his whisky money every morning, and drinks it every evening (afternoon)." The loafer merits special description, because, as one Plainviller phrased it, "Uncle Ab absolutely never done a day's work. He's an institution here. If it wasn't for him we wouldn't have a *real* loafer." The honorific "Uncle" is applied to him ironically and with a kind of perverse respect. Ab's wife supported him by "taking in washing" and hiring out for housework at ten to fifteen cents an hour, until he became eligible for Old Age Assistance. He enjoys the fact that opposition failed to prevent his acceptance for "the pension." "They tried to keep me from gittin' my pension, but I draw it just like anybody else." These men are sometimes called the "charter members" of the club.

The club "sits" throughout most of the long summer on two iron benches under a shade tree in one corner of the square. In bad weather and in winter they move into stores; only two or three stores lack benches or chairs where people may sit. The club is joined fleetingly or for several hours at a time by other men of equal and lesser ages, even by lounging youths and boys, all of whom listen and all of whom—except the boys, who speak rarely—contribute to the conversation. Here daily the society of forty and fifty years ago is reconstructed, as they remember it, and the frontier society of their fathers, as these oldsters heard it described when they were children. The old times are lived over, and lamented (and pitied, for the "ig-

---

read" the newspaper, but holds it upside down. His most famous malapropisms are (1) "—a hypodermic of measles;" (2) "I'm gonna put a *condition* (addition) on my house if I have to *crucify* (sacrifice) a cow."

norance of them days, and the way people had to git along"). Genealogies are recounted ("jist to git things straight—to show how people are all connected up—to show why people done the things they done.") The tragic and comic events of the past—especially "killings" and practical jokes—are relived. Gossip and scandal concerning people already dead are remembered and revived. Work tasks are performed again, and the personal strength and self-sufficiency of earlier days boasted of. "Under the tree is where they grow all the big corn, and chop all of the wood, and pull the horses (that is, haul the heavy wagonloads)." And "stories" are retold as they used to be told. "Stories" are generally tall tales about impossible events. Their characters are real people, however, who still live or once lived in the community.

The present also interests the Old Men, who are far from being the intolerant and meddlesome critics old men generally (and locally) are assumed to be. Only one or two (and they are not among the "charter members") are "as sharp-tongued as women"; they are "carping" and meddlesome "busybodies," but most of the "damage" they do is through their wives, not through their loafing club of old men. The rest, while certainly not themselves "reformers" and often ridiculing the efforts and "mistakes" of reformers,[17] have seen too many changes in technology, morals, and taste, and are perhaps too well aware of their own social uselessness, to exert a very active influence in community affairs. The iron benches control a view of the street and everyone who enters it from any direction. The Old Men daily gather up all the threads of current events and gossip. They talk it all over, tie it up with the past, and "bring it all up to date." They laugh, satirize, complain, approve and disapprove. But their attitudes are more tolerant than is assumed by the women and girls who on each trip down the street have to pass by the Old Men, endure their scrutiny, and "wonder what they're saying now." The Old Men are

17 For example, the county agent and the vocational agriculture teacher. (Preachers are not thought of as reformers.)

more tolerant than intolerant. Their chief function is to entertain themselves and other males. No woman approaches nearer this group than the town pump, about twenty feet away from the iron benches.

Across the street from the Old Men, and viewing them from concealment behind the glass windows of the Notions Store, sit several old women. These are the "Old Women," [18] the "Widows" (not all are widows, and not all the widows gather here), the "Gossips," the "Old Gossips," the "Busybodies," the "Snoops." These terms as applied to them by men and younger women are arranged in order of ascending resentment. Women who loaf in the Notions Store speak of it as a place "where ladies gather." A widow inherited this store from her husband and continues to run it. She is often called "one of the worst old gossips around here." If a man enters the store, the conversation ceases. All eyes regard him. The proprietress asks, "Did you want something?" The purchase finished, the man leaves, or he stands a moment to chat—the chairs in the Notions Store are for women. Such chatting is either "kidding" or news, an exchange of news between the man and the woman, or a solicitation of news from the man: "What were the Old Men talkin' about just now? . . . Are your folks all well? . . . What do the children write? . . . Did you see the accident yesterday? . . . Did you hear the particulars?"

The most frequent kidding with men in this place is a form of sexual byplay: the proprietress says, "I thought you were some old widower, comin' in to make a date to take me to church tonight—anyhow, I've got a date." She then tells of proposals, rejected and heart-broken suitors, and imaginary intrigues and romances, adulterous or otherwise, among the old, but chiefly among the old widows and widowers. She carries on similar kidding by telephone with certain old men,

[18] It need hardly be said that the majority of old women do not gather here. Nor do most of the old men sit frequently "under the tree." Many old people make a point of "stayin' at home," of being "busy at something useful," and especially of not being seen frequently in these groups of the old.

including frequent impersonations of other women, as a form of practical joking. It is as if the taboo system which prohibits free sexual conversation and relationships is relaxed among people considered too old for real sexual interests.

Other women say (and men believe) that the Notions Store is a clearinghouse for exchanging and garbling all news, especially scandal and any other gossip discreditable to individual reputations. Here adult men are condemned for "not working hard enough" or for "neglecting their families"; youths, for "wild oats," real or fancied; women, for extravagance, ostentation or poor taste in dress, moral missteps, and delinquency in the management of children, kitchens, or gardens; young girls, for the clothes they wear, the company they keep, the certain bad ends they are coming to if they don't "show a change"; children, for idleness at home and school, bad manners, disrespect to their elders.

The gossip of these women is often laughed at but it is also dreaded and hated. They are said to "fight every progressive thing in this community." [19] "They are against schools . . . against good clothes . . . against being the least bit modern . . . against anybody having a good time." Their attitudes "show why young people want to leave here." "They're too old to enjoy anything themselves and they don't want anybody else to." Such comments are frequent from young people (of the "sparking age"), from married adults of various ages, and even from the Old Men. A young married woman who runs a restaurant near the Notions Store said, "They pretend to be *for* you; they talk nice and seem to approve everything people do, but you know that the minute your back is turned they start tearin' you to pieces!" They do, indeed, I think, connive against more modern (and functional) education, against the agricultural program, against free and open youthful enjoyments, and against most progressive attitudes. They are a chorus of restraining voices

[19] As many people also say of the churches, and as church people often say of "the people who don't respect the law." And as people "who don't have anything" sometimes say of those who do ("they are too stingy to spend it"). Everybody is *for* "progress."

against change. Their techniques are the same "grapevine" techniques that politicians use.

Other "gossip cells" are equally well known, but they are groups of only two or three women who "work together." The headquarters for one is a porch on the west side of the square. This particular gossip cell is better known for its malignity than for any harm it actually does. Its "leader," the owner of the porch, is an old woman with poor eyes and an inaccurate memory. She mistakes people and their actions as she watches the street from across the square. Men passing her porch who find her alone often pause to tell her "whoppers," which she transforms and retells, to the frequent discomfiture of the gullible who pass her stories on, and to the delight of her tormentors. "If Old Miz —— tells it, then you know it ain't true." Two other women are considered very evil gossips although they rarely visit or talk with anyone but each other; people who walk or drive past the house of either say that "their faces are always stickin' out through the windows and the doors." Another pair of women "canvass the town daily for news, and then they both have to visit every house again to spread what the other one found out." Several of the "Old Women" also canvass the town, that is, "visit people," with great regularity. The role of old women as gossips is partly mythical, but they do collect and scatter a good deal of news. One reason for the great resentment against them may be that they are so numerous in the town. Twenty-one of its residents are widows (there are only three widowers), and many other householders are old. It would take a whole book to describe all the ways in which old women (or any other group) exert social control. One Plainville man stated that two elderly women (sisters-in-law), who board teachers and who visit the Notions Store daily, "run the whole school and keep every modern idea out of it." Certainly through the dread and fear of them which exists, old women exert a great restraining influence against deviation from stricter and older moral patterns. One man said, "They drive sin into the timber." It seems rather curious to find, in a society in which all people say that "a man's best friend is his mother," little respect or even tolerance felt toward any old woman except one's own mother and, by extension, one's own grandmother.

An important and highly visible clique, with a strictly defined membership, is a group of young married women living in or very near Plainville. The influence of this group on the community is very great. They call themselves "Our Set," or "The Girls," or "The Young Ladies," or "The Younger Women." Others call them the "Young Married Women (Ladies)" or the "Leaders," or the "Would-be Leaders," or the "Style-Setters around Here." One man called them "Our 400 —only they ain't but a dozen of 'em." They are an "exclusive" clique—they "dress nice," "fix their hair pretty," "run around lots," and "like to be up to date." They are not the women who behave in the most "modern" fashion, however. Another "young set," of four married couples, whose women dress equally well, are more modern. They drink cocktails together, and sometimes even get drunk and gamble at the parties they hold. They are a "wild set" and are condemned, though one of their women is also on the fringe of the "Leaders." She is sometimes "invited when somebody that was invited can't come and you need an extra person." The Leaders however are not in close relationship with the wild set. They and other young women who are not quite eligible to be themselves considered leaders belong to the much larger Plainville Women's Club which is called the Boosters Club. Thus the Leaders are, beyond their own doings (exchange of luncheons, going shopping together to larger towns, and so forth), in close contact with other women in the community, including those guardians of tradition, the older women. The Young Ladies "try to be leaders" in all progressive matters. They also attempt to live and set a scale of living like that in larger centers. Yet they try to avoid criticism on all grounds, including that of too great modernity. Though most of the husbands of these women stand high in the community, they participate in almost none of the social activities of their wives. Men, in general, do not like "parties."

Scores of adult cliques exist, of course, other than those described. Families, both immediate and extended, groups of neighbors, the work gangs, several groups of men who "follow the hounds" at night, one group of gamblers at dice, poker, and blackjack, the congregations of each little rural church and of the four churches in Plainville—all these are cliques, functioning socially both for entertainment and toward social control and social action. Through all this multiplicity of social grouping a great variety of purposes and aims—even disparate social aims—operate. Forces are under way, with clique leadership and backing, to maintain without change the old mores—morally, technologically, and so forth. Others attempt to lead, persuade, bribe, cajole, betray, or compel people to abandon old attitudes, scorn old ways, "practice scientific agriculture," "be up to date," "become like city people."

SEX AND AGE GROUPS

In Plainville, as in all human societies, the most fundamental social division is into the two sexes, male and female. Almost from birth the infant begins to receive differential treatment in accordance with supposed inherent sexual differences in personality. Within at most a year or two, the individual is expected to demonstrate the personality traits that are attributed to its own sex. At "the walking age," throughout childhood and youth, in the time of full maturity and adult life, and during the period of old age and decline, Plainville males and females enjoy privileges and are bound by duties, interests, and viewpoints that are theirs by sex alone—or more accurately stated, by sex and the age-status to which at any given time they have attained. Effort will be made in a later chapter to explain how family and community connive in the task of creating the personalities considered suitably male and female.

Yet Plainvillers group themselves by age alone, regardless of sex. The age categories for younger members of the society are especially numerous because childhood is the period of growth and of both formal and informal education. A listing of these categories follows, in frequently used local terms.

"Babies" ("babes," "infants") are ordinarily infants in arms. By extension the term also frequently applies to toddlers; also to any child of preschool age. Also, in pity, or in forgiveness for a misdeed, to later childhood, or even to middle or late youth. "She married when she was only a baby (perhaps she was sixteen) . . . How can you expect him not to destroy things, when he's only a baby? (He is eleven, and breaks more cultivator pins at plowing than his father does.)" Again, the term "baby" may be used as a severe disciplinary "insult" by a parent who wishes with finality to put an "upstart youngster" in its place: "Let a baby drive a car? You can drive it as soon as you quit wearin' didies (diapers)!" (The victim may be a sixteen-year-old son who wants the car for a date.) An "infant in the eyes of the law" is any boy under twenty-one or any girl under eighteen.

Children ("kids," "young-uns," "little ones," etc.): these terms connote, by one usage, all offspring of whatever age. ("My young-uns is all grown up and got kids of their own and some of *them's* got children."). They mean ordinarily, however, any children big enough to run about and play informally outdoors with other children and not "too big to be ashamed just to play." Children leave off most informal outdoor play shortly after adolescence. After that, girls begin to "talk" more than they play, and boys confine most of their "play" to formal games like baseball. Hunting, swimming, and certain other boys' recreations are not called "play." "Children," in the ordinary sense, are sub-categorized into "small children," including "tots," "toddlers," or "little bitty (teeny) children" and "large children." Children are also categorized as "school children" (and by extension "high school children"), "kids big enough to help (or work)," etc. Another way in which natives "describe" children is according to school grade or high school class; this is an extension of an earlier method of telling what "reader" (Primer to Fifth or Sixth Reader) a child was "in." Children themselves, though in some activities they "play in herds," in other activities grade themselves very narrowly by age or size to the exclusion of other children.

There is a significant gap in clear local terminology for the age just after adolescence before full growth and maturity have been attained. The word "children" is felt to be inadequate or at least vaguely pejorative ("they don't like it") for young-sters at this stage, yet they are still too young to be included clearly among the "young people." The latter term means primarily the marriageable but still unmarried people, and secondarily the young married people—particularly those still without offspring. This gap in terminology doubtless re-flects several historical and social factors, for example: (1) the historically recent retarding of the approved age for marriage; (2) "high school education," which keeps half the youngsters in a subordinate role later than the age at which many of their parents and grandparents "married and settled down"; (3) the partially recognized anomaly of being sexually old enough for adult work and parenthood without having the social and economic privileges of adults; and (4) the fact that intense discriminations based on age or size, or both, are felt and practiced by all members of this group. In these dis-criminations envy is directed toward others a year older or "a size bigger;" contempt is often felt toward inferiors in age and size.

The gap is bridged partly by the loosely restrictive word "youngsters" (which insults nobody from age two to age twenty and flatters people in their early twenties), partly by extending the sense of the phrase "young people" somewhat downward in time, and partly by adding modifiers to the word "children," for instance, "older children," "great big children," "children nearly grown," "high school children" or "high school age children," "children nearly big enough to start sparkin' (courting)." Boys of this age are sometimes called "lads," though the word "lass" is seldom applied to girls. The noun "adolescent" is lacking in local phraseology. The word "youth," meaning "a young man," is also lacking. The age under discussion is sometimes called the "shy age," or the "timid age," or the "age of greatest embarrassment."

Those whom the community calls primarily the "young people" are "at the sparkin' age." Boys of this age are also likely to be at the "wild oats stage," though "nice girls" are not privileged to "sow any wild oats." This is the age of "good times," "dates," and "courtship." It is the age when people "used to have parties and enjoy 'em," before automobiles, motion pictures, and religious sanctions ended parties and dances. Nowadays it is the age when girls "like to read love stories and see them fool movies," and boys "like to see just how *fer* and how *fast* they can drive." It is also the age when it becomes "quite a problem" for parents to provide spending money for boys. Both "children" and "grown people" are on the whole strictly excluded from the recreational association of young people, though slightly younger brothers and sisters, and mothers, often receive reports from a family member in this group. These reports cover "who all was there and what everybody said and did," and are considered very interesting. For younger members in the family they serve as a spur toward growing up, and to parents they provide a check by which to judge and control, or attempt to control, the conduct and morals of dating youth.

At marriage, people become "married people," though this phrase includes in primary connotation neither the "young married people" whose functional participation in community life as married adults has not fully begun, nor the "old married couples" whose similar participation has begun to wane. The term "married people" primarily means the heads of families who are "in the prime of life." Their children are in school, and they are interested in maintaining the schools. They go to church and take their children to church, or "they should." They vote and are interested in the outcomes of elections. They work and "manage" as full adults. Were it not for the "strangle hold" which a few old people have on much of the money and land in the county they would "run the community."

"Old people" are those whose children have married and left home, whose physical vigor has begun to decline ("they can't do as much as they used to"), whose "minds are not as active as they used to be," whose "interests" are becoming less alert, whose opinions are no longer received with the respect once given them. They are usually "no longer interested in the schools" except to "try to keep taxes down," but they are "more interested in church than they used to be." They continue to vote "as long as they can get to the polls." Most of their social life is with the old. They are, in order of descending respect, the "old couples," the "old widows and widowers," the "old bachelors" and the "old maids." A term of either kindly pity or respect for the old is to call them "the agèd." A term of either pitying or callous contempt is the term "the old and childish." An "old person" with property, or still able to work and manage, is considered somewhat "younger" than one of the same age who "draws the pension" or who is "failing" physically.

People who pass through life unmarried are "old maids" or "old bachelors" from the age when they cease being "eligibles." In Plainville, as everywhere else, people become old maids or old bachelors later than they used to. Fifty years ago it was not uncommon for a girl to marry at fourteen or sixteen years old, and for a boy to marry at sixteen or eighteen. A girl became an old maid if she failed to marry by twenty, and a boy was an old bachelor at twenty-five or thirty. Girls are now relatively safe from the label "old maid" until they reach thirty; men become old bachelors at thirty or thirty-five. Very few people, however, remain unmarried, and few marry later than at age twenty or twenty-five.

All these categories are bisected (and often further subdivided) and relabeled by sex: there are "girls" and "boys" —and "girl-" and "boy-babies," "little girls" and "little boys" (or "little fellers"), "big girls" and "big boys," "great big" or "half-grown" girls and boys. There are "schoolboys" and "high-school boys" and "schoolgirls" and "high-school girls." Children, with or without sex labels, are also classified as "old enough to mind," "to reason," "to know right from wrong," "to want to help," "to want to own something," "to do a grown-up's (or boy's or girl's or man's or woman's) work." Boys, again, are spoken of as "old enough to do chores," "to want to be with boys," "to want to hunt and fish," "to need a gun," "to 'cuss'," "to want a girl"; and girls as "old enough to want to help their mother," "to stay in the house," "to wash the dishes," "to sew and cook," and to "want a feller (beau)." During the twenty or thirty years when people are full members of the adult society of married people, they are, by sex, "married men" and "married women," "the fathers" and "the mothers," or "the husbands" and "the wives." Later they become the "older married men (or women);" still later, the "old (married) men (or women)," and for a while before death the "(old) widows" or "widowers." The list of such categories could be extended almost indefinitely; if so extended, it would show a greater richness and complexity in the terms referring to males than in those referring to females. This, in turn, would reflect the greater freedom and mobility permitted to males, and the greater "value" placed upon their personalities, their work, and their very lives.

People at different stages of life are apt to look with different eyes upon age and various matters connected with age. My own "telling" can be said to be from the viewpoint of an adult male, "in the prime of life." The actual telling by an adult female would not be much different, though the "emotional charging" of it might be. An "old" person might sometimes consider a forty-year old adult as "young" or "almost young." Old people may refer to young married people as "still children"; they sometimes think of themselves, the old, as particularly "wise" and "respected." "Children" and "young people," however, view age with the greatest variety in "differential attitudes." Children tend to consider all middle-aged people as "old," the very old—for example, their grandparents—they may consider "younger" in many ways than their own parents. A sixteen-year old may think of himself as "grown," of his eighteen-year-old brother as "a real man," and of his fourteen-year-old brother as "a child." The oldest brother may call both younger brothers "children," and treat them as such, while the youngest boy may say and think, "I'm as near grown-up as *they* are." The system may look different to children also in terms of sex. For example, to girls the word "boy" can serve oftener as a satisfactory label under which to group all boys than it serves to a boy himself, whose association with other boys is bound narrowly into a very limited age group. To a boy the word "boys" usually means "boys my age." The situation is exactly reversed when boys and girls, respectively, use the word "girl."

A Plainviller's passage from one stage of life into a later stage is marked by various events, acts, rituals, or ceremonies and by conventionalized sentiments and verbal statements. At his birth there is "rejoicing" by kinsmen and interested neighbors; his mother may receive a pre-birth or post-birth "shower" of useful articles. His first tooth, step, "pants," long pants, chore and work proficiencies, paid job, barber-shop haircut, "whiskers," date, and so forth—all symbolize stages in his development and identify him with an age-group. Most of these are "small events," but emotions about them are felt, stated, and shared. His first day in school is a "high point" to himself and to his mother, who "always cries" when she sends him, dinner bucket in hand, down the road to the schoolhouse. Everybody jokes and brags on a "first year scholar." Annual promotion cards are important instruments of age-grading, but the first great "high point" after starting school is "finishing the eighth grade." Here he gets a diploma. Another high point comes in the following fall, if he enters high school. If he doesn't, he falls into a limbo without progress until he "starts working for himself," or marries. In high school, however, he passes from Freshman to Senior, and finally receives another diploma, an extremely important ritualistic event. Meanwhile, he has probably been "saved" and baptized, at age twelve or fourteen.

Dates, appropriate clothing, permission to use the car, symbolize his passing into the group of young people. Acceptance by limited sectors of his new group may come through "starting to drink" or by proving his "manhood" through sexual intercourse. Marriage is a high ceremonial, symbolized by a license, a certificate, a "shivaree," and much "joking." Later events of great importance in "placing" him are: the births of children, a first child especially; the "first-child-to-leave-home," the "last-child-to-leave home"; the "first signs of old age" (graying hair, baldness, inability to do as much work as formerly, inability to "make his children mind like he used to"); perhaps widowerhood; occasionally "retirement"; and finally, death.

3 Social Structure: The Class System

THE class system of Plainville might well be called a "super-organization," because it provides for every person living there a master pattern for arranging according to relative rank every other individual, and every family, clique, lodge, club, church, and other organization or association in Plainville society. It provides also a set of patterns for expected behavior according to class, and a way of judging all norms and deviations from these norms in individual behavior.

Yet many, if not most, Plainvillers completely deny the existence of class in their community. They are aware that class distinctions exist "outside," and speak of city dwellers as divided rather exactly between two unevenly sized categories of "rich" and "poor" (or an "idle class" and a "working class"), or among three classes which they call the "rich," the "middle class," and the "poor." About Plainville and most of Woodland County they often say with some pride, "This is *one* place where ever'body is equal. You don't find no classes here." In equating themselves loosely with members of the greater society, they identify verbally with the "working class," or with "the poorer people in cities," though they contrast unfavorably the lot of city wage earners, who "work (or slave) for others," with their own "independence" and "freedom," whether as merchants, farm owners, farm tenants, or odd jobbers. Further, their respect for "property" is so intense that they in general disapprove heatedly of unions, strikes, collective bargaining, or any other devices by which city workers organize or act to further their own interests against those of ownership or invested wealth.

According to their individual rank people tend to recognize the local class system for what it is, or are at least more able or willing to verbalize regarding it: "higher ups" speak more clearly and frankly about the system than do their inferiors. Politicians, mortgage entrepreneurs, traders, professional men, and socially ambitious people seem to understand the system better than many other people do, because they have had to study it and use it, in manipulating people to their own advantage. The strongest preventives toward full recognition of class as it exists and operates here are these: (1) the deeply rooted American moral attitude that class distinctions are wrong; (2) a traditional conviction that rigid class distinctions occur only in cities (or in the South, where Negroes constitute an "inferior" class); and (3) the local etiquette governing inter-class relations—no one must be reminded overtly of his "inferiority" ("Everybody here is treated equal").

"People know their place" well enough, however, and in actual daily life few errors are committed against the rules under which people meet, work, transact business, talk sociably, and maintain before inferiors the fiction of living in a classless society.

THE CATEGORIES AND CRITERIA OF CLASS

The Plainville class system, as it appears to the average "better class" adult who "bothers to think about it," is represented in Figure 3, which suggests a diamond-shaped numerical distribution of the population according to class.[1] The labels on the diagram, except the designations "religious" and "non-religious," which are added for convenience in this discussion, are the most frequently repeated terms, among a wealth of synonyms, by which upper-class people classify both themselves and others. The diagram was drawn, and its labels were selected and appended, after listening during fifteen months to hundreds of Plainville people discuss, criticize, ridicule, condemn, and approve their neighbors. I believe that the nearly 300 household units of Plainville and its trade area

[1] I am indebted for this concept to Robert K. Merton's review in *Survey Graphic*, October, 1942, of *The Social Life of a Modern Community*, by W. Lloyd Warner and Paul S. Lunt.

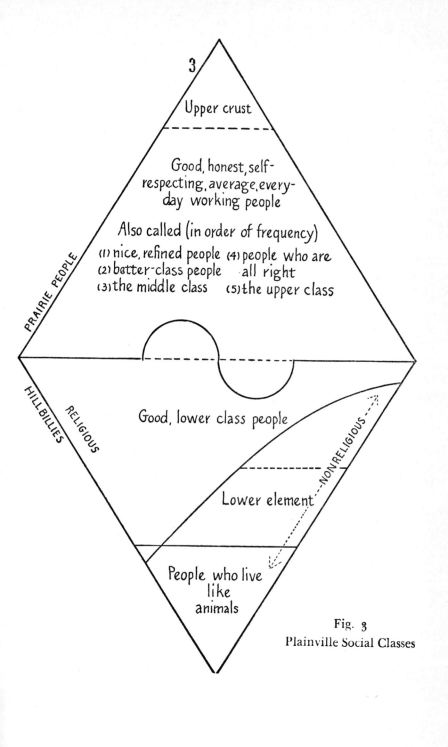

3

Upper crust

Good, honest, self-respecting, average, every-day working people

Also called (in order of frequency)

(1) nice, refined people
(2) better-class people
(3) the middle class
(4) people who are all right
(5) the upper class

PRAIRIE PEOPLE

HILLBILLIES

RELIGIOUS

Good, lower class people

NON-RELIGIOUS

Lower element

People who live like animals

Fig. 3
Plainville Social Classes

could be evenly distributed over the diagram without grave injustice to upper-class opinion regarding the relative rank of each family head.

People do not always agree on just how "high" or "low" an individual deserves to stand within the sector of the society where he "belongs"—no two people control exactly the same facts about an individual, nor do they weight the facts equally —but upper-class people do not disagree in identifying an individual with one of the two main classes. They disagree seldom, if he is "lower class," in locating him definitely in one of its three sub-categories. In fact, people are much more willing to use the word "class" in reference to others whom they consider inferior than in reference to those whom they consider equal or superior to themselves.

To an observer who patiently listens to Plainville gossip, the criteria of discrimination by which Plainvillers judge and rank each other seem at first to be nearly infinite, because every item of human possession and behavior seems to be involved. Due to the society's muting of the concept of class, and also to the peculiar styles followed in local humor and gossip, comments suggesting class ranking are more frequently made by inference and innuendo than by outright statement. Another fact at first confusing to the observer is that few people agree verbally on what traits count most in assigning status to a neighbor. What the Plainviller says he does in judging another is "add ever'thing I know about him up in my head and strike an average." What he usually really accomplishes by this process, however, is not the assignment of class status, but the designation of the "respect" which he feels is due that person *within* the ranks of the class where he "belongs." Respect and class are separate aspects of the prestige system, as will be seen later.

Before examining the criteria of class, let us look briefly at the classes themselves.

The "backbone" of the Plainville community is said to be the "good, honest, self-respecting, average, everyday, working people." Various adjectives from this lengthy label can be applied to people in "respect," without indication of their class status, but when the whole phrase is rolled off the tongue to describe an individual's connections, there is no doubt about his position in the community. He "belongs." The phrases "people who are *all right*," "nice, refined people," "better-class people," "the middle class," and the "upper class (here)" are rarer and more daring designations of members of the upper class.

This upper class includes about half the people in the community. Though its members vary in relative rank, the class does not break up into clear subdivisions. A few families "near the top" are sometimes called, satirically or resentfully, the "upper crust" or the "would-be upper crust," but people who "stand out," or "try to hold their heads up" above what people choose to call the "average level of life around here," are condemned, and no one would admit to upper-crust classification for himself or family. The upper class prides itself on being "plain," "average," and not outstanding. It sets the tone for the society.

The other half of the people belong to the "lower class," and there is no doubt in upper-class minds regarding who these people are. The lower class, however, unlike the upper class, does not present a single uniform "average" front or tone to the world, but is subsected, in upper-class eyes, into three sub-classes. Those members of the lower class whose mores most closely imitate—especially in financial honesty, willingness to work, and personal morals, the main criteria of "respect"—the stated ideals of the upper class, are called "good lower-class people." A somewhat less numerous group, considered deficient in these respect-worthy qualities, is called the "lower element." Still lower is a small group of people who are considered almost sub-human; their behavior is not judged by the conventional standards of "responsible people." They are often called "people who live like the animals." How the society appears to each of these groups will be described in due course.

Let us now examine the criteria by which people actually

fall into their proper ranking by classes. The diamond of Figure 3 is bisected laterally by a line which separates the Prairie people from the Hill people. The line is drawn because the "better class of people" live out on the prairie; the "lower class" live "back in the hills." That is what people say, and the statement is almost exactly true at present. One exception to it lies in the fact that the very best land is the bottoms; the homes of the "rich bottom farmers" can be reached only by traversing the hills. If the bottom farmers "live like prairie people," they are "better-class people"; if they "live like hill people," they are not. The two curves in the central line, however, refer mainly not to the bottom farmers, who are very few, but to certain hill-farm families who are "better people," and to people actually dwelling on the prairie who are not. The former, again, "live like prairie people," the latter, "like hill people," and both rank accordingly. The most visible and obvious criterion of class status, therefore, happens to be geographical.

The second criterion relates to the first, and can be called "technology." The prairie land is better than hill land. It is less rocky, and in all ways is better suited for tillage by modern farming practices. Those who farm it imitate the technological patterns of Midwestern agriculture. The bulk of the modern machinery, whether powered by teams or motors, is on the prairie farms. Prairie fields are larger than hill fields and a greater variety and acreage of crops are grown on the prairie than are grown in the hills. There is a similar difference between the livestock of the two areas: more domestic animals and more kinds of animals are found on the prairie farms; "pure-bred stock" as opposed to "scrub stock" is valued more by prairie farmers than by hill farmers. In the hills "old-style patch farming" has survived better, as has the even older pattern of living from stream and woods—from fishing, hunting, trapping, and gathering, and from woodchopping. The "way a man makes a living" is an important item of social discrimination. The better-class families who actually live in the hills follow farming practices more modern than those followed by their neighbors, and the lower-class people who live on the prairie "scratch out a living" with little regard to the predominant styles of prairie agriculture. No "hunter and trapper" or "patch farmer" or "wood chopper" belongs to the upper class, and no prairie dweller who "farms the way people farm nowadays" is lower class.

A third and very important criterion is lineage. "Good families" (so labeled by any number of synonyms) are contrasted with "poor families," or "low-class," or "lower-element," or "no-account," or "trashy" families. So rigid are the restrictions governing courtship, visiting, worship, and so forth, and so firmly set are the patterns of behavior expected from each member of the society according to "what kind of a family he comes from," that lineage can almost be described at present as an absolute criterion. However, many of the "good prairie families" are connected by various links of kinship with many hill families, and since people have no hesitation in "stating their kin," the present arrangement of families in the class structure must have arisen since 1870–90, when the prairie was brought under cultivation.

A fourth criterion, as might be expected, is "worth" or wealth. Its extremes are, on the one hand, "real wealth" (say, property worth $20,000–$50,000), or more reasonably, "independence" ("They own their own home . . . They are independent . . . They have enough to *do* with"); on the other, "poverty." Degree of wealth again correlates with residence on the prairie or in the hills. The average wealth per prairie family exceeds that of hill families in land value per acre; in size, quality, and appearance of houses and other improvements, including fences; in number and quality of livestock herds and poultry flocks; and in many other items of use and appearance on which discriminatory judgments can be made, such as implements and tools, cars, clothes, furniture, and food. Many people, when asked outright, "What gives a man his rank among his fellows?" will answer, "The only thing that counts in other people's eyes is, how much money has he got?" The facts partially belie such an answer, however, because fully a third of the lower-class people living in the hills are better off financially than the poorer third of the better-class prairie people.

As a fifth criterion, "morals" is given much local lip service. The common moral traits which most people agree in stressing are "honesty" (which primarily means regularity and promptness in the payment of debts), willingness to do hard work, "temperance" (regarding alcohol), and performance of all domestic duties. Traits most commonly condemned as "immoral" are dishonesty, idleness or laziness, family cruelty or neglect, gambling, drunkenness, and, of course, any serious "law breaking." Other, and severer, moral points are also stressed by many. These include church membership, or "salvation," and negatively, complete taboos against drinking beer or spirits, dancing, cardplaying, smoking (especially cigarette smoking, and particularly cigarette smoking by women), other uses of tobacco, swearing, obscene talk, ostentation in dress, and so forth. Regarding these severer norms of moral behavior, there is much difference in opinion and in intensity of opinion. A good many people, including some who do not stress all the severe taboos listed, say and apparently believe that "to live right and do right" is the one critical criterion by which people are and should be judged. Actually, however, no one ever crosses the main class line, from lower class to upper class or vice versa, as the result of moral distinction or moral delinquency alone. Within the upper class, morals are a critical criterion only for approval and "respect," and therefore only for relative rank within the class.

Morals count for more in judging lower-class people. Except for its lowest and smallest group, the lower class is subdivided mainly by the criterion of morality. Most "good lower-class people" past the age of adolescence have been "saved," and the majority of them are members of the Holiness Church. The life of this large group is active, neighborly, and moral, by all the positive traits and taboos that have been given. Though they "strive to better themselves" financially, of course, no other criterion of status is as important as morals in their social judgments of themselves or of others. Upper-class people would include in the list of "good lower-class people" a group of families who are not affiliated with churches but whom they still consider "good citizens," inasmuch as they work hard, pay their bills, and cause no trouble in the community, but who are lower class because of lineage, living in the timber, and old-fashioned ways.

Beneath "good lower-class people" is the "lower element," a group of hill families who range from a reputation for "backwardness" in regard to modern ways, downward to a reputation for outright criminality. Few lower-element people "ever darken a church door." The best of these people "are good enough citizens in a way," though "mighty rough" or "mighty ignorant." The less respected "absolutely won't do a day's work," or "they like to come to town and get drunk and get into fights," or "they get arrested and get into jail" (for fighting, disturbing the peace, drunken driving, etc.). The least respected "run hounds all night in the timber," or they "steal chickens and meat."

The word "morals" is useful in describing the "people who live like the animals" only because they are considered too lowly and too "ignorant" to be accountable either morally or legally for what they do. If a man and a woman of this class choose to live together without marriage, everybody else in the community considers this breach of convention to be comic but not reprehensible. No one would "have the law on" a man of this class for chicken stealing or corn stealing. The owner of the stolen property would instead scold the culprit "like a child," or attempt to frighten him out of further ill-doing, preferably with a practical joke. Favorite jokes of this type are shooting "at" the thief, with no intention of injuring him, or loading a shotgun shell with salt instead of shot, and "letting him have it in his backsides where it'll sting a little and scare him a lot." A few whole families and several individual men are in this class. All are believed to be, and seem to be, somewhat subnormal mentally, though most mental subnormals are classed socially with their immediate families.

The sixth criterion of class is of enormous complexity, because it involves all the other criteria, renders them meaningful, and in a sense supersedes them. At the same time it governs interclass relationships and is critical in matters of class mobility. This criterion is "manners." The number of traits associated with manners is so nearly infinite that no effort can be made to describe them all. All relate in some way to the fundamental division of the society into two main "ways of life": the older, more isolated, and more self-subsistent hill life, and the newer, more up-to-date life on the prairie. To begin with, the thousands of traits connected with prairie versus hill residence, technology, and average wealth should be considered, not only as items of functional use, but in the additional light of "manners." People on the prairie have better and more modern cars, improvements, farming implements, livestock, furniture, clothing, etc., than the hill people have, but such things represent not only the greater productivity, or wealth, of the prairie; they represent also the habits and tastes of prairie people, and their "feelings" of what it is appropriate for their class to possess, use, and display, in their increasing efforts to do things as they are done in better farming regions outside. They represent "manners," in short. For example, tractors are increasing on the prairie, though all the agricultural experts agree that tractors can be profitably used on few Woodland County farms. The frequent purchase of new automobiles by many prairie farmers also puts a great and unnecessary strain on their limited financial resources, carrying them further and further from the real independence of subsistence farming into the web of debt that is here connected with a cash economy. Yet relatively good cars, in contrast with "jalopies," are a part of prairie manners. Certainly many "old-style" backwoods people are in a better financial position than many of their social "betters" to afford material possessions regarding which discriminations are made. People say of them, "They ride in that old big-wagon, drive that jalopy, live in that unpainted hill shack, wear them old clothes, eat the grub they eat, because they *like* it better."

Of lower-class life and manners people also often say, "Them kind of folks live the way they live because they don't *know* any better." "Knowledge" is one of the most important discriminatory traits that appear in local conversation. People say of those they consider "ignorant"—and the upper class considers the lower class to be very ignorant—"They don't know how to live . . . farm . . . take care of their stuff (stock, crops, houses, money) . . . dress . . . cook . . . eat . . . talk . . . talk proper . . . talk to people . . . act . . . act in public (or in front of people) . . . act in town . . . act in church . . . act anywheres outside of the timber." "They don't know what to raise . . . buy . . . feed their children (or stock)." "Half of 'em don't know enough to take a bath over once a year." "They don't know nothin' except houn' dogs, huntin', and fishin'—and runnin' the timber. . . . They don't know nothin' except cornbread and molasses. . . . They don't know nothin' except hoes and axes, and doin' it the *hard way*. . . . They don't know nothin' excep' ignorance!" "Lots of them women and children back in the hills and timber is afraid of strangers. If a stranger goes up to one of them houses, all the dogs start barkin', and then you see the women and children, and the chickens, hogs, and dogs all start runnin' for the brush." Contrarily it is said, "Them's the happiest, cheerfulest people in the world, because they don't want anything more'n they've got."

The lower element is described in similar terms, with phrases of moral reproach added. "They are rough (that is, profane or obscene) . . . their men and boys cuss right in the house. . . . Their women cuss just like men . . . their boys and girls talk the same language and tell the same kind of stories. . . . All they know is just drink, dance, and carouse. . . . Some of them children don't know who their own daddies are. . . . I wouldn't want to live among people as lazy as them: some of 'em would rather steal what they eat than raise it. You'd have to put locks on your house, your smoke-house, and your corncrib if you lived in *their* neighborhood."

As upper-class gossip progresses downward through the personnel of the lower class, the spirit of ridicule increases, and condemnation in general tends to decrease. The people who live like the animals are subjects only for mirth. They "don't hardly know nothin' only just how to get along, if people help 'em a little." Most of them live in cabins or shacks on other people's property "way back in the timber," sub-sisting from meager gardening and hunting, from occasional odd jobs at wood chopping, brush cutting, or field work, and sometimes aided by gifts of home-grown food by neighbors who "keep an eye on them to see that they don't starve." For all its love of malicious gossip and anecdote, the community is "kindly" in seeing that nobody "really goes hungry."

Enough has been said to show the importance of manners as a criterion of social ranking. Manners separate the two main classes much more effectually than any other criteria. Residence on the prairie or in the hills, like lineage or family or wealth (if accompanied by appropriate manners), merely establishes at birth an environment, with an expectancy that the new-born individual will learn specific patterns of be-havior that belong to his class. The children of families that live in the hills are expected to grow up "ignorant" of many things which prairie children know. They are expected to learn a different and "inferior" technology, to be "content with less," to have different "morals"—either the stricter, "fanatical" taboos of lower-class religious people, or the less strict, sometimes "criminal" morality of the lower element. They are all expected to grow up with "backwoodsy" man-ners.

This description of classes has dealt only with Plainville "country people." It would serve with some modification for other farming communities in the county, and with more modifications for other farming communities in adjoining counties. The salient peculiarity for Plainville is its surround-ing prairie, about which a whole cluster of "modern traits" has been localized. The same prairie traits are important for Stanton and for the town "A" in the northeast corner of the county. The "best people" who trade at Discovery (and several other little towns) are the bottom farmers. The "best people" *in* Discovery, however, are the county officers and the federal employees. The best people in Stanton are the town "aristocracy" of merchants, an aristocracy which is sneered at throughout the rest of the county for "trying to hold its head above," and which tends to sneer at the other trading centers as "hillbilly communities."

Plainville "town people" belong to one or another of these classes as their lineage, wealth, income, morals and whole way of life (their "manners") fit them in. The family a man "comes from" (if a local family) counts extremely high in judging "what you can expect from him." ("His *family* lives in the hills . . . on the prairie.") Modernity of life, as indicated by cars, clothes, language, extensive use of electricity, etc., and its opposite largely replace the prairie-hills diagnostics where, as among "newcomers," these are not sustained by active kin ties. Professional people (the doctor, the Christian preacher, the undertaker, the vocational agriculture teacher, and other teachers) stand high. Among many people "respect" for the undertaker diminished greatly when he became involved in a scandalous lawsuit; respect for the doctor diminished among the other half of the people when he "sided against" the undertaker in court—but respect is only one aspect of prestige: no one is declassed for simply losing the moral respect of the community. Owners of the more "modern" business houses rank high, provided they do not sell beer or spirits; other business owners rank according to the conventional criteria. Odd-jobbers rank low, and WPA workers and "reliefers" rank lower; I doubt if over a dozen upper-class people in the county ever accepted relief or WPA jobs, except foremanships, or office or managerial work. Until recent years Plainville, like Stanton, had its little "town aristocracy" of dominant business men—a banking family and several important owners of "general stores"—but with the passing of these families and the decline in small town business this distinction has disappeared. The social difference by which town people *as town people* once outranked country people *as country people* has also disappeared almost completely. ("There ain't no country boys any more.")

DIFFERENTIAL ATTITUDES
TOWARD THE CLASS STRUCTURE [2]

Figure 3 shows how better-class Plainville people rank the members of their community. It is necessary to show how the class system appears to certain other Plainvillers.

To tell how "everybody sees the classes" would, of course require many diagrams, because the tradition of denying class enables individuals to attach more weight to one criterion than to another. For example, the "pure money-grubber" may sometimes view his neighbors as arranged only in a prestige-diamond of hard-won wealth—inherited wealth, it may be said in passing, carries less respect than earned wealth. For women, throughout the community, the class lines are much more sharply drawn than for men, because men cross the lines freely in business dealings, trading, loafing, and all other activities lying outside the "home," while women, confined more sharply to the home, have much less contact across the class lines. For small children there are almost no distinctions. The ideas of how they are expected to "treat children from other families" are only gradually implanted in their minds, through home and other influences. Girls have learned "most of the differences" before adolescence, while it is not important that boys learn them so accurately until they start "going with girls." The techniques for teaching children their "place" and the place of others are very subtle in a society where people seldom say, "We are better," but often say and oftener infer, "They are worse."

2 For an excellent analysis of differential attitudes toward a class system in a Southern community, see Allison Davis, Burleigh B. Gardner, and May B. Gardner, *Deep South*, (University of Chicago, 1941).

The most significant modification of the class diamond appears in Figure 4, which suggests the valuation placed on "salvation" by all the "good religious people." Distribution of the community's families on this diagram would be determined first by pious morality, and second, by some summing up of the criteria of residence, technology, worth, and family. The placing of families would differ considerably according to the church of the informant.

Among the entire Holiness congregation and among most rural Baptists and Methodists, the criterion of morality would be supreme. "It makes no difference what you've got or who you are. The only question is: how do you stand with God?" Only Holiness people, however, have set up an integrated social system of neighborliness, by which they are able to deny wholeheartedly for themselves the standards of the dominant class. They would include all "real believing" church members of any denomination among "good religious people." They would also grant high "worldly" status to a good many upper-class "good citizens—though they don't live right." Thus they are aware that their own main criterion does not agree with the dominant standards of the community, though they live as if it did, and "hope that a day will arrive when all will live godly lives." The "lower element," as they see it, agrees pretty well with the lower element as seen by upper-class people, though they draw the line more sharply, at any given time, between themselves and the lower element than upper-class people draw the line between lower-class religious people and the lower element. As for the "people who live like animals," even the Holiness people, more eager than any others in the community to welcome new members into their fold—regardless of "past sins and past lives," provided that a sinner is properly "converted"—even the Holiness people treat this sharply set-off group as if it has no souls to be saved. Most preachers of any sect, if asked to tell what kinds of people constitute the community, will set up categories similar to those in Figure 4, but the Christian preacher would hardly visit any "lower-element" sick, or "pay his respects" to their

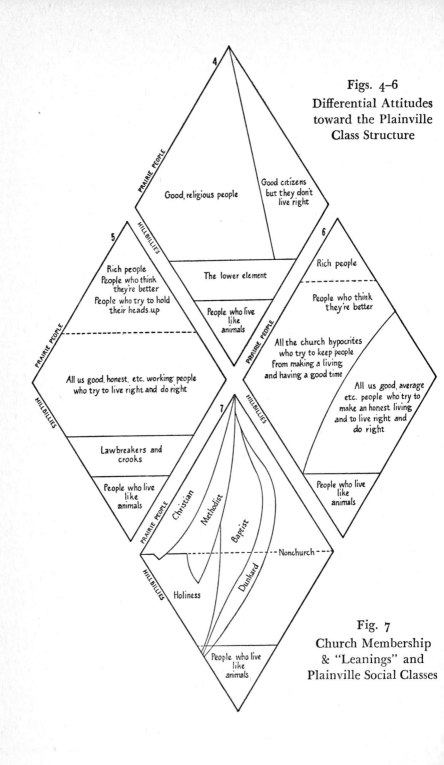

Figs. 4–6
Differential Attitudes
toward the Plainville
Class Structure

Fig. 4
Good, religious people
Good citizens but they don't live right
The lower element
People who live like animals

Fig. 5 PRAIRIE PEOPLE / HILLBILLIES
Rich people
People who think they're better
People who try to hold their heads up
All us good, honest, etc. working people who try to live right and do right
Lawbreakers and crooks
People who live like animals

Fig. 6 PRAIRIE PEOPLE / HILLBILLIES
Rich people
People who think they're better
All the church hypocrites who try to keep people from making a living and having a good time
All us good, average etc. people who try to make an honest living and to live right and do right
People who live like animals

Fig. 7 PRAIRIE PEOPLE / HILLBILLIES
Christian
Methodist
Baptist
Dunkard
Holiness
- - - Nonchurch - - -
People who live like animals

Fig. 7
Church Membership
& "Leanings" and
Plainville Social Classes

dead by attending one of their funerals unless asked to preach it. Then, of course, "he could hardly refuse."

The fact that more ways and more varied ways of ranking members of the community exist among nonreligious lower-class people than in any other sector of the society seemed at first very surprising. The main reason why they do so, however, is their great social isolation, not only from exposure to prairie technology, attitudes, and manners, but from the unifying influence of a church. They are "unorganized" on any community-wide basis, but live "back in the hills" in knots of two or three families (often kinsmen), with whom they do their main "neighboring." The leading symbol of unity of all their kind in the community is "resistance to authority," including particularly "churches" and "law" (especially game laws and the law for compulsory school attendance). Their pattern of life is the "oldest" in the community, in that they have resisted money economy, modern technology, education, and law more than any other group.

Some lower-class people, lacking any religious pressure to see the community in "the Holiness way," describe the class system as it is viewed by the upper class. About their own position in it they may laughingly say, "They call people like *me* 'lower class' around here because I don't break my neck tryin' to make a livin' the way I don't want to . . . They call me 'lower class' because I don't roll an' moan an' make a fool of myself in church."

Others, more resentful of the dominant class, lump together the "main bulk" of the community into "all us good honest average everyday working people who try to live right and do right." Above them are "the rich people," or the "people who *think* they're better," or the "people who try to hold their heads up." Beneath them are the "law-breakers and crooks." ("Of course *every* community's got a few of *them*.") Still further beneath are the people who live like animals (Figure 5). Others, still more resentful, especially of the important role of churches in dictating and criticizing moral conduct, describe the society as it is pictured in Figure 6.

Most striking, among the lower element, is the number of cultural traits which are condemned or ridiculed by the dominant class, and to which this class attaches positive prestige values. All the "hound-dog people" belong to the lower element. No sound is sweeter music to a "hound-lover's" ears than the baying of hounds at night. No sound is uglier to average "better-class" ears. No Holiness people keep and run hounds; hounds are owned without much condemnation by a few upper-class men of impregnable status, but few men between these two extremes will tolerate hounds. Yet a lower-element man skilled at raising, training, and running hounds is highly admired by "his crowd."

Similarly, ability to "live out of the river and timber" is esteemed among the lower element. They place a great positive value upon numerous "pioneer" traits, no longer much respected out on the prairie. These include hunting, trapping, shooting, (a "good shot" is admired by every one, but "a man shouldn't spend his life at it"), "living without much money," and "living without much hard farm work." Knowledge of nature is more respected among this class than any other.

A good many "immoral" traits even have positive value to "more reckless" lower-element people. They respect good dancing and fiddling. Some of them respect "a good fighter." Some respect a "good hard drinker." Some not only respect freedom from the authority of religion, but condemn and ridicule church people. Most of them respect game-law evaders, though this trait is not unique with them. A few must respect the idea of living as much as possible through thievery, because most of the petty thievery is done by this class.

The small group of people who "live like animals" have no very clear picture, or, at best, a very garbled picture of the society about them. One reason why they "understand so little" lies in their real or apparent mental subnormality. Another lies in the fact that through practical joking their "betters" deliberately fictionalize the world for these people, as well as their role in it. For example, at a "wood-sawing" where Lafe Drumm was hired to help, the sport of the entire day was baiting Lafe in a way designed to convince him that he was a man of great talent and social importance. His wife— according to local folklore he had bought her from his brother for "a shotgun and six dollars to boot"—was discussed as "a wonderful woman. Why don't she join the woman's club in this neighborhood and show 'em how to *do* this pressure-cannin' and chicken-raisin'?" Lafe's "timbering" was treated as a "great enterprise." "If you could just git the contract to haul wood to the schoolhouse, you'd be one of the biggest business men in this country." Finally, he was urged to run for office—"if people thought you'd run, you wouldn't have an opponent." Lafe receives such remarks with some suspicion, but he is also flattered and puts some credence in them.

CLIQUES AND ASSOCIATIONS AND CLASS

All the special groups that have been described, whether formal or informal in organization, occupy definite positions in the class system. The only exceptions are the Republican and Democratic parties, but even here important social discriminations are involved. The first is the party to which "most of the good people that have lived all their lives around here" belong. Some very "high" people are Democrats, but Democrats are considered by the majority to be on the whole less dependable, and less desirable citizens, than Republicans. Newcomers who are Democrats are viewed with slightly more suspicion than Republican newcomers; both the county agent and the Plainville vocational agriculture teacher (Democrats) were advised by a local machine Democrat to call themselves Republicans when they were being interviewed for their jobs. Socialists are considered "wild and atheistical" and somewhat outside the class system. The Old Men who loaf on the iron benches are also placed by age and functionlessness into a kind of classless limbo, but each reflects a small light from his former class status.

Plainville's clique of young women "Leaders" is very near the top of the upper class. Some call them the "upper crust."

The Boosters Club includes all the Leaders, plus various older women and other younger women somewhat less "stylish" than the Leaders. The Boosters rank very "high." The only farm women who join the Home Economics clubs are securely of the better class, and the 4-H clubs are composed only of upper-class farm children. For the most part only upper-class men and women meet with the county agent to formulate plans involving agricultural reform. Lower class people would feel "silly" and unwanted if they appeared and spoke their minds at meetings. High school children usually break up into conversational groups and social cliques according to parental class. A boy or girl who can play superior basketball is given a position on the team without class favoritism, and in this activity lower-class youngsters frequently seem for a time to pass as local "heroes" into the upper class, but when high school days are over, and serious courting begins, the former hero is again restricted to his or her "born class." Groups of kin who keep up very close contacts with each other are of a single class. Branches of extended families who are in separate class groups often "keep up appearances" of family loyalty, too, but the lower branch usually allows the superior branch to set the pace and quality of the contact. The upper-class branch "takes things to" the lower branch, and does most of any visiting that is done between the families. Cliques of families who "neighbor" extensively and exchange visits are of the same class. The butchering and threshing gangs are composed of people who rank about equally. No lower-class man or woman is a Mason or an Eastern Star. Almost no lower-class man is an Odd Fellow or a Woodman, though these lodges always ranked somewhat beneath Masonry. Even the churches are arranged in a strict hierarchy of class.

MOBILITY WITHIN THE CLASS SYSTEM

One of the proudest points in the Plainville credo is the point that "Anybody can rise. Any feller can git just about where he wants to be if he's got the grit and determination." The ideal of vertical mobility as practicable for "anybody that'll work" was transmitted to Plainvillers from the days when free land was available for all who wanted it, and when everybody knew of "poor boys who made millions" out of rapidly expanding urban industries. The ideal of upward mobility is still stated as a "dream," but often rather ruefully. As a Plainville man said, "They used to say any boy could be President. A boy's got about the same chance of bein' President nowadays as he's got of bein' Charley McCarthy—or as a girl's got of gittin' to be a movie star." He added, "Still, you find some of 'em thinks they can make it. And their *folks* thinks it's better for 'em to try than to root, hog, or die like they've got to if they want to just git along."

Practically, the two main classes are rigidly exclusive systems into which people are born. Movement across the line separating the upper class from the lower class is virtually impossible, without leaving the community. It is not easy even by way of migration, because local manners, training, viewpoints, and the initial contacts of migrating Plainvillers with the outside world are pretty apt to place them in a first job or social setting from which no very great "rise" is likely.

An upper-class youth who migrates has only a slight advantage in education and manners over a lower-class youth, but he enjoys the advantage of considering himself the equal, or at least potentially the equal, of "anybody anywheres," simply because he is "as good as anybody around here." He may fear that "some people will laugh" at his grammar, table manners, and clothes, but he assumes that if circumstances require he can learn to speak and act "like city people." His main erroneous conception of city life is that there is only one kind of urban prestige—in which "money counts for everything." The myths and facts about city people and city opportunities are so garbled in the heads of Plainville youth that very few of them even "strive" to become anything except wage earners. The few upper-class boys who "succeed," however, usually become "money-makers."

Migration presents somewhat different problems to lower-class youth. Most of them are so well indoctrinated by the time they migrate with the sense of their own social inferiority that the best they "expect or hope for" is "a job with good wages." For a few, however, humiliation regarding their social position at home is intense enough to provide a powerful drive toward success outside. Furthermore, simply because they are "lower class" they are likely to set forth with some inkling of the fact that there are other kinds of urban prestige than "what money will buy"—for example, professional prestige, which can be equated roughly with moral prestige at home, and which can be striven for through "education." Most of Plainville college students come from lower-class families. When they leave home they know they will not only have to "watch" language and table manners, but will "have to learn everything." Their adjustment to city life sometimes amounts "almost to a conversion."

It should be stated here that urban social classes do not equate well with rural social classes.[3] City people tend to class all rural migrants together as "countrified," or as "hicks." However, they suppose some young newcomers from the country to possess admirable rural traits of "honesty" and intelligence or shrewdness which will enable them to "learn quickly" and to "succeed." The rural background of the few who actually do "learn and succeed" often comes later to be highly self-cherished, and honored or even envied by their city-born friends, as a factor in their success.[4] Traits that con-

[3] For an analysis of classes in an urban community, see W. Lloyd Warner and Paul S. Lunt, *The Social Life of a Modern Community*, Yale University Press, 1941. Plainville's "upper class," "good lower class people," and "lower element" can be only very loosely paralleled with Yankeetown's Lower Middle, Upper Lower, and Lower Lower classes, because of many great dissimilarities between urban and rural culture.

[4] When *Main Street* was a popular novel, rural boys in urban colleges "regretted" their rural background, and others "pitied" them for growing up "without opportunities." In the 1930's, Eastern college students from the country and from the Midwest were envied as "true Americans." This shift in attitude came with the great depression and might be described as a metropolitan "nativistic" movement, attempting to recapture "pioneer" and "rural" values and virtues to supplant those lost with the slow-down of urban expansionist economy. At the same time, many rural people were trying to recapture lost "neighborliness" (of frontier days) and lost "godliness," through a wave of religious revivalism.

tribute to the "rise" of some country people who migrate to cities are youth, good looks, charm, tact, intelligence, shrewdness, self-esteem, ambition, quick adaptability, further education—and sometimes resentment of great social rejection during childhood. They feel they "have to succeed so's they can come back here and *show* them ol' boys." Social discrimination and personal maladjustment as factors in rural-urban migration have been less discussed than the factors of overpopulation and land scarcity, but they are equally important.

Many Plainville migrants have been lost to memory, and a handful have lifted themselves to high or relatively high city status, but among people still living, or recently living, in and near Plainville, only three real shifts in class status have occurred. It may be instructive to see how they were accomplished.

The mail carrier, Wilson Bird, rose from "the worst hillbilly stock" to a position of respect, affluence, and full participation in upper-class affairs. He did so through the following main procedures: He came back from the Army after the first World War as a second lieutenant [5] ("one of them three-months wonder boys") and rented a room in the hotel in town, instead of returning to his family. The hotelkeeper "carried him for his room and meals" until Wilson got a job as clerk in a store. Wilson developed a reputation for "honesty and no bad habits," and began to save his money. Later he passed a civil service examination and secured the profitable job as rural mail carrier. Meanwhile, through native intelligence and experience, he had acquired the "manners" of the upper class. He gradually abandoned close contact with his kin, except enough measured attentions to avoid criticism as "hardhearted." As soon as he had saved a considerable sum of money, Wilson married the daughter of a prosperous farmer. They now have three children, all of whom go to high school and to the Christian Sunday School. The family owns two or three farms, and one of the best houses in town. A lower-class kins-

[5] Military organization ignores many traditional social discriminations and sets up new ones. In the present war about as many bars and chevrons have gone to lower-class Plainville boys as to their local superiors.

man tills one of the farms. Wilson's immediate family are distinctly upper class, and Wilson's success in view of his antecedents and living kinsmen is often cited in proof of what "anybody that wants to can do."

Ora Bolles's rise was even more outstanding and is oftener cited, though he did not rise so high. Ora died a few years ago, just after winning election to a county office. He was a son in "one of the biggest and worst and most ignorant families in town." His mother has already been mentioned as an ardent exploiter and hater of the New Deal, and as the widow of a man who committed suicide with an ax. Ora was "bright in high school"; he "worked every chance he got, if it wasn't nothin' more'n cuttin' grass"; he "showed himself to be absolutely reliable"; he was "sociable"; he "kept away from all bad company except his family." When he "got past the grass-cuttin' age," he became a store clerk. With this stable and respected job, he courted and married a "good moral girl" from the upper edge of the lower class. He saved his money, bought a home and started raising a family. He made many friends, and finally he ran for office and won. "People give Ory lots of credit for what he done, and when he needed help they voted for him. He showed what anybody can do that'll just try."

Elmer Simmons accomplished what is even harder—he descended during his lifetime from the upper to the lower class. When his father's prairie farm was sold and the money distributed among his heirs, Elmer moved to a cheap hill tract back in the timber. He quit serious farming and "trying to do something," started "hunting, fishing, and idling," and "took up with the lower element." He married a backwoods girl, and settled into the lower element's pattern of hill life. His children and his prairie brother's children "look alike but you'd never know from the way they act that they was cousins." People expect "laziness," "lack of ambition," and hill manners from his children as they do from any other children born into families of the lower element.

It is more difficult to lower one's class status than to lift it.

because the upper class is varied enough to retain any one who retains its "manners," and because it is apparently almost impossible to lay upper-class manners aside, once they have been acquired. There are people in the upper class who have "lost everybody's respect" (through idleness, dishonesty, drunkenness, or other vices); some have even "disgraced themselves and their families," but they are not considered as having changed class. They may have "gone to the dogs," but their position is reclaimable at any time through "reform." Similarly, there are "good, hard workers . . . honest, reliable people . . . moral people . . . smart people . . . and clever (accommodating) people" in the lower class, but these approved traits do not change their class status, unless they also "learn how to act." A few more people "rise" than "fall" because people are attuned to the ideal of "trying to rise." No one actually "tries to fall."

The case of a fourteen-year-old boy, Roy Summers, illustrates the practical difficulties that accompany attempts to rise in status. During the winter of 1939–40, an unsuccessful effort was made to lift Roy from the lower element into the upper class. An old couple in town named Handy hired Roy to do chores, when Mr. Handy became ill. Roy moved into their home. He was a good worker, and Mrs. Handy grew maternally attached to him. When Mr. Handy recovered, his wife suggested that Roy stay with them permanently, "choring" for his keep, and earning whatever money he could at odd jobs for others. She "learnt him how to eat, talk, take baths, and act in front of people." She decided that he should live with them and "go through high school just like my own sons done." The idea appealed greatly to Roy. The first friction with Mrs. Handy came over the question of Roy's visiting his father and smaller brother. Mrs. Handy wanted him to "treat his folks good," but she objected to his visiting them, because "Roy always comes back here dirty, and I have to start over again with him clear from the beginning." Mrs. Handy frequently commended Roy warmly before people on "how well he was doing" in contrast with how little she could expect from any one "with his family," which was indeed among the worst in local reputation. His mother had deserted husband and children and was said to be a "hotel whore" in Metropolis; a sister was in the "reform school"; an uncle was in the penitentiary; Roy had been living in a hill shack with a younger brother and their "worthless" father. One day, in testimony of Roy's surprisingly excellent character, Mrs. Handy patted his cheek as she said to a guest, "He don't steal!"

Another point of friction arose from Roy's smoking. Mrs. Handy first "broke him" of smoking in his room or around the property; then she ordered him not to smoke anywhere. When she caught him perched on a stool and smoking in the cafe which sold beer, she told him he'd have to decide whether he wanted to "live like nice people live" or "go back to his people." Roy felt injured and went home, disliked "the dirt" there, begged and gained permission to return to the Handy's, but stayed only a short time longer. A sixteen-year-old lad of equally "low origin" invited him to ride in a "jalopy" to Metropolis to "hunt work," and Roy left Mrs. Handy "without even saying good-bye." When the boys came back "broke" two weeks later, Roy went home to his father.

Many people in town had wanted Roy to succeed, and had "encouraged" him with odd jobs at ten cents an hour. During the time he was at Handy's he saved eight dollars toward buying "a suit for school." He *could* have moved up into Mrs. Handy's class, if the strain had been less severe. He was learning most of its "manners" successfully enough, but as one under constant scrutiny, and under the expectation of failure, he could practice none of the "bad boy" traits, like smoking, which are common to boys of all classes. To succeed, he would have had to steer carefully between a Scylla of excessive "morality" and a Charybdis of "sissiness." It would have been easy enough for any adult with full knowledge of the system to plan a campaign for Roy's advance, but the boy was not blessed with enough insights to live carefully through the two or three years during which he would have been "on trial." He "lacked the moral strength."

Status-shifting between the two sectors of the lower class is relatively easy. Even repeated shifts are made between "lower-class religious" status and the "lower element." "Salvation" and its reverse, "backsliding," are the two main devices. The Holiness Church, particularly, provides a mechanism for quick social acceptance by members of its congregation to any one—regardless of family, reputation, or past "sins"—who confesses sins, is saved, and shows by conduct that "his conversion meant business." Indeed, Holiness people will accept a new member quite completely even before he has been able to demonstrate in deeds the fruits of his salvation. They apparently believe that social acceptance in itself may encourage the recently saved to translate salvation into "correct" daily behavior. Many people in all churches view salvation as equally important, though they express more skepticism regarding its validity until proved by honesty and good morals. This skepticism is highest among members of the Christian Church, and is especially directed toward adults who have been saved during revival meetings in the more emotional churches. Ultimately, however, even upper-class people are apt to recognize an individual's shift from the "lower element" to the "good religious lower class." By backsliding, a lower-class person moves from the "good religious lower class" to the "lower element." An upper-class backslider, however, is in the eyes of his class only a backslider. He has lost some respect in the eyes of most of his equals, but he has not been declassed.

4 Religion

THERE are many nonbelievers in Plainville. Perhaps a fourth to a third of the people have been so permeated by rational ideas from the outside world that they no longer believe the received tenets of fundamentalistic Protestant theology, or they at least discredit any literal interpretation of the Bible. More men than women are disbelievers, but there are a good many of both. The total number at first appears to be smaller than it actually is, because people fear social condemnation as "atheists," if they express open doubt or disbelief regarding the existence of heaven and hell, the Bible as a "divinely inspired Book," and the doctrine of eternal salvation through the rebirth of baptism; but when people feel confident that a listener "won't tell," many state their heresies freely. Disbelief takes many forms. One hears outright and hateful condemnation of the churches as instruments of darkness which "rob the people here and keep them in ignorance"; ideas that "the Bible is just a kind of history"; and statements of belief in "*some* kind of a God, but not the kind the preachers talk about." Disbelievers are scattered among both main social classes. Some upper-class nonbelievers belong to the Christian Church, as a matter of policy or testimony of "good citizenship." Such people like to say, "If it wasn't for churches and schools, land here wouldn't be worth ten cents an acre." Lower-class people seem never to be obliged to "belong to the church" as a conscious matter of policy. They are generally either emotionally religious or wholly unreligious. Among the lower element, irreligion "runs in families." It is possible to join the Christian Church, but hardly possible to join the Methodist or Baptist or Holiness church without a preliminary intense emotional upheaval of conversion. In the more emotional churches, the struggle of seeking "salvation" is often very painful indeed.

As Figure 7 (page 130) shows, the churches form a local

social hierarchy. The Christian denomination stands highest, the Methodist next, the Baptist next, and the Church of God Holiness lowest. This is the ranking as it appears to all "Christians" (members of the Christian Church) and to most nonreligious people. Methodists and Baptists sometimes accuse Christians of only "pretentions" to highest rank, and often speak resentfully of their larger church. The ranking by Holiness people would be almost exactly reversed: the vitality of their own faith sets their church highest, even socially, since they deny the validity of "worldly" standards of judgment. They consider worship in the Christian Church as too "cold" to be properly called religion. The same criticism of the Christian Church as cold and worldly is offered by Baptists and Methodists, who poke fun, however, with the rest of the community, at the "ignorant going-ons" of Holiness meetings. Emotional excitement, expressing itself in personal testimony, singing, sermons, shouting, prayer, and the sobbing of mourners struggling for salvation at the mourner's bench, often reaches as high a pitch in crowded Methodist and Baptist churches as it does in the Holiness church.

There are people of still other faiths in the community. Most numerous are the Dunkards, who are omitted here because they have no church in town. One important Dunkard church stands on a rocky hill ten miles north of Plainville, its congregation composed almost entirely of families of the Ballou "nation." Several facts about these Dunkards are remarkable: (1) The Dunkard tenets traditionally stress "nonconformity to worldly standards," including certain peculiarities in dress, and, notably, refusal to accept military service. Yet the Woodland County Dunkards pride themselves on conforming to "all recent changes in the community." Their youths do not request military exemption. (2) Although most Ballous are "hill people," Dunkards discourage and condemn religious emotionalism. They say, "The Dunkards who wanted to shout have all gone over to the Baptist Church." Several other Dunkard (and predominantly Ballou) churches are in the adjoining county north.

A scattered handful of people are "Russellites" or "soul-sleepers," who have no church but meet occasionally in two's and three's in homes to discuss their faith. They "disbelieve in churches, in hell, and in capitalism," and the most faithful of their sect "believe that they have already died and been resurrected." They are considered "radical" and ridiculous, and they "live to theirselves." The widow of the most prosperous Russellite ever to live in Plainville still occupies a pretty cottage her husband built a few years before he died. The house is surrounded by a large garden and orchard, with a splendid variety of fruit trees and berry vines and bushes. The hotelkeeper said of the builder of this home, "When Old George was a-buildin' that place, I said to him, 'You're makin' an awful fine property, for an old man that can't stay here long to enjoy it.' He answered me, 'Oh, I'm gonna live here always, because I've done died and be'n resur-rected!' But it wasn't long till the undertaker drug him off to the graveyard." The small Russellite movement sprang up about thirty years ago among dissident members of two or three rural Baptist congregations, which at that time met in country schoolhouses. Russellites have little contact with the national organization of Jehovah's Witnesses, beyond buying a few periodicals.

An immigrant colony of the Reorganized Church of Jesus Christ of Latter Day Saints moved into one rural neighbor-hood about forty years ago and founded a church. They were not persecuted, but they found the land or the community unsatisfactory, and moved away again. Only two or three of them remain. A Russian Jew for many years ran a general store in Plainville, where he died some years ago. People re-member him affectionately, but as "odd": he "talked funny" and enjoyed "gabbing with every Jewish peddler or drummer that come to town," but was a Mason and a pillar of society. The myth that has grown up about his memory stresses his kindliness and financial generosity but, more remarkably, his gullibility. People say, "Several of the business men around here got their start in life, clerkin' in Old Henry's store, and stealin' from his cash drawer." A Polish family of Catholics once moved to Plainville to start a bakery, but people considered their bakery products to be "dirty." Now they are farmers, and completely outside the local social system. They go to mass occasionally in a rural Catholic community in a neighboring county. Of all the religions in the world, Catholicism is considered by most Plainvillers to be the most "non-Christian."

Until about 1925, it was the Methodists and not the Christians who were the religious "ee-light" (elite) of Plainville. Their church building was the best in town. The Christians were a small and unimportant new congregation, who owned no church of their own, but met for worship in a vacant store building. The Methodist leaders were three or four upper-class families who owned the Plainville Bank and the most prosperous business in town. "For a good many years, the Methodists made all the money," and they constituted a genuine little aristocracy. The facts that brought about this shift in status are interesting.

The Christians set up a tent on the Square and imported a preacher from Largetown for a series of revival meetings. The revivalist happened to believe that, because of cars and improving roads, the church of the future must be a "community church," serving a large area and furnishing recreation facilities for the young. A building fund was started. A request for money was sent to an ex-Plainviller named Harlow Jackson, who had "made millions in Oklahomy oil." The preacher's ideals for a community church appealed to Jackson, it is said, and "of course he wanted to do something for his old home." Others say that he still resented the suffering he had endured in youth, as a member of a Christian family which the Methodists looked down on. Whatever his motives, he offered $25,000 toward building a church if a similar sum was pledged locally. The full sum was not collected, but enough money was found to build a large brick church. The circular seats of the auditorium will seat a thousand, and there is a balcony. The basement is divided into Sunday-school rooms and a large "recreation hall." There is a furnace. People remember that men who solicited building funds said, "Let's build something that'll make that Methodist Church look like a woodshed!" (Instead of "woodshed," some said "backhouse.") At the same time, also partly "on Jackson money," a Christian bank was financed to compete with the Methodist bank. In the great wave of mortgage foreclosures which swept rural America when farm "values" of the first World War were deflated, the Methodist bank failed. The Methodist aristocracy died off or left Plainville in disgrace,[1] and the new Christian Church triumphed. The Christian bank also expired later, but more gracefully. At considerable sacrifice ("to avoid disgrace"), the doctor, Jackson, and one or two others guaranteed its liabilities, and it was merged with the Discovery bank. The depositors lost nothing.

The whole spirit of the Methodist Church has changed since its original leaders left town. It retains more prestige than either the Baptist or the Holiness church, but according to many, including the retired preacher who served it in the old days, it has been overrun by people who prefer the more emotional kind of worshiping. Several local Methodist preachers are recent "converts" from the Holiness Church. The retired preacher says of them, "They like Holiness ways, but they like the Methodist pay. Of course, I still have to *go*, but it's a disgrace to listen to them." The county agent's wife, a Methodist, said, "I never did hear people anywhere else shout in a *Methodist* church."

The Christian Church won out in the socio-financial competition, but it failed to become the important community-wide religious and recreation center that its promoters dreamt of. Its main nondenominational use is for high school commencement exercises. No other place is large enough to seat the crowd which gathers for commencement. Sunday-school classes are taught in separate rooms in the basement, and the

---

[1] One of them fled to Metropolis, where he now "peddles tea from door to door." The hotelkeeper said, "It seems pitiful, after all he had, and as old as he is, for him to have to carry them heavy samples up and down the sidewalk. But I guess he had it all comin' to him."

recreation room is frequently used for fund-raising church dinners or bazaars, but seldom for the games and young people's parties for which it was intended. Older and conservative church members criticize its use for such purposes. Several of them objected strenuously to lending the church as a temporary schoolhouse, in 1940–41, when a WPA schoolbuilding was under construction, but yielded when it became apparent that all the other churches were willing to cooperate.

The Baptist Church is the least active of the Plainville churches, chiefly because there are several very lively rural Baptist congregations in the trade area. The preacher who conducts services once a month in Plainville preaches to much larger country congregations on each of the other three weekends of the month. His Plainville revival meetings are also generally less successful than those in the rural neighborhoods, where he sometimes "saves" twenty or thirty people during a revival. He considers his Plainville church to be his "deadest" congregation.

Holiness people, as no others in Plainville, have a "strictly seven day a week" religion. The members seem bent on "living out every day" what they talk and hear preached in church on Sunday. Their individual "confessional" talks in church stress positive neighborly ideals as well as the strictest of moral taboos on personal conduct. Only the Holiness people gather frequently in homes to pray over the sick: they believe that only prayer, and not medicine, can cure. All their social life is permeated by religious conversation and prayer. Theirs is the only congregation still practicing material charity for the poor. Their mutual helpfulness, in exchanging work and food, exceeds that of all other Plainvillers. The social aim of the Holiness congregation is to deny all "modern" values and to restore various pioneer and early Christian virtues, as they conceive these to have been. Their primary religious aim is to save as many individual souls as possible from Satan, but they also believe in "planting with prayer" and "harvesting with thanksgiving." A driver on roads that pass Holiness farms often hears men singing or whistling, from barn or hog pen or field, the hymns they sing in church. A rural school teacher said, "I think they tell their children about Jesus and all the other Bible characters, as people like themselves, who once walked the earth and might have plowed corn right here." They think of the other churches, and of the Christian Church especially, as centers of "Sunday religion." Indeed, religion as "only a Sunday duty of church-going" is at the maximum in the Christian Church; neighborliness as a religious duty, accompanied by a kind of sacred joy in its performance, increases as one moves downward through the hierarchy of churches.

While emotional behavior and religious hysteria are highest in the churches that rank lowest, it is difficult to judge whether emotionalism is currently increasing or decreasing in Plainville churches. Certainly the Holiness manifestation of emotionalism has mounted greatly during the last ten years, not only in Plainville but in the whole region. Holiness camp meetings in a near-by county are widely attended by campers from as far away as Metropolis. These camp meetings are important cultural centers from which traits connected with this essentially nativistic religious movement are diffused among many rural communities, and even from rural into metropolitan areas.

Before "the coming of Holiness" to Plainville, all the country churches, Baptist ones especially, seem to have been "hotter" and "wilder" than now. "Everybody shouted, and most of them rolled, in real *good* meetings, until the last ten years," some people say. Others say "You never hardly ever *heard* any shouting until the Holiness people started it." Aunt Lou Handy, now a light among older "Christian" women, said to me, "folks are ashamed for you to see and hear what goes on in them ignorant churches." A former neighbor said of her, "When Aunt Lou was a girl, she used to be the loudest shouter in her Baptist church. You could hear her for miles—through the timber." In regard to the ebb and flow of local religious enthusiasm, one man said, "When two or three good crop years come in a row, people begin backslidin', but after a couple of drouths, they come crawlin' on their bellies back to church."

The Christian preacher is better paid than any other. For preaching two sermons in Plainville on one weekend of each month, he receives $30. His three other churches in neighboring towns each pays somewhat less. He receives in all about $1,500–$1,800 a year. This sum includes voluntary fees for weddings and funerals, and the value of occasional gifts of food. No church in the county supports a preacher for more than one weekend a month; he usually preaches two Sunday sermons: one after Sunday School at 11:00 A. M., and the other at about 8:00 P. M., after Prayer Meeting. The congregation generally meets on all the other Sunday mornings, however, under a superintendent, for Sunday School, and on a weekday evening for Prayer Meeting. The Baptist preacher is paid $10 monthly by each of his four churches. On his Plainville weekend, he preaches three sermons, one on Saturday night and two on Sunday. At one or two country churches he preaches still a fourth sermon on Saturday morning. Revival meetings augment his income somewhat, but his funeral and wedding fees do not pay for the gasoline he burns in driving to funerals. One of his churches is twenty-five miles from his home. This means that he drives a hundred miles for his weekend services there, if he comes home at night to do his chores. His main income is from farming. He works hard every weekday on his rather large farm, when he is not interrupted by funerals, visits to the sick, and other occasional pastoral duties. "I'm about the only man in this country," he says, "who works hard seven days every week." During the revival season he "works night and day." When his house and nearly all its contents burned a few years ago, members of his several congregations all came to his aid with many contributions of money, furniture, work, and foodstuffs. "Counting gifts and insurance," he says, "I probably made a profit from the fire." The Methodist preacher's situation resembles the Baptist preacher's, except that he farms less (and much less effectively). He augments his income somewhat (since the undertaker's "court scandal") by selling burial insurance for an undertaking firm located at "Y," and is considered a more canny manipulator of the collection plate at revival meetings than any of the other preachers. The Holiness preacher receives in money only the free-will offerings of the collection plate. These amount to little—seldom over four or five dollars a Sunday, and sometimes not over a dollar—because the Holiness Church is the gathering place of the religious poor. He receives many gifts of potatoes, canned fruit ("sweetened," if the giver can afford the sugar, otherwise "unsweetened"), and garden products, however, and in times of stress—for example, when he is busy with summer revival meetings—Holiness men make up work parties and travel over to his farm in the next county to cut and shock his corn fodder or do any other necessary work. Sometimes he is given a load of hay or other feed for his livestock. All preachers receive many free meals, but Holiness preachers and their families spend much time traveling around as guests of members of their congregations. Many such visits are undertaken to conduct protracted sessions of prayer for healing sick people. It is considered an honor to "entertain the preacher."

In addition to weekly prayer meetings and Sunday school, and monthly sermons (called "regular services"), each church has a young people's organization and a Ladies Aid. The former meets weekly in the church, ordinarily early on Sunday evening, for "good clean entertainment," including song, prayer, and discussion of a topic selected at the previous meeting, under a youthful "leader" chosen at the same time. Some topics that received discussion at these meetings were: The People of God, The Place of Education in a Democracy, The Place of Religion in a Democracy, Faithfulness to God and Man, Unbelief, How to Use Our Radio, Sin, Condemnation, Taking a Christian Stand against Drinking, and Peter, the Rock.

The Ladies Aids meet mainly in homes. The Christian and Methodist Ladies Aids combine a good deal of secular pleasure with their religious duties. The members exchange luncheons with fellow members. They donate clothing, fancy work,

home-made jellies, etc., for bazaars, the money from which
goes to the church. They also raise money from big church
dinners, held in the church or in a vacant store downtown, to
which the public is invited and pays twenty-five cents per
guest for unbelievably large servings of food donated and
served by the members. They serve, at "restaurant prices,"
short-order luncheons and soft drinks at public sales on farms.
They sell quilts, and the "quiltings" at which these are made
are famous gossip occasions. The money they raise goes for
church furniture and repairs, and helps to pay the preacher,
though "paying the preacher" is considered primarily the duty
of men. The Methodist ladies are said to have made money-
raising an end in itself: they are reputed to have "hundreds of
dollars in the bank, drawing interest." An interchurch wom-
en's organization called the Missionary Society includes leading women from all the churches except the Holiness. Its
membership is about the same as that of the Booster Club.
Its function is "to raise money to convert the heathen" in
China and elsewhere. Once a year, after complex fortnightly
exchanges of entertainment and gifts, the Missionary Society
sends five dollars to its national office.

Each week the *Discovery Beacon* prints a special column
of "Plainville Church Activities." Here are reported: the number attending preaching and Sunday school in each church;
the names of former residents and other visitors from outside
who attended each church; the names of all people who
dropped birthday pennies—presumably one for each year of
life—into the special box kept for birthday offerings in each
church; the subjects or texts of the sermons that were
preached; a list of titles and performers of any special musical
numbers; and a report of songs, readings, and any other "cute"
performances by very young children.

The climax of the religious year is the revival. The Baptist
Church holds two revivals nearly every year. The Holiness
Church often holds several. The Christian and Methodist
churches ordinarily hold one each. Each revival is scheduled

to last a fortnight, with nightly services, and occasionally (except at the Christian Church) with morning sermons too.[2] If the revivalist fails to arouse interest, the meetings sometimes close within the fortnight. More frequently, however, they last longer, if conversions are coming in fast toward the end, or if it is felt that a few more sessions might "bring through" any mourners who are having a particularly "hard time" at the mourner's bench. Four extra services were held at the end of the Methodist revival in 1939, to try to bring through the fourteen-year-old daughter of a member. Several lasted far past midnight, and the girl suffered extremely from a sense of her "lost condition," but all her own prayers and the prayers of others, including several preachers, failed to "save" her. A year later she was "saved" with apparently little difficulty.

Revivals may be held at any time, but the main revival season begins in late July after the corn is laid by and the haying and small grain harvest are finished; it lasts until late October or early November, or about time to begin cornshucking. Although revivals fall during the summer slack season in farm work, farmers who attend have to cut their corn (during dry years) and do their threshing as best they can. The meetings work a greater hardship on preachers who farm than upon most other farmers, who feel obliged to attend faithfully only the meetings at their "regular" church. The Baptist preacher preaches revival sermons on probably a hundred nights during each year. Attendance at these meetings is not limited to the sect holding them, and religious people (as well as many others for various motives, inluding a desire to "have a good laugh") attend many services at all the churches. Only the Holiness

2 The Methodist revival evangelist in September, 1939, railed in the pulpit against the superintendent of schools for not dismissing school each morning to allow the children to attend meetings. "I'm not *against* education," he preached, "but I'm *for* God. If the people and the teachers here was interested in their children's souls, they'd have 'em here in church." The school superintendent was distressed, for he shrank from criticism from any quarter, but he could not dismiss the schools, for fear of greater criticism from other church members than he was receiving from the Methodist leaders. The preacher also railed against farmers who worked in their fields during the mornings when there was preaching. "God wants 'em to save their soul more'n he wants 'em to cut corn."

Church, however, draws spectators and listeners who do not enter the church, but watch and listen from outside, through the open windows.

The arrangement of the various portions of the ritual or ceremonies for a revival sermon resembles that for any regular meeting which includes a sermon, though the repeated meetings of a revival series bring about a gradual crescendo of emotion, which mounts night after night, if the revival proves successful. Families begin arriving at the church about 7:30 P. M., having done up rather early their milking and other chores. They file into the church and find seats, husbands and wives sometimes sitting together, but often separating, the wives to sit on the left side of the church and the husbands on the right side. Small children sit with their parents, or in groups near the front; bigger children and young couples who "are going together" sit far back in the church. Pious older people like to sit well "up in front." In the three lower churches old people often punctuate the sermon with "Amens" and other approving exclamations. The choir occupy places at the front of the church, facing the crowd. The preacher opens services, sometimes with a prayer, but more often by leading the choir and audience in several hymns. In all but the Christian Church, initial hymns are followed by personal confessions or "testimonials," sometimes alternated with further hymns. The sermon comes next, and usually lasts from thirty minutes to an hour. The sermon ends with an "Invitation" by the preacher to "come forward, confess your sins, and be saved." At this point the congregation breaks into an invitational hymn, such as, "Come to Jesus." From now on anything may happen. If no sinner comes forward the audience is dismissed with a prayer pronounced by the preacher or by one of the elder members. If there is a convert, all the church members shake hands with him and a hymn of rejoicing is sung before dismissal. At revivals, however, many invitational hymns are sung and the preacher pleads repeatedly for sinners to come forward. Further testimonials may be recited, and the preacher and other members may start searching through the congregation for sinners with whom to plead. Sometimes prospective converts are embraced tearfully in exhortation. If sinners are at the mourners' bench—only the Christian Church lacks a mourners' bench—various members, and visiting preachers, may kneel with them in prayer. Occasionally a dozen loud prayers ascend simultaneously to heaven.

Sermons preached in the Christian Church are usually prepared in advance and are coherent, but many revival sermons are utterly incoherent. These excerpts are from a typical Holiness exhortation:

> There are ninety-six known anti-Christs now in the United States. One of them is Father [X] in New York City. If I was to go there I sure wouldn't let *him* push me off no sidewalk . . . I'm a-gonna spend my first five thousand years in Heb'm just a-listenin' to the angels sing . . . I've got sympathy for the godless. I'm agin the things they do but I have sympathy for *them* . . . The sins of the people in this town—it's enough to run a man wild. . . . Some people may be ashamed to come up here [to the mourner's bench] because they're afraid some woman will laugh at 'em, but a woman never turned no man down for being saved. . . . The devil says to people, "Sow your wild oats, have a good time, and *then* settle down." . . . Any woman you see suckin' on a cigarette wouldn't make no decent companion [wife]. It's divorces that's a-ruinin' this country. . . . Why ain't they been any souls saved at this meeting? It's the cold hearts of the people here. . . . Father, truly I'm sanctified, Father, tonight. [Here the preacher, in shirt sleeves, was punctuating his speech by stamping his feet.] . . . See', God', I'm a-try'in' to show' 'em, God', the er'ror of their ways', God'. . . . Open your heart and let God in! I'm sanctified, tonight,God; and I pity the people that don't know the love of God! This town is full of beer jints and ain't fit for a decent man to live in or to take a decent woman down the street.

The words vary but are always rhythmic. They always stress

an inspirational acceptance of the spirit of God, the terror of hellfire, and strong condemnation of "the sins of this community." The sins most commonly attacked are cardplaying, drinking (and tolerating the sale of beer and whisky in Plainville), car-riding, cigarette-smoking by women, failure to attend church, and the possession of "cold hearts that will not let God in." From afar, also, the "sins of the cities" are condemned: dancing, red-light districts and "white-slavery," and the "lures and temptations held out for the young." Sometimes cities are attacked as places where "everybody is money-mad." The "going away of our youth" is sometimes attributed, not to economic necessity, but to the "sinful call of the cities" or as "a punishment to parents for not bringing up their children right." "Education, beyond what it takes to read and understand the Bible," is often attacked, by Methodist, Baptist, and Holiness preachers. Holiness preachers also attack with special vigor (for women) bobbed hair, cosmetics, showy clothes, and short skirts; and (for men) tobacco, evil thoughts and language, and sometimes neckties. An odd Holiness taboo is that pop must not be drunk out of a bottle, but must be poured out into a glass first, the bottle evidently suggesting beer. The most frequent positive exhortations in sermons are: "Open your heart and let God in . . . Feel the burden of your sins and repent before it is too late . . . Know the greater joy of living with God in your heart than living with the devil there." "Salvation" occurs when one "knows that God has entered" one's heart; at this time the "burden of past sin" rolls away, and the convert "knows that he is saved."

The following revival service in the Baptist Church was conducted by Reverend B. At the end of the initial singing, the preacher invited everybody to tell anything that they had in their hearts regarding their relationship with the Lord. Reverend X, a farmer-preacher who was that year without a pulpit, arose first to testify and talked for nearly an hour. (Some months later, Reverend B complained to me that he had feared Reverend X would never finish. He explained that Reverend X, having now no pulpit to preach from himself, was trying to "steal the sermon.") Reverend X described how one evening shortly after midnight twenty years before he had been saved. He had long been penitent about his lost condition and was conscious of having sinned. He had been attending a revival meeting, like this one, where he had been praying over his "lost condition," and others had been praying for him. Suddenly, one night, when he had almost lost hope, the Lord entered his heart and he knew that he was saved. The proof of salvation, he said, is simply knowing in your own heart that salvation has come. "People ask me how I know I'm saved forever," he said, "and *that's* the way I know!" Additional proof came later, he said, through noticing that although he still sometimes sinned, he no longer *wanted* to sin; he no longer *loved* sin as he had loved it before he was saved. Reverend X then exulted that this life will not last forever, that the saved can one day leave this life of sorrow for the life of joy. After he had finally finished, a number of members testified briefly. One woman told of her conversion years ago: It took place in the barn after midnight, "in a big wagon with the side boards on," where she had gone to pray alone after returning home from meeting. Another said, "The Lord has brought such peace to me . . . his love will save others too, if they want him to. Lord, help me take care of my family; I'm trying to raise my family right."

Now Reverend B began to preach. He chanted: "I am glad' God has given us the way to eternal life. I'm glad' this earthly life is just for a short time. I'm glad' God has shown us how to defeat the Devil, I'm glad' God is not a respecter of persons [that is, does not select those he saves according to earthly place or rank]. I'm glad' the way to heaven is not through good works but through the grace of God." He preached for several minutes on the theme that "grace is a free gift," isolated from "good works" (community ethics). "How you stand with God is the only important thing. No matter what good works you perform, these count for nothing unless the spirit of God has entered your heart." He also developed a corollary point, namely, once saved always saved. The "backslider" is a person who once only *thought* he was saved. He who has once been saved is unable to sin again, though the Devil tries to convince people falsely that they are saved, only to keep them among his fold.

He next told how he had been called by God to preach the gospel and how God tells him what to preach and how to preach. "I preach only what God puts into my mouth." Another preacher once offered him a two-year scholarship at a divinity school, tempting him with the idea that a preacher without a degree would soon be out of a job. But Reverend B refused, saying, "If God wants me to go to school he'll tell me. God called me, and he will tell me where and how to preach."

Next he told several stories as a warning to sinners: At a country church house near Plainville, thirty-five years ago, two young men agreed to go up to the altar and pray, just to see what would happen. To one nothing happened. To the other God spoke; not loudly enough to convert him, but enough to disturb him with the conviction of sin. As the two youths walked home they had to cross a bridge. When the one that had been "partly saved" stepped onto the bridge he decided to dance—again "just to see what would happen." He "danced on that bridge and he danced away the spirit of God. He died just awhile back, after all the years had passed. On his deathbed he repented and said he would give away everything he owned to feel again the way he felt that night in church. But then it was too late."

Another man whom the preacher once knew laughed in the face of a man who was trying to save him. Two weeks later he took "pneumony fever" and died, crying, "God have mercy on my soul." From these two *exempla,* he passed directly to the invitation, at which point a sinner who already feels the grace of God inside him can walk forward and say so to the preacher. Sinners, however, who feel only the burden of their sins, are supposed to come forward and kneel down at the mourners' bench to pray and be prayed for.

Reverend B shouted, "Where would you be tomorrow, sinners, if you go to bed tonight and fail to wake up in the morning?" Reverend B preached little "hell-fire" on that night, though the burning agonies of hell are often vividly described in sermons. The congregation began to sing, "Come to Jesus," as the minister left his platform and started walking up and down the middle aisle of the church, peering into faces in search of signs of emotional stress, and calling upon sinners to come forth.

No souls were saved that night, though there was hope for a while of saving the hardened soul of a man whose wife (converted long ago) arose, passed across the aisle from her seat to his, threw her arms around him, and sobbed on his shoulder. He hung his head in great embarrassment.

Various mental states seem to be possible as preliminary to the revelation of grace, or conversion, depending somewhat on the church and on the age of the convert. The most common feelings that people describe as preceding their own conversions relate to a great "burden of sin" (the "feeling of a lost condition") which they bore for days, the fear of hell, and the fear of "death without a promise."

Most children brought up in religious families join the church between the ages of twelve and fourteen. At about this age pressure from kin, preachers, and congregation seems to stimulate the required "feeling of sin," and the children are generally saved, after appropriate mourning and prayer, during a revival meeting. In telling of their conversion people remember well their old "burden of sin" but few remember any definite sins that burdened them, as children, before conversion. Very few people of any age, but especially few children, join the church during the rest of the year. More anxiety is felt regarding the unsaved souls of boys than of girls, when children are at the proper age to expect their conversion. This anxiety relates to the fact that boys are considered to be more sinful by nature than girls, and more stubborn, and to the knowledge that boys will suffer some "shame" through ridicule by other boys when they "get religion." No one laughs at girls for being saved. The souls of boys may also be unconsciously valued higher than those of girls: people sometimes maliciously say that the Bible nowhere expressly attributes souls to women, though most people believe that the sexes are equal in the eyes of God. Fewer girls than boys fail of conversion during adolescence, but most children join then. For children of religious families, joining the church at about the "proper time" is a necessary preliminary to establishing their own expected status in the community and is a protection to the status of their parents.

A good many adults are also saved, either for the first time, or after backsliding from a previous conversion or conversions. Adult conversion often follows a serious illness. A member of the Holiness Church said that during a long illness he was delirious; he dreamed of seeing Hell as a lake of fire "with just the arms and legs of people sticking out." "I decided right then," he said, "that if I ever got up again, I was a-goin' to be saved and not go there. And I was. I'm a changed man." The changes he listed were these: The Lord had delivered him in turn, since conversion, from (1) "gittin' mad at people and wantin' to fight ever'body ever' few minutes," (2) "wantin' to tell and listen to them rotten dirty stories they tell in the back room at the garage," (3) "needin' tobacco," and (4) "wantin' to wear a necktie." Another man, a rural Baptist, said, "I joined the church so's my children would be brought up in the church." He (oddly) did not, and does not, believe in the Bible as "anything more than history and morals," though he prayed at the mourners' bench, endured several nights when he tossed sleeplessly and sobbed on his pillow, and finally felt the burden of sin roll away. He has "felt better ever since. When I got saved I felt good all over." His wife and three daughters joined the church at the same revival series, but she said, "I still feel ashamed at how he and the girls carried on."

The adult ordeal of conversion (conversion may or may not be accompanied by an "ordeal" in the Christian Church) is often a device by which the convert removes himself from a situation of "disrespect" in the eyes of the community to one of "respect." Through salvation a drunkard, a gambler, or a man who has been considered sexually immoral, financially dishonest, or a "worthless worker," can set his footsteps on the road toward social acceptance by the religious sector of his own class. Members of all churches "rejoice when a sinner is saved," but upper class people await practical proof of "a changed life" before their earlier opinion of him alters much. Rejoicing is greatest in the Holiness Church, when a man of the lower element comes into the church. The road of salvation is difficult for such a man, however, because for all the warmth of welcome he receives, he must give up many warm earlier associations and bear the contempt of his old friends for "backslidin' into the church." Not all such conversions "stick" (are permanent). Sometimes a lower-class wife is converted and later brings her children and husband into the church. Not much hope is felt for the permanence of such a woman's conversion, unless that of her husband follows rather soon, because her husband is apt to ridicule her faith and to put obstacles in the way of her participation in church activities.

A few people try to cross class lines through religion, but none succeeds. Theoretically no obstacle keeps lower-class people out of the Christian Church, but "they wouldn't feel comfortable there." One upper-class widow had identified herself with the Holiness Church, whose great light and leader she was until her death in 1940. Members of her class criticized the affiliation, and she lost respect in their eyes, but her class status remained unchanged, though upper-class people tried to visit her on her deathbed at times when they would find her surrounded by the fewest of "them ignorant Holinists."

A few people are converted repeatedly. One woman (once Baptist, but now Holiness) has been baptized so often that a man said, "You'd think she'd 'a' be'n washed plumb away." Sometimes repeated conversions are the result of repeated backslidings—sometimes they result from the search, among the churches, for "the truest faith," or the "true baptism," and so forth. More poor people are converted repeatedly than wealthier people, and more women than men.

The method of baptism is still a point of some controversy among the churches, though less so than a few years ago, when the "wrong kind of baptism" was considered tantamount to damnation. Christians, Baptists, and Dunkards practice total immersion (Dunkards immerse three times); Methodists ordinarily "sprinkle," though they will "dip" (immerse) if the member desires. One Methodist woman said, "I had the preacher *merge* me, just to be on the safe side."

A sermon was preached at the Christian Church on the meaning of the word "baptism." The preacher argued that baptism meant total immersion. Sprinkling, he said, is not baptism. ("Sprinkling," some people say, "ain't washin' your sins away. It's just dry-cleanin' 'em.") The Greek root of the English word "baptize" means total immersion, he said. He quoted Wesley himself, the "father of Methodism," as admitting that it means immersion. How then can anyone be saved by any other method? Such was the gist of an hour's sermon. Members of the other "total immersion" churches sometimes criticize the Christian baptism because it is done in a "tank" (a baptismal font in the church) rather than in running water. Whatever form is followed, the baptism of new church members occurs about a week after their conversion, or at the end of a revival series. Outdoor baptisms are performed at any season, even if ice has to be broken from the river, and large crowds gather on the bank to watch. A universally held belief is that "nobody ever heard of anybody catchin' cold from bein' baptized." Membership can be changed from one church to another, by "letter," and without new baptism, if the person concerned feels that his earlier baptism was valid.

Few technical theological points, except the right method of baptism, are often argued between the sects nowadays, though religious arguments were once heated and frequent. Most religious people now think "you can get to heaven through *any* church." Some think you can get there "even outside of churches." A man said, "You can be saved in the timber." The old arguments over "infant damnation" are over. Arguments over "predestination" are almost finished. The doctrine of "once saved always saved" is still sometimes debated: one branch of the Baptist Church adheres to the doctrine, against all the other churches (except the Holiness Church), which believe that a man *can* sin, even after salvation, if he so wills. The Holiness people believe in the possibility of sin after conversion for all except a few who "know they have attained Holiness" or "Sainthood" on earth.

It is difficult in a few words to assess fairly the role of religion and churches in Plainville. The daily interests of most people, aside from some Holiness people, a few more primitive Baptists and Methodists, and one or two preachers, seem to be not religious at all, but work ("making a living"), sociability, and gossip. Yet religion seems to permeate the daily air, not as a stress on discriminating the "saved" from the "sinners"—as all the sermons preached in church might lead one to expect—but as a vital concern with the negations on moral conduct which the churches set up. The religious control of morals operates mainly through gossip and the fear of gossip. People report, suspect, laugh at, and condemn the peccadilloes of others, and walk and behave carefully to avoid being caught in any trifling missteps of their own. A half dozen men wanting to share a half pint of rock and rye on a cold morning in the Produce House look out through the plate-glass window to see who is passing that might observe and tell. The few women who smoke do so on the sly. Young people who want to dance drive to a road house in another county, so no one at home will know.

On Sunday most stores are closed, and the movement of cars and people is mainly to and from the churches and on "after church visiting." "There is no place for people to go except to church. . . . There's no place for *young* people to go except to church. . . . The old see to it that the young have no place to go except to church. . . . The church aims to provide a good clean place of entertainment for the young." Not even in the Christian Church, which stands proudly aloof from the emotionalism distinguishing the others, are discussed any of the important problems of agriculture, ethics, and human relationships that actually face the community. The real resident "reformers" (for example, the county agent and the vocational agriculture teacher) all go to church as a way of keeping "in" with the community, to lessen criticism of their work, but not one of them would dream of attempting to make of any church, or of any preacher, an instrument or ally to help further their work. One of them said of the churches, "They control everything. Nothing can be taught in school because the religious people would rise up in wrath. The only thing the churches do for young people is give them a chance to rub hands in a holy place. They oppose science, even in farming. They control all conduct and prevent all progress. But they provide a social center for people, especially for women."

Many natives share or partly share his feeling. An elderly grocer to whom the above quotation was read, without naming its author, said angrily, "That's a lie! Without churches there'd be no progress! But I guess that's right about the churches being a place for women to meet and look at each other's clothes and find out what happened." The retired Methodist preacher spoke sadly of the present day role of the Church. "The Church does nothing. It's bound to a formula. There's no inspiration to do anything except increase the membership. It's just an insurance policy for the old, and a gossip center." I asked, "Do churches save souls?" He replied, "Oh, I guess they try to save souls, but even preachers aren't agreed on personal survival any more." An old man (and non-believer, though he "went to church and supported churches" when his wife was alive) said, "If it wasn't for the churches real estate would be worthless, and we'd all be like the animals." The ideas that churches (and schools) preserve real estate values and that churches keep people from being "like wild animals" appeared often in native discourses on this subject, but less often than the statement that their primary role is as a "social center, especially for women." Actually, while women outnumber men somewhat in church activities, they are not the "main pillars" of the churches here. The frequent statement that they are is a borrowed urban stereotype.

The idea that churches resist progress is remarkably common among all non-church people and many upper-class church members. It is curious that the opinion that churches save souls was not advanced voluntarily by any upper-class informant.

In the eyes of more emotional religious people, however, the church is the instrument of neighborliness and mutual help on earth, and the avenue to eternal salvation, which is worth more than pearls and rubies or "all the education that money can buy." The first point usually mentioned by these people, when queried, is the role of the church as a saver of souls.

5 From Cradle to Grave

ABOUT one hundred babies a year are born in Woodland County; "new lives" number about twice those of all ages who die.[1] The arrival of a new baby is attributed—when people "bother to think about the matter"—to parental desire for a child, to "laziness," "pure carelessness," or an "accident," to "ignorance" of preventive methods, to "nature," or even to "God's will." Most married couples want children, as "heirs," playthings, companions, or as instruments toward attaining full family status in the community. People also say that they "like to watch young life grow," and that "children bless a home."

Not all want as many children as are born to them, however, and many would wish the intervals between births to be longer than they are. "Planned families," that is, families in which the number of children and their approximate arrival dates are planned, are less frequent in the lower class than in the upper class, where people feel strongly that parents should have no more children than they can "afford to take care of" properly. Families of six to twelve children, commonplace only forty or fifty years ago, are now rare, even among the lower class. Such large families are both ridiculed and condemned, and are attributed to selfishness, laziness, or carelessness on the part of the husband, or, in some very religious lower-class families, to an "old-fashioned" idea that children are the gift of God, whose will should not be interfered with. Only a few people are ignorant of simple commercial contraceptives. Contraception may apparently be practiced freely without compunction, although even men are abashed by

[1] The live birth rate per 1,000 population was 15.76 in 1939; 14.1 in 1940. Stillbirth, infant (under one year old), and maternal death rates, per 1,000 live births, were for 1939, respectively, 58.25, 29.13, and 9.71. Corresponding figures for 1940 were 65.2, 10.9, and 10.9. The total death rate for the county was 8.11 (1939) and 8.9 (1940).

discussion of the matter on any level except the ribald. "People here don't like to speak about that." Any "sexual" subject, including pregnancy, is "delicate" and embarrassing, unless discussion is confined to one's own sex group and, loosely speaking, to one's own age group, and is couched light-heartedly in a special and obscene "male" vocabulary.

Most pregnant women are embarrassed at being seen in public and they often blush when "spoken to" (greeted) on the street. Women are criticized for appearing publicly "in that condition." The only women who seem to feel that pregnancy is wholly "natural" are a very few "modern" and educated women and certain backwoods women who "don't seem to even understand" that pregnancy gives them grounds for embarrassment. The latter will even "offer the breast" to their babies publicly, without effort to conceal it from the gaze of bystanding men and children. Most women, when they become pregnant, keep the fact secret as long as possible from all except close adult relatives.

There is a large and waning folklore about prenatal influence: "She has a strawberry (grape, cherry, etc.) mark on her body because her mother craved strawberries so, while she was carrying her. . . . He is hare-lipped because a craw-daddy pinched his mother's toe and scared her." Everybody knows people who bear birthmarks attributed to the fears, frights, or food cravings of their mothers, but few women are "careful" about such hazards. A very few attempt to bestow a particular "disposition" on a child prenatally; a woman might, for example, try to predetermine her child toward a "good religious disposition" by reading her Bible attentively during pregnancy.

More practical concern is felt regarding a pregnant woman's health than about any magical influences on the child. A prospective mother should not "work real hard" right up to the last. She does her own cooking and housework, of course, "until her pains begin," but she should not wash or iron, or lift heavy buckets full of water, or hoe in her garden, during the last week or two. The mores further prescribe that intercourse between the parents should stop two or three months before a child is born. Yet many men are said to be so "selfish" that they continue until two or three days before the birth. Restraint in this matter is ordinarily phrased as for the protection of the mother, though several informants stated that intercourse continued too late may predispose a child toward abnormal sexual desires. Intercourse should not be resumed until the mother is "well" again, but here again many husbands are said to be selfishly urgent. Traditionally a woman leaves her bed on either the seventh or the ninth day after childbirth, but many "rest" longer nowadays. As for the proper interim between births, fifteen months were formerly thought adequate. "They figured in them days that a woman needed that much rest between children, but lots didn't get it. I've seen 'em with one child in their arms, a-leadin' another by the hand, and carryin' a third one inside." An interval of two or three years is now considered better.

A Plainville baby may be born in a Largetown hospital, or it may be born in a hill shack with no attendance whatever. Both situations are rare, however, and apply to only two or three births a year. The latter, while more frequent than the former, is deeply condemned. The doctor officiates at most births, which take place in the mother's home. Sometimes, especially for a first birth, a young woman returns instead to her own mother's home to receive the latter's care. An older woman, either a neighbor or a kinswoman, is usually present to "keep plenty of water boiling" and otherwise help the doctor, and to care for the mother until the husband feels that he can manage things alone. The doctor often refuses to attend cases on which money is still owed "for the last baby," a refusal which most people consider perfectly just and ethical, no matter what the situation. In such cases, and in others where the family is too poor even to think of sending for a doctor, the elderly woman helper takes full charge.

Up to twenty-five years ago many, if not most, births were attended only by midwives or "granny women," who were specialists and often received pay or gifts for their work. In those days the granny women also practiced as general curers, in which role they were called "witches." Many of them communed with ghosts, knew love charms, and occasionally were reputed to control certain harmful spells also. None are living any longer, though some of their practices are remembered. One used to burn cobs in a pan under the bed to hasten parturition; the doctor enjoys telling how he was once called late to a birth scene, and scolded her for burning white cobs instead of red cobs. He also remembers having seen granny women feed the newborn baby a drop of blood from its own umbilical cord, "to prevent colic."

Childbirth scenes, as described by people who have witnessed them, do not seem particularly cleanly or sanitary, but most of the babies and mothers manage to live through them. No rituals ordinarily attend birth. The afterbirth is simply buried or burned, without any other notion than to dispose of it. All family and community "rejoicing" is in the secular realm. If the mother belongs to any well-established clique, her friends often "surprise" her with a party and a "shower" of inexpensive useful gifts some weeks before her child is born, and soon afterwards her friends visit her to "see the new baby." When a baby is born into a good family, everybody is supposed to "feel glad."

Brothers and sisters are supposed to be greatly excited and jubilant over a new baby, as soon after the event as they have come home from the neighbor's or kinfolks' house where they were sent for safekeeping and have recovered from their surprise at learning what has happened. Every one denied that an older child is ever jealous of the new arrival in a home. That questions on such a subject should be asked seemed astonishing, nonsensical, and rather shocking. People were familiar enough with situations of jealousy between older children, especially grown children (over, for example, chronic parental favoritism toward one child, or an inheritance), but "Everyone loves a baby!" they said. All older children, they say, love the new baby, like to brag about it at school, and are proud of their responsibility in helping take care of it.

Children are named without ceremony, ordinarily immediately after birth. Alternative names, male and female, have often been decided on long in advance. Occasionally there is a delay in selecting a name and rare cases are remembered of calling a child by some term like Babe, Bud, or Sis, until it is old enough to choose its own name.

There have been many vogues in names. For men, biblical names like Abraham or Isaiah and high-sounding old-time names like Napoleon, Ulysses, and Lycurgus (usually abbreviated to Poley, Lys, and Curg) have died out with the very old. Simple names like Robert (always called Bob), William (Bill), and John (the favorite name) were always popular and still are. A few of the names now frequent among men and youths are Alva, Asa, Orle, Oral, Merle, Delbert, Hobart, Byron, Virgil, Omer, Homer. A new fad has begun of calling boys by double names, like Billy Fred, James Alvin, Walter Monroe. This imitates an earlier and still popular vogue of calling girls by such names as Ina Faye, Wanda Lea, and Rose Mae. Girls' names are extremely varied, because people like to give them rare or even unique names. There are girls named Columbine, Yolanda, Lorine, Belvine, Orfa, and Willa. Flower and gem names were once more popular than they are now: Rose, Violet, Lily, Ruby, Pearl, and Jewel. Names like Mary, Anna, and Jane are considered old-fashioned.

Actually, both males and females have always received two "given" or Christian names, a "first name" and a "middle name," but for males the middle name had function only after they were grown to provide a middle initial for use on legal documents and in signing checks, while the middle names of females were hardly remembered after childhood. Nicknames are popular for males, often supplanting the real names. There are men called Slim, Fat, Squinty, Squeaky, Big'un, One-Eye, Snake-Eye, Skunk, River Bill, and Fy-fy (imitating a speech defect). Some derogatory nicknames are used only "behind a feller's back."

Most people "hope for a boy" as their first child. This hope may possibly reflect the fact that boys were once a great eco-

nomic asset in farming. Their labor became valuable when
they were about nine years old and grew increasingly more
valuable until they married, left home, or became of age and
independent on their twenty-first birthdays. Even now many
a farm boy "does a man's work" from the time he is eleven
years old, though school interferes more with his labors than
formerly. If the first-born is a girl, however, she is welcomed
with the same love and pride that a boy would have received.
Even "unwanted" children, sometimes called "little accidents,"
are usually cherished, once they are born. If the hope for "a
boy first" is satisfied, people then generally begin to hope for
"a girl next," though a "houseful of boys" is preferred to a
"houseful of girls," when children in a family all happen to
be of the same sex. The ideal family of today is considered to
be a father, a mother, and perhaps two children, a boy and a
girl. The father should ideally be a year or a few years older
than the mother, the son a year or two older than the daughter.
Larger families, of four to six children, are also admired,
"when people can take care of them." Poorer people are condemned and ridiculed for having numerous children: poverty,
backwoodsiness and "a pack of hounds and ignorant children"
are associated together in the minds of "better-class people."
An "only child" is greatly pitied for lacking brothers and sisters
to play with and grow up with. "Its folks can buy it more, of
course, but only children most always grow up selfish. They
don't learn how to give and take." Cases of adult selfishness
and lack of social or business tact are sometimes explained as
the result of an "only childhood."

Parents claim to love all children equally. None ever admits
"favoring" one child over another, though many are accused
of favoritism by neighbors and kinsmen, including their own
children (usually in retrospect, after growing up). Actually
the youngest child, or "baby" (so-called up to any age) in a
household is very often favored. Occasionally an eldest child
is favored, or a single child of one sex born into a household
of children of the opposite sex. In the latter case, some favoritism, not only by the parents but also by the other children,

seems to be approved and considered natural. When an eldest
child is favored, it is because he or she assumed a partially
parental and managerial role toward the younger children
and special responsibilities in the family's economic life.
Several factors conduce toward favoring a youngest child.
First, the older children, as partial caretakers, filling an im-
perfectly defined mixed role as siblings and substitute dis-
ciplinarians, have a hand in "spoiling" them when they are
very young. Second, younger children are in general much less
strictly disciplined than older children. And third, the youngest child comes to be especially cherished by parents because
he generally remains at home for some time after the older
children have married off. The second point is a matter of
agreement and frequent comment in Plainville. "They certainly don't make *him* mind the way I had to . . . People are
always easiest on the younger children." Older children often
express resentment, even long after they are grown, at the
fact that "the younger ones" received less punishment in
childhood than they themselves suffered. Married children
are also frequently very watchful of the youngest child's
spending habits and fearful that he may get into a favored
situation regarding the parental property. As a matter of fact,
property is almost always divided among children with rigid
equality.

There is as much variation in routines for babies as there
is in the rest of Plainville life and technology. Some babies are
"raised by the book," others by old or hit-and-miss methods,
others by every conceivable combination of granny lore and
modern methods of child care. One informant said concerning
her four children (now thirteen to nineteen years old) that
she had raised them all in "the old way." She had in recent
years read books on child care, and "always knew something
(from magazines and hearsay) about book practices." Even
when her own babies were small she "agreed with what the
books said," but she raised them in the old way because it was
easier.

Babies are breast-fed. According to the vocational agriculture teacher's wife, there had been only two or three bottle babies in the community since she moved there in 1937, except her own two (aged two and a half and three and three quarters in 1940), whom she was raising "scientifically" in every respect, under the guidance of a Largetown pediatrician. This was unique for Plainville. Her children were admired for their good looks, "cute ways," and healthy bodies, but they were rather pitied for having received too little "attention." Older women thought that the mother had needlessly deprived herself of numerous small pleasures natural to motherhood in having played with them and fed them "by the clock." It was thought especially strange that she owned no rocking chair, in which to "sit and rock her babies." An interesting fact in connection with "bottle babies" is that with the bottle comes the whole complex of modern child training: food formulas, heating of food to proper temperature, and regular times for feeding, play, sleep, and affection. The average baby is nursed whenever it wants food, sleeps in bed [1] with its mother and father, and tugs at the mother's breast at will during the night. When it cries it is lifted up, cuddled, and carried in an effort to comfort and "quieten" it. It receives attention whenever it demands it, at any time of the day or night.

Weaning was done in the old days at almost any age from one to six or seven. For practical reasons, however, only the youngest child or an only child was generally allowed a late weaning. Sometimes a child was weaned just before starting to school, at age six, so it wouldn't "cry for its dinner" in school. Children weaned before age two or three were weaned so young to allow the mother to "dry up" a few months before its successor came. That much "rest" between lactation periods was considered good for her. When pregnancy occurred soon after the last child's birth, weaning obviously had to be initiated when the child was under a year old. Very seldom did

---

[1] People say that in the old days of cord-bottomed beds, many babies were smothered to death. The cords sagged, and parents "overlaid" the baby by rolling to the center of the bed in their sleep.

an older child have access to the breast after a younger child was born.

Children who "nursed late" were of course ridiculed, and they were generally nursed in privacy to spare them from laughter and shame. There is a folklore about late weaning. It was told in front of a middle-aged man who had been a "late weaner" that once when he was seven years old he became very hungry while visitors were in his house. He sulked and whined for awhile behind a door, but was unable to attract his mother's attention. Suddenly he popped his head out and said, "God damn it, Maw, I want to suck." He was asked, "Did you really say that, Willie?" He replied, "I guess I did. They say I did." A story is told of another boy (now a man) who whimpered in front of company until his mother gave him her breast. In a minute or two he loosened his hold on the breast and said, "Give me the other one." It is told of an old-time and successful doctor (now dead) that when his little girl reached school age, he moved near the school, so that she might run home two or three times a day to be nursed.

The nursing period in general has been shortened to between twelve and twenty-four months, despite the fact that the old pressure has largely ended for weaning one child to make way for the next one. The few backwoods families who still produce "a baby a year, like animals," are greatly ridiculed. Actual weaning ordinarily follows a gradual introduction of other foods quite early, while the child is still being nursed. When the child is six or eight months old, the mother begins to offer it food from the table, where she sits holding the baby at meal times. She gives it sips of milk from a glass, and tastes of gravy, potatoes and other vegetables, and sometimes meat, from her plate. She sometimes pre-chews the harder foods before putting them into the baby's mouth. A man said, "The first thing we used to give our'n was som'p'n soft to chew on, that we knowed wouldn' hurt 'em, like a little fat side-meat." Meanwhile, to discourage the child's interest in the breast, various techniques are employed. The intervals between breast feedings are lengthened, and the feeding period is often

shortened. It may be told, "You eat *real* food now, you don't
want to suck any longer." Sometimes it is shamed severely each
time it asks for the breast. Most children are allowed to suck
at night later than in the daytime because they sleep with
their parents. Finally they are taken from the breast entirely.
An effort is usually made to end breast feeding gently and without shock, though some people initiate weaning, and others
terminate the weaning problem of a persistent child, by
methods intended to arouse revulsion toward the breast, such
as painting it with black stove soot or with quinine. Sometimes (by an old and now rare practice) "sugar tits"—cloth teats
filled with butter and sugar—are given to a weanling to
"pacify" it, but the standard use of pacifiers is to assist infants
in teething.

No form of bodily self-play is ever induced to quiet a child
during the ordeal of weaning. Thumb-sucking by infants is
sometimes not immediately discouraged, but efforts are always
made to shame larger children out of the habit, if it persists.
They are told that the thumb won't grow, or that *they* won't
grow; a few people actually believe that thumb-sucking will
stunt a child's growth. The commonest aids toward "breaking" a persistent thumb-sucker are thumbstalls or gloves tied
on at night to prevent contact between mouth and thumb.
Sometimes the child is forced to wear the stall publicly to
"shame" it. Stove soot and quinine are also sometimes rubbed
on the thumb to arouse distaste, as on the breast for weaning.
In weaning a child, bantering and shaming techniques, especially shaming, are particularly effective because weaning is
instituted at an age late enough for the child to understand
conversation. If a child with a smaller sibling still wants to
nurse he is told that the breast is for his little sister or brother.
"The baby needs that, and you can eat potatoes like mother
and daddy. . . . You'd be ashamed to be a little baby. . . .
A great big boy (or girl) like you don't want to suck!"

Sphincter control is introduced, except by the most "modern" people, when the child can understand through language
what is expected of it. The mother who had raised her own

children in the "old way, though she believed in the book way," said that when each child was about two years old, she began to take it to the outhouse with her. She would sit on one hole and set the child on the other. She would grunt and induce the child to imitate her, waiting beside it until the movement took place. Then she would praise the child. "I reasoned with my children in everything more than I ever punished them," she said. Her husband explained her great "motherly kindness" and "understanding" as a rebellion against her own childhood. Her mother was "an unreasonable hellcat, that beat her kids nearly to death, for the *least* things they'd do."

The vocational agriculture teacher's wife decided, because eating causes peristalsis, to set her children on their pot and serve them their meals there once a day. She also by grunting induced them to grunt, urged them "to try hard," approved when they succeeded, and scolded them or "tried to shame them for being little," when they failed. Many children are scolded severely for "making a mistake" after sphincter control is initiated, and some are spanked harshly. Mothers do not seem to believe that any special problems are ordinarily encountered in teaching sphincter control to their children, full control being usually established at about the age of two or two and a half years, but not often before. Urethral control meets apparently with more difficulties, since a considerable number of large children and grown people are known as bed-wetters. All of the known adult bed-wetters are males, and they suffer a great deal of shame from their "failing."

Differential treatment of children according to sex begins very young. Little boys, it is thought, are "just naturally different from little girls," and the supposed and expected differences are accented and encouraged "from the cradle on." (Cradles, by the way, are no longer used.) Boy babies, as "naturally stronger," are offered fingers to lift themselves up by earlier than girl babies; girl babies who lift themselves up young by older people's fingers are "strong as boys." Girl babies oftener than boy babies are admired as "pretty." Girl

babies are "dolls." Boy babies are "little men." Girl babies
are dressed "prettier" than boys. The same first clothing is
worn by both sexes, because it was acquired before birth, but
in all clothing made or bought for them after birth there is
a tendency to distinguish between the sexes. More lace and
ribbons are put on girl babies' clothing; boy babies' clothing
is made plainer. Men like their sons, as soon as they can
walk, to have at least one pair of blue-denim overalls pat-
terned as closely as possible on the working garb of men.

This differential treatment, as will be seen later, applies
in every department of a child's life. It seems to be the purpose
of the society to establish very early separate sets of behavior
habits for boys and girls—habits which have to do with clothing, work, morality, and personality—especially with the development of aggressiveness and domination in boys, and
with passivity and submissiveness in girls. Such patterns breed
in boys feelings of their own superiority, and of contempt for
the work, interests, and intelligence of girls and women, but
of admiration for their physical attractiveness. Most girls
subscribe, with the boys, to the superiority of being a boy.
These mores hold, with few exceptions, for all classes. Boys and
girls are treated "equally" however in one important respect.
From both is "expected," though not always obtained, im-
plicit obedience to the will of their parents. All children are
supposed to "obey" without question, yet even here there is
a difference: a boy is often spoken of as having a spirit like that
of a colt, which must be broken to obedience as a colt is
broken. Girls are "naturally more willing" to obey, and "give
less trouble" in management and discipline.

In most families, children of opposite sex (and sometimes
in prudish families, sisters also, but never brothers) are taught
not to undress in front of each other after they are old enough
to change their own clothes. It would be inconvenient for the
mother to separate them earlier. As they begin learning to
dress themselves under her supervision, she begins to teach
them the principles of modesty, both by verbal instruction and
by backing one out of sight of the other behind a stove, a

chair, or some other piece of furniture, or off into another room. Children begin to try to undress and dress themselves at about two years of age, but they do not often become fully competent at the task before about age five. Yet with all this early stress on modesty, the mother frequently bathes children of the opposite sex together in the same tub until they are four or even five years old. Here, however, she is faced with a problem of efficiency, since water has to be carried in from the well and heated on the stove. She is more apt to bathe her children in turn, using the same water; if she follows this plan she is likely to bathe the larger children or the girls first, the smaller children or the boys last.

The strictures on modesty, especially concerning the exposure of sexual organs to the sight of others, are very rigid. Most married couples would consider it immodest to undress completely before each other in a lighted room; many married couples are said never to have seen each other undressed. Siblings must never see siblings of the opposite sex (except very small children) undressed, and children, as soon as they can bathe and dress themselves, begin to conceal themselves carefully from the eyes of parents. Boys of any age strip off freely in each others' presence in a room or at a swimming hole, and boys micturate before each other, but not before adult men, without turning their backs. Adult men ordinarily turn away from others when micturating.

Modesty is often carried in Plainville to extreme ends of squeamishness. Two grown sisters living in town who share a room and sleep in the same bed were said by a neighbor woman never to undress for bed at the same time "without either turning out the light or setting up a screen between them." One woman told her married son as an oddity—he said he would not have thought it so—"As long as your father and I have been married, we have never once gone to the toilet together." Preachers criticize sun suits for small children as immodest. Slacks for women moved from the realm of extreme "immodesty" in 1937 to free acceptance as "decent" if not recommendable attire in 1939. Language considered "slangy," but "not really rough for boys" (phrases like "darn it," "the dickens," "thunder!") is immodest when uttered by girls. The average upper-class woman is "modest" about nursing a child in front of people.

There is a good deal of variation in standards of modesty according to class. Some very "modern" families make a point of teaching their children not to be prudish regarding nakedness, either their own or that of their parents, though they are careful to teach them to obey the standards of other people when away from home. And among certain "lower-element" families there are said to be no "restrictions" whatever: "They think nothing of nakedness. . . . A girl will show her brother her body and she can see his." Among Holiness and other lower-class religious families, however, the conventional taboos of modesty are intensified and extended, like other moral taboos. Short skirts, low-necked dresses, and even bobbed hair seem immodest to many Holiness people. It should be said regarding nonreligious and even antireligious people of any class, that there is no necessary correlation between lack of religion and failure to observe and sanction the community's moral taboos. Many nonreligious people train their children to rigid sex morality, "guard their daughters' reputations," and are otherwise "just as moral as anybody."

Techniques of securing obedience are whipping, spanking, slapping, shaming, teasing, scolding, nagging, threats, privations, rewards, encouragements, demonstrative verbal approvals, and physical affection. For whipping, razor straps are sometimes used; buggy whips were often used "on big boys" —when there were buggy whips; and a great variety of switches, in size, name, and ability to inflict pain, are employed. Hickory and willow switches are especially dreaded, because they are thin and flexible, and of great tensile strength. To "hickory" or "willer" (willow) a child means to whip him severely. A "peach-tree stick" is not much dreaded. A special punishment is to force a child to cut and trim the switch to be applied to his legs or bottom. If he "rings" it with his pocket knife, to cause it to break at the first blow, he is "apt to get a worse one than was intended." A whipping is also called a "licking;" a severe whipping a "larruping," a "hiding," or a "rawhiding." A "tanning" may be severe or not. To "touch a child up a little" with "any old stick that comes to hand" is not supposed to hurt the child physically as much as it hurts its "feelings." Spanking is with the hand, on the bottom, legs, or arms. Slaps are similar smart blows on the face. There are also ear-boxing, ear-pulling, head-thumping with knuckles or thimble, hair-pulling, and several other formal methods of physical chastisement.

People differ in opinion about the amount of corporal punishment children should receive, and about how and by whom it should be administered. A "reasonable amount" of whipping is recommended and practiced by most parents, especially on boys, but children "should not be whipped till the blood comes, or every day like they used to be." The average boy gets perhaps a dozen or two actual "lickings" during his childhood. He is seldom whipped after the age of twelve or fourteen. The average girl gets less. Some children get "one a day" or "one a week"; some get none. The idea is not un common that a parent should not punish a child while angry; but few parents are credited with so much restraint. Parents, however, who "seem to enjoy whipping their children" are severely condemned, though serious physical injury would have to be done to the child before there would be legal or even neighborly interference. It is told satirically of some parents that "they never whale a child without saying, 'This hurts me more than it hurts you.' "

Teasing, kidding, and shaming, alone or in combination, are among the most effective means of molding a child to the patterns desired in the community. Of these three techniques, however, only shaming is recognized as of formal disciplinary and instructional value. ("I *shame* oftener than I *whip*. And I *reason* as often as I *shame*," said one mother.) A child is ordinarily shamed on the grounds that it is not living up to the standard expected of its sex, its size, or its age. Girls are told that they are supposed to be modest and not act like little boys. Boys are reminded that as boys they are supposed to be able to do things, and not act like girls or much smaller boys. "You're a big girl (boy) now. You don't cry (fall down, spill things) any more. . . . You (said to a girl) don't want to go with Daddy. Boys go with their daddies, and *girls* stay with their mothers. . . . You (said to a boy) don't want to play with Sister's doll. Boys play with wagons . . . You're big enough (said to either) to mind (or work) now. . . ." A child is rewarded for doing what the parent wants it to do by a smile, by fondling, or by approving words: "That's a big boy (or girl) . . . That's a good boy (or girl)."

Common privations for disobedience (or other bad conduct) are keeping children indoors from play, or at home from play with neighboring children; or depriving them of an expected trip to town or elsewhere, or of some desirable foodstuff or "treat" (cake or pie at home; candy, gum, or an ice-cream cone in town). Threats of privation, however, are more frequent than the privations themselves. Parents often secure obedience by threatening a dilatory child, "If you *don't* do that you won't get . . . etc." Yet even when a child has been "bad" in the face of a definite threat of deprivation, the parent often "forgets" or the child secures the desired treat anyhow as a bribe to "stop whining and wheedling," especially if it takes advantage of a conversation between the parent and a friend in town, to start "pleading." Plainville children are never "sent to bed without their suppers," or locked up in a dark closet for their ill deeds, but many are threatened with the "bugger-man" (bogey-man) who "lives outside in the dark" to punish or "git" bad children. The bugger-man is a great unseen ally of harassed mothers, and most children develop a fearful dread of the dark.

That teasing and kidding are not considered "instructional" is perhaps due to the fact that mothers seldom kid or tease a child. They are instead a "refuge" to which children return for comfort and security when the teasing becomes too severe elsewhere. Other children and adults (especially males) are delighted to fill in any gaps in this direction. Fathers so often tease and kid children for mere pastime that a child sometimes becomes confused about just what the father expects of it. The produce dealer's daughter, aged three, was accustomed to his kidding her about everything. To the question "Who's little girl are you?" he had trained her to reply, "I'm a boy!" (Her real "given" name was "Billie M.") One day in the Produce House he was playing with her a "spanking" game which they often played. She would say, "Spank me, Daddy!" He would spank her lightly, and both would laugh affectionately. Suddenly he asked her to run an errand to the store next door. She thought he was kidding, and in a kidding manner she refused. He threatened to spank her if she did not do his bidding. She said, laughing, "Spank me, Daddy!" He spanked her hard. She was amazed and grief-stricken to discover that he had become serious. He said to a bystander, "She'll have to learn when I'm kiddin' and when I mean it." Some Plainville fathers, though not Billie M.'s father, seem to take conscious pleasure in even torturing their children (especially small sons) cruelly through teasing. These cases are rather extreme, but every Plainville child that wishes to live comfortably has to learn when people are kidding and when they really mean it.

Certain little boys about three years old who learn this lesson best assume an astonishing role as "favored children" in the eyes of the whole community. The vocational agriculture teacher's son and one little farm boy were two such cherished children. Everybody thought they were the cutest and sweetest children in the community. Both had learned to distinguish between serious conversation and kidding. Both had learned to answer kidding with "wise" and "smart-alec" comments by which they gave as good as they received. Asked, "Have you got a girl?" the first might answer, "Yep! I've got seb'm (seven)! How's your old woman?" The second, if asked, "Did your Dad help you plow corn today?" might reply, "Yes, but I had to give him a lickin' before he'd work." The small son of a restaurant owner suffered endless torture and interference with his play, which was necessarily on the sidewalk in front of the restaurant, until he learned not to cry or fight back when teased by all the male street loafers, but to take teasing in good part and answer kidding with "cute remarks."

There are some rather interesting differences in the relative disciplinary powers of mothers and fathers. A few mothers are reported to be more severe with children than their fathers are, but most children regard their mothers as some measure of protection against severe punishment from fathers. Children do not ordinarily mistake for more than a threat the mother's frequent threat, "If you don't obey me, I'll ask your father to punish you when he comes in from the field." They know that her patience will have to be frayed in the extreme (or the offense must be very grave) before she will substitute a "big trouble," involving the father, herself, and the child, and perhaps her other children too, for a "small trouble," which will quickly blow over even if she fails to solve it. The majority of mothers do their own punishing, and the father his own. A father generally gets quicker obedience from a child than its mother does because—though he actually has much less role than the mother in rearing and disciplining the child—punishment from him when it occurs is more sudden, sure, and severe. He is less apt to "threaten first," and he will stand less argument or "back-talk." That many mothers will plead, cajole, nag, urge, and threaten but not often actually punish a child above seven or eight years old is a fact so well understood by most children that as a form of sport they often deliberately arouse the whole process "just to see how far they can go." When a mother does actually carry out her threat of reporting a child's misdeeds to the father, the latter ordinarily hears out from her the details of the case before executing punishment. The details are sometimes accompanied by denials or counteraccusations from the child, and sometimes by informal testimony from its brothers and sisters.

So many variations occur in the disciplinary system that it is impossible to describe them all. Some children "would not be allowed to say a single word" while their mother is reporting an offense to the father. Some are not allowed ever to "correct a parent," even on a parental misstatement of an everyday fact. Some, perhaps the majority, are nowadays allowed what older people consider to be shocking license in "speaking their word" and in doing what they like. Of one family with many children, living in town, a neighbor said, "Whatever either parent tells one of them childern to do, you know that the child is gonna do exactly the opposite."

It can perhaps be said that while the father stands in the background as a final judge and power—and for boys an ideal of male competence and superiority which they are urged to imitate, the main tutelary and executive power for very small children is the mother. Her authority is in many ways a reflection of the father's position as "lord and master," but the early ideal for *moral* imitation is probably the mother. In her role as an "obedient and dutiful" wife, she inculcates in young children the ideals of goodness, obedience, and all good conduct. Most men will say, "I leave all this (that is, discipline and early instruction) up to my wife." The situation is altered greatly for boys, when they start "follering" the father about his work. It is altered also for both sexes when they start to school.

Not all of the whole "socialization" process, of course, is in the hands of mothers or even of parents. The school and even the Sunday school, but more especially play groups, brothers and sisters, other children of various ages but especially older children, and many adults outside the family all have a hand in "socializing" each child. A listing of what children "learn" and where they learn it would fill several books. The formulation of personality, especially the personality of boys, begins very early to pass away from the mother. A fact well worth mentioning in this connection is that rural children and small town children of both sexes, for all the "isolation" of rural life, know warmly more adults (though usually fewer children) than most urban children know. Through schools and parental interests, urban children are segregated much more rigidly than country children into very narrow age grades. Many learn to know intimately only two adults: their parents. This fact must be of enormous significance in the personality development of urban children and in their understanding of adult life in general. If the city child's parents are "peculiar," "neurotic," or badly adjusted to each other, then he must get a very strange idea of normal adult relationships. Country children, in observing rather intimately the patterns of domestic and economic life in other families, have innumerable opportunities to correct through comparison any misconceptions of "normal" family or other adult life which they receive in their own homes.

From brothers, neighbor boys, and other males, including adult males, the growing Plainville boy begins gradually to learn, as soon as he is old enough to toddle or be led away from "his mother's apron strings," a great number of things that boys (and usually only boys) are "supposed to know." Here too age grades are of great importance, because males (like females) are gathered informally through play, and formally through school, into a rising series of narrow age groups. Until he is fully "grown up," his own age group is a group of boys whose ages differ from his only by a year or two. These are his "equals." Older age groups, however, while "exclusive" in certain ways, not only "welcome" him as he rises from one age to the next, but reach downward to influence him, both directly and through the intervening age-groups, which pass on downward what they learn from above. From much of what a boy learns from other boys, his mother, and often also his father, would gladly protect him. She would spare him when very young the teasing from older males, which begins very early to teach him combativeness and aggression. She would later spare him the rough and dangerous play and "dirty talk" of boys' gangs, and still later his "wild oats" period. If he follows her instructions, however, and rejects those of his male companions, he will be a "sissy."

Among girls there is less conflict than among boys between what the mother teaches and what the society outside the home teaches. The little girl does not get teased very severely. Girls' age groups, while formally and theoretically similar to those of boys, are less rigidly exclusive. The girls' "gangs" are only a weak imitation of boys' gangs. For a growing girl, the task of the society is to teach her how finally to pass from a situation under her mother to one resembling her mother's. All the techniques and ideals learned from her mother will apply in the new situation. She can, and often does, make the whole transition, from infancy to "a home of her own," without serious inner conflict. The growing male, however, must learn, as the Danish fairy tale writer phrased it, that "the world is not like what one's mother says, but what the neighbors say." In league to prevent his learning this are his mother and other women, the church, his schoolteachers, all "genteel" and "respectable" forms, stated ideals, and rituals in the community, and usually the "spoken word" of his father. In league to teach him, however, are the older boys and men, gossip, actual observation of trading practices and the like, and often the tacit connivance of his father. He must learn all that he is supposed to, "sow a few wild oats" without acquiring any fixed bad habits, and finally break away from the domination of his parents and settle down, into a new situation either "outside" or in his home community, where *he* is dominant in at least a matrimonial situation. To attain fully approved adult status he must finally subscribe anew, ostensibly at least, to the fictions of "respectability" which overlie the bringing up of the next generation.

The earliest work techniques are taught by the mother; little boys and girls first learn simple chores: putting their playthings away (from the middle of the floor), hanging their coats and caps up, fetching objects for mother, bringing in chips and cobs for kindling; later, carrying in wood, at first a stick at a time; still later, picking berries or fruit, gathering in the eggs, feeding and watering the chickens, working in the garden (hoeing, weed-pulling, and gathering the vegetables). These are the "common tasks" which all children are taught, regardless of sex. The teaching of them is seldom called "teaching," however, though the learning is called "learning." It may be significant semantically that in native vocabulary "learning" means either teaching or learning. The efforts of local school teachers to clarify the distinction between the two words is as illogical functionally as their effort to convince Plainville children that a double negative means a positive.

It is considered that, except in moral matters, where "most children would naturally be bad, if you didn't learn 'em better," the motive impulse for learning lies with the child. Children "want to learn." They "like to help." They "want to *do*." They like to "foller and watch and help mother (or daddy) when they can." Boys begin very young to follow their fathers and "help him at his work," more often than girls are allowed to. Children often "want to do more'n they know how to." The "patient" parent permits them to try their hand frequently at new tasks, even when their "help" slows down the work itself or botches it. Children's play often imitates the tasks they can already perform, the tasks of older children, and adult work and social situations.

By age six to nine, girls can dry the dishes; a little later they can wash them. Most boys also learn to dry and wash dishes, but "they don't like to." It is girls' and women's work, and boys don't want to be "caught doing it." Girls often begin to sew at about the same age; a little later to sweep and dust, to make the beds, to wash and iron and mend clothes, and sometimes to cook. Mistakes in cooking "ruin good food" and bring "complaints from the menfolks," however, and many girls do not learn to cook until much later. Some girls learn to do "fancy work": tatting, crocheting, embroidering, and sometimes fancy quilting. Gardening work begins for both sexes at age nine or ten.

Boys begin to milk at eight to ten. Girls sometimes do too, though milking is "men's work." At about the same age boys learn to split and chop wood, to keep the water bucket filled and the wood box full, to do "barn chores" like feeding, and they begin to work in the field. Few girls learn to do these men's tasks except for carrying water into the house. Yet girls do not scorn "men's tasks," as boys scorn dishwashing, sweeping, and bed-making, nor would they be ashamed to do them. Many girls envy boys their work, their greater mobility of action, and their future roles. No boy ever says, "I wish I was a girl." Fathers and brothers however are criticized for letting women and girls do "heavy work," especially for letting them "chop wood" or "work in the field."

Many girls are fully competent to "take care of a home" (including the "mothering" of smaller children) by the time they are eleven.

Most boys are fully competent to do all but the heaviest of field work at the same age. Boys learn first to drive a team, then in turn to harrow, plow ("break") ground, ride a rake, cultivate corn, ride a mower, etc. Hay-pitching and other tasks require greater strength. The order of learning is shifted somewhat on tractor-run farms, but the average boy knows from observation very early how tractors and cars are operated, and boys are often allowed to handle gasoline-run machinery as early as at age eleven. The father teaches all these skills; the boy "begs to learn" and is encouraged to learn. In learning to handle team-operated farm implements, he first follows the father. He then "takes the lines" (by which the team is controlled) himself. He next is allowed to harrow or plow a round by himself, watched or accompanied by the father. Finally, he is able to "make a full-time hand."

In the old days he would from this point on have made a full-time hand in the fields. Any schooling he got would have been got when he was not needed at home. Now, however, compulsory schooling interferes at age six with the full exploitation of children's work. Boys and girls alike must attend school, theoretically, until they are fourteen or until they have "passed the eighth grade." Almost all better-class children and many lower-class children now go on to attend the high school in Plainville. Thus "the work their parents get out of them" is mostly limited to "before and after school," to Saturdays and to the seventeen or eighteen summer weeks of school vacation. They perform many labors during these times. During the summer, most schoolboys living on farms work about as much as their fathers worked at the same age. Their work is limited somewhat by the fact that a father is unable to put in as big a crop as he might have planted if his sons had been available for work in early spring. Modern machinery, however, for planting corn and drilling small grain, tends to speed up the early spring and late fall work more than it speeds up the work of cultivating corn, haying, and harvesting. Many boys also stay out of school a few days at a time to help with pressing tasks. Winter Saturdays are often spent in the timber at wood chopping. Most farm boys and girls have numerous chores to perform before and after school. Their teachers assign them little or no "homework."

Very few children live in town; for those who do, the "common work" techniques for young children are about the same as for country children and are taught in the same way. Town people have gardens, often a few chickens, and sometimes hogs and a milk cow. Wood and water are to be carried in. For girls, the household tasks are nearly identical with farm housekeeping tasks. For boys, however, there are fewer techniques to be learned, and town boys are accused of growing up as "lazy, worthless loafers," unless their parents own places of business in which they can start "helping" at a young age.

The school is the first important formal disciplinary institution which the child enters outside his own home. The teacher is a new "parent," often cherished as "younger" than the real parents, but often regarded through folkloristic devices which induce fear of teachers and dread of school as more unsympathetic and formidable in authority than parents themselves. A teacher can "love" a child, but she (or he) can also "whip," in all schools outside the consolidation, despite a state law against corporal punishment. In school, by processes bearing little resemblance to suggestions in the state syllabus, most children are somehow taught the rudiments of reading, writing, and figuring. In school also, the common moral sentiments on which all "nice people" agree are again reiterated, though "nothing is said in school" (outside the vocational agriculture classes) either to reinforce or weaken any "fanatical" moral strictures, or any superstitions or magical ideas which the child may have learned at home. The school "tries to serve the whole community" without offending anybody.

A more important aspect of schooling, however, is that here the child is drawn partially away from the mother's apron strings and begins long periods of contact with more children than he has been accustomed to. All the children in a neighborhood are gathered into a rural school; most of those from a wide area into the consolidated school. In either case, the children are thrown together by age, regardless of sex, for formal class work. Outside of classes, the boys play mostly with boys, the girls with girls. Until recently, most rural school grounds were divided into two areas, for mutually exclusive use by the sexes.

The social organization of children, even in a small rural school with not more than ten or twenty "scholars," is extremely complex and discriminatory. One important division is of boys against girls. Girls "like to play with boys," and "want to know what boys know," but boys admit them only discretely into their games and their counsels. Boys tease girls and profess disregard for them. Boys say, "girls are a nuisance." "If a girl tags along or bothers, twist her arm and get rid of her."

But this is not the only important division or discrimination. An older boy is greatly superior to a younger one, in strength, skills, and valuable knowledge. The age lines between boys are very narrowly drawn. Younger boys desire acceptance by older boys; older boys admit younger boys to their society only when they are "useful," in games, for teasing, and as an audience for the ostentation of superior knowledge. Considerable cruelty is practiced by older boys on a younger boy: they attempt to shame, tease, or torture out of him any weakness, cowardice, or "babylike" quality he manifests. A boy becomes aligned most closely with the group of boys whose ages are within a year or two of his own. While such align-

ments are in many ways exclusive, they also overlap with
similar alignments of younger boys and of older boys: an
eight-year old boy who is a leader and impressive "big shot"
with the six to eight-year old group is at the same time often
an underling among the eight to ten-year olds. From these he
collects, as a tolerated spectator or object of condescending
enlightenment, habits, attitudes, and information and misin-
formation, which he passes on to the awestruck members of his
younger group. The main process of male socialization takes
place in this fashion. Male traits and "knowledge" are passed
down and inculcated, from age-group to age-group. This is
one of the main social functions of the boys' gangs and age-
groups.

Something similar, but weaker, happens among girls. Among
girls, however, the teasing patterns are negligibly evident.
Girls are "taught to be nice" to younger girls; this fits in with
the doll pattern, with the ultimate roles of girls as mothers,
and with the single developmental line followed by female
lives.

From boys, boys learn "not to be a sissy." They learn to
hammer, whittle, make pop guns and sling shots, fly a kite,
shoot a gun, hunt, fish, swim, skate, and play many approved
games. A country boy is also supposed to "learn the timber":
to know where all the wild foods grow, the traditional names of
insects, snakes, birds, trees, weeds, and vines, and the habits
of wild animals and birds. He is no longer, however, "really
supposed" to acquire nearly so much of this nature lore as his
father's generation learned when they were boys.

A boy learns from other boys how to fight—how to "hold
his own," at least. He does not have to know as much about
fighting as his male forebears did, because fighting, especially fighting among men, but also even "real fighting among
boys," is beginning to be disapproved.

From other boys he further learns a great number of "dangerous" or "outlaw" traits—these are the traits his mother
especially discourages and disapproves. Teasing or torturing
girls or smaller boys is one of them; so is cruelty to any form of

life, but he plucks the wings from horseflies and tosses them into the air to hear them buzz. He kills every snake he finds (this is approved). He climbs to dangerous heights in trees, jumps off barns, takes risks. He learns to "break things" and "destroy things" ("boys are just naturally destructive"); to have contempt for bathing and the cleanliness of girls and women. He learns to cuss and "talk dirty," and to tell "dirty" stories. The themes of these stories are scatology and sex. He "learns about sex" from boys. He learns "how to steal water-melons" from patches, fruit from orchards, and hickory nuts from other people's timber. He learns to think "it's more fun to *take* something like that than to ask for it, though he knows nobody'd mind him having it." Prestige accrues to him among boys for learning the outlaw traits along with "useful knowl-edge." The outlaw traits are only feebly developed in girls' gangs, though girls are reproached less than formerly for ac-quiring some of the more harmless boys' traits. Little girls who "whistled," "walked fences," turned "summersets," or —worst of all—"straddled a horse" were once considered "tomboys," a hated and dreadful label. Nowadays some par-ents are proud of a tomboy.

Sex education for Plainville boys is largely left up to "na-ture" and, tacitly, to other boys. Sex is a subject which neither mothers nor fathers "feel they could discuss" with their sons. Parents teach small children no names for their sex organs (beyond perhaps the words "that" or "it"), and tell them no facts about childbirth.[2] When a new baby is expected, the other children are generally bundled off to a neighbor's until after the birth. They may be told that mother is "not feeling well." They are supposed to be greatly surprised at seeing the new baby when they return home. About it they are told one of several customary myths: the doctor fetched it in his satchel, a stork brought it through the sky, swinging in a big diaper, Mother came across it in the grass, or Daddy found it in the orchard.

[2] Very "modern" people, of course, explain childbirth, though the cult of explaining it in terms of birds and flowers failed to reach Plainville. And again, some lower-element families tell their sons frankly "where babies come from."

Only very young children, however, subscribe to these myths. The average six-year old child has frequently observed intercourse of animals (boys have especially—it is easier to protect girls from such sights), and most of them have seen the births of kittens, puppies, pigs, calves, or colts. They have asked questions, first of their parents, whose hush-hush dissemblings have indicated that these are no proper subjects for adult-child discussions. Later they have sought and learned from other children a body of information in the main correct, though some garbling naturally occurs as taboo knowledge is circulated downward through the age-groups. The average seven- or eight-year-old child has learned to integrate fairly well what he has seen with what he can learn from other children. Most children of that age "know where animals come from and where *they* come from," though they still know nothing of periods of gestation. A common early misconception regarding birth is that every act of coitus results in offspring, and that offspring follows coitus almost immediately. "Lots of girls used to believe that till they got married—if they knowed *any*thing."

The total lack of realism with which fathers face the problem of instructing their boys about sex is curious. Either they tell them nothing whatever, or, when the boy is fifteen or sixteen years old, they manage to transmit the popular notion that "self abuse" will cause pimples, or general debility, or insanity. The boy, more likely than not, has already heard this story from other boys, as a discredited myth (but not sufficiently discredited to remove all fear) which adults either actually believe or wish youngsters to believe. At about the same time the father is likely to become less guarded with his son—he may tell a smutty story to him or in his presence, or relate sexual gossip, as a form of "treating him more like a man." Many fathers say, "Boys really ought to be told about things, but I wouldn't know how to start." Considerable constraint regarding discussion of sexual matters persists between most fathers and sons until after the son is married and has children of his own.

Mothers or older sisters, on the other hand, generally prepare girls to expect menstruation, and sometimes they tell girls "about men" before marriage. Sexual explanations arouse less embarrassment between mother and daughter than between father and son. At one time, however, according to several women, "Girls were told absolutely nothing. That was considered the duty of their husbands." Menstruation is a fearfully taboo subject. Even women do not like to say the word to each other; they prefer to refer to it by euphemisms like "that way," "not feeling well," "indisposed," or "in that sickly way."

What all this taboo on sex actually means is difficult to say. It is undoubtedly related to the fact that sexual relations between husband and wife are said to be usually unsatisfactory. A common complaint about marriage relations is that "the old man likes sex but the old lady don't." Perhaps the comparative ease with which mothers can teach their daughters the "facts of life" (in contrast with father-son constraint) may have something to do with the widespread feminine attitude that sex is predominantly a male interest—something that girls should be warned against, though taught to accept as a later wifely duty; an interest which women are tacitly banded together to resist as strongly as they dare. Many people think that the majority of women are frigid.

To return to childhood, boys ordinarily are "taught" by slightly older boys, at about age ten or twelve, to perform their first "sexual" experiments. These manual pastimes seem sometimes to become a featured activity of boys' gang life, in addition to hunting, swimming, fishing, and "roaming the timber." Several men rather humorously told of such, though they had "never mentioned such things to anybody else in their whole life," and found it extremely odd that they should be quizzed on this subject. One man told how his "club" used to sit on a log on the river after swimming, and "compete with each other" on the point of speed. Many folkloristic jokes and narratives treat further boyhood experimentation with domestic animals, especially calves, and occasionally with

little girls, even with sisters. When names of real people are
attached, they are usually the names of lower-class people, but
nobody seems to take such stories very seriously as truth. All
early sex experimentation is carefully concealed from parents
and all other elders, and children, if caught, would expect
severe punishment. Grown men, however, in looking back
upon it, generally regard it as rather harmless, or as they say,
"just natural." After puberty is fully established, such self-
play, when practiced, is practiced in solitude.

Actual sex experience, when it precedes marriage, very
seldom occurs at an age younger than seventeen or eighteen
years. Pre-marital experience seems to occur oftener, and at
an earlier age, among "tough" lads of lower-element families
than among any others. The community's stated sexual ideals
are the same for boys as for girls; chastity until monogamous
marriage. As a matter of fact, however, so much restraint is
hardly expected from boys. What is expected of a boy is enough
secrecy to avoid gossip or scandal, and enough "sense" to avoid
"trouble"—trouble meaning to catch a venereal disease or to
impregnate a girl. Relative secrecy regarding a venereal disease
can be guarded through treatments by the local doctor or an
outside doctor, but "serious girl trouble" can result in expense ("hush money" or the cost of sending the girl outside
the community for an abortion or for childbirth), family disgrace, or an "unfortunate marriage."

It is expected however that most boys will acquire a limited
amount of sexual experience before marriage, as they are expected to experiment with drinking and "running around."
All these "outlaw traits" are associated with a young man's
"sowing his wild oats." It is better if he sows his wild oats
outside the community, if possible, and Plainville boys sometimes pick up girls, or occasionally even patronize prostitutes,
in towns as far away as Largetown. A girl who sows any wild
oats, at home or abroad, is disgraced, and her parents are
disgraced. But a "disgraced" girl, even if she becomes pregnant and has a child, is accepted again into the community
when she gets married, and "the talk has had time to die

down." Women now respectable are the mothers of babies whose arrival gave rise to much finger counting ("and nobody ever got to nine"). The stigma of bastardy was once so intense that even the grandchildren of a bastard still suffered some disgrace. Bastards are now considered unfortunate, but not themselves blameworthy; and if their mother marries, their dubious origin is nearly forgotten.

The courtship system is only remotely connected to the data just given, though the term "going with girls" can cover any variety of youthful intentions. Courtship grows out of the conventional and approved "dating" relationships between youths and girls, and it is directed first toward entertainment and later toward marriage, "settling down," and attaining full adult status. Sexual play in conventional courtship does not go beyond kissing or "necking," because courtship is between social equals. Parents are very careful, regarding their children, of the "company they keep." Class lines may not be crossed in approved dating, courtship, or marriage.

Dating begins at age fourteen to seventeen; the age depends on size, maturity, and parental consent—and, for boys, on when they are allowed use of the car. Couples used to go places together afoot, and on horseback. A later generation of dating couples went about in buggies. Now no boy can hope for a "date" unless he has access to a car. Double-dating is popular, until "a couple gets really serious," because money is scarce, and it costs money for car rides and trips "outside" to movies—the two chief pastimes for dating couples. The dating situation in the Plainville high school somewhat resembles that in any typical American coeducational college. The majority of both sexes (even barring very young or small children) have no dates. Fewer girls than boys have dates. The very "popular" girls are sought after by a considerable number of boys; about fifty percent of the boys old enough and big enough to date compete eagerly for about ten percent of the girls. How both sexes finally resolve the problem of personal choice and decide to pair off and get married is a mystery, but they do. Almost no Plainvillers fail to get married. The thirty-four "surplus women" in Plainville are nearly all widows; only two or three are old maids. The situation in the countryside is similar. Yet it is considered hard for a woman to get a mate, though easy for a man to get one.

A further point should be made about how the social organization of youth fits into the class system. The restriction against cross-class dating has been mentioned. When a better-class boy dates a lower-class religious girl, his family is only greatly disturbed, and fearful of a possible alliance with the girl's family. If he dates a lower-element girl, they are ashamed and scandalized, because "everybody knows what he's after." For an upper-class girl to have a date with a lower-class boy would be inconceivable. All children are obliged to learn a very complex set of rules regarding their proper relationship with socially inferior or superior children. For young school-boys there are almost no restrictions, though their parents "teach them the difference," or gap, that exists between families of separate classes. In later childhood, boys of almost any class can play, hunt, swim together, visit each other, and even "stay all night" together. A preacher's son on vacation from college spent one of his first nights at home illegally "noodling" for spawning catfish on the Apple River, together with two "absolutely lower-element" brothers (named Billings) from a neighboring farm. The fathers of these boys "neighbor." They exchange work or tools, chat at the line fence, and visit each other for an hour or two both outdoors and indoors, ostensibly as equals. Says the preacher, "You couldn't ask for a better *neighbor* than Old Albert. He kids me about preachin', and I kid him about goin' to hell!" The two mothers draw a sharper line. They "treat each other with respect," but they would visit only in case of serious sickness or need. The preacher's daughters were not allowed to play with the Billings girls after the age of about eight. If his oldest daughter (now sixteen) meets a "grown" Billings boy in town, she "speaks to" him pleasantly, but she would not dream of pausing a moment to chat.

Upper class methods of teaching children how to treat inferiors are observable daily by people who have access to the homes in which upper-class children are reared. These methods are about as uniform and inexorable in their application as they would be if all upper-class people freely and openly subscribed to a "class theory" regarding social organization of their community. Discriminations against inferior people are usually inculcated in terms of family names, or at most, the phrase "people like that," a phrase which can be used either pejoratively or approvingly. The child is told, *"You* don't want to play with Johnny *Jones! He* (his family, people like *that)* don't know how to *act* (talk, play, play right, play nice, play *your* kind of games). . . . Why don't you walk home from school with the *Smith* children? You'd like to be *seen* with people like that. . . . The *Joneses* keep hounds . . . are dirty . . . have bedbugs . . . won't work . . . live back in the timber . . . have nothing (the appeal is only rarely to relative wealth or property) . . . don't go to church . . . are rough . . . are not *our* kind. People would *laugh* if they saw you at Joneses. . . . The Smiths are nice (or 'nice average') people like us . . . they *live* right and know how to *treat* people right." It doesn't take much talk of this kind to teach Junior and his sister who the Smiths and Joneses are, but they hear enough to drive the lesson firmly home against the contradictory axiom that "ever'body here is equal." At the same time they are "cautioned" repeatedly never to "show" the Jones children that they "feel any difference," and never to "tell away from home anything they hear at home that might hurt anybody's feelings." A lady mentioned her chagrin when a neighbor woman once "bawled her out in town" for saying that the latter's family "had bugs." The informant said, "I just told (my little boy) that so he wouldn't want to play there, but he went and told it. I fixed (punished) him, and he never told anything like that again."

It is harder for a field worker to observe how lower-class children learn their share of the same lesson, though they learn it equally well. Certainly all lower-class parents teach their children as a fundamental dictum regarding their status, "You're just as good as anybody." When their children complain, however, of rebuffs or neglect from other children this dictum is apt to be softened into an appeal to them through self-pride to *"act* like you're just as good as anybody." Or they may hear the following, "I wouldn't want to go where I wasn't wanted." Real or fancied slights suffered by these children are often explained away by compensatory statements of contempt toward the families of the offenders. "They're *selfish* people . . . cold people. They don't have no manners (don't know how to treat people). . . . They're stuck up, uppity, persnickity . . . They think they're *good* (above, rich). . . . They're too 'nice' for us. . . . They're Sunday school folks so of course they think they're above . . . They're church hypocrites." By comments related to prestige points valid only among the lower element, the pride of children is often reinforced toward the parental way of life. *"You* know how to shoot (hunt, fish, trap, swim) better than *any* Smith boy . . . You could outfight any Smith your size." It is through such "timber" traits and the common "outlaw traits" of all boys that the Smith and Jones boys often become and remain "good friends" in a male life carried on mainly outdoors. It begins in boyhood play and continues in the line-fence neighboring, loafing-group intimacy and trading and "political" maneuverings in which all men move freely about the community. The social integration of the community rests on the easy intimacy of men. The community *is* a community because men can associate freely beyond the walls of their homes.

Marriage comes generally, for boys, at about age twenty to twenty-two; for girls, slightly earlier. In order to marry, a boy "by rights" should have a means of livelihood figured out in advance, but many marry first "and then figger out how to make a living." The economic opportunities in and about Plainville have already been described.

I must at this point go back a number of years and suggest

how a young man has attained enough knowledge of property and economic procedure to undertake the hazard of starting a new family.

By the time he was fifteen, at latest, the farm boy was equipped with all the skills and techniques for making a living, except the skill of "managing." When not in school he did a man's work. In fact, one of the first important blows to his self-esteem and happiness probably came about then with his discovery that through his own early eagerness to learn he had been jockeyed into doing a man's work, without gaining any voice in planning or helping to manage the family enterprise. "As soon as he learned to do things he got to do 'em, but nobody asked him what ought to be done next or how." His parents also very early taught him frugality, "the proper respect for money," by telling him how scarce and valuable money is, by doling out small sums of spending money to him painfully (as if "somebody was pullin' a tooth"), and by urging him, "Don't spend it. Save it." From other boys he learned the art of "swapping": pocket knives, marbles, toys, string, broken bits of farm machinery, anything he carried in his pockets. "Swapping," in the boys' world, is a duplicate of trading among men. Boys learn by swapping to be "smart traders" who make a profit, or "suckers" who get cheated, or the more average property owners who "keep what they have" without risking it on a gamble or a trade. Yet real money or property beyond small spending money— a nickel or dime at a time, begged often from his mother— were, like planning and managing, very probably outside his domain. A few girls are allowed to raise a setting of eggs, to sell as fryers; some boys are given a pig or a calf to raise. The proceeds, in either case, usually go for clothes which they would get anyway, yet children seem very proud when allowed ownership and management even to this limited degree. People often comment on how "children love to own something." Most people agree that "they *should* own something," but few own anything.

Some are allowed to "claim" a calf or pig, until it is sold

or eaten, but without voice in its disposal or any share of the money it brings. Children are never paid for work they do at home. Boys, however, have the right to "work out," when not needed at home. They are paid about half of men's wages when they are, say, fifteen, and of average size and strength for that age; a year or two later, they get full wages ($1.00 to $1.50 a day in 1939–40) for the days they work. Boys and girls both have a right (though no exclusive right) to any salable wild products. For girls this means that they can gather and sell wild blackberries and wild gooseberries beyond family needs, if they can find anyone who wants to buy them. Boys can trap and hunt. Not all boys trap and hunt—prairie boys generally live too far from the timber to set a trap line. But many a boy, in good trapping years, earns all his spending money, clothes, and sometimes school supplies, by trapping, skinning, and selling the hides of skunks, muskrats, 'possums, and perhaps a few mink and raccoons. Until 1939 he also had a sale for rabbits (shipped away as meat), at ten to fifteen cents per carcass. (The upper-class contempt for "hunting and trapping" does not apply to boys; it applies only to adults who hunt and trap as an old-fashioned way of livelihood or a way to "escape honest work.") Two girls from the hills were rather admired for having earned the money for "high school clothes" by "trapping just like boys do," in 1937–38. Children are in general allowed to spend whatever they earn even though it may be well understood between them and their parents that they have to spend it all for necessities.

Before a youth gets married, then, he knows how to farm. He has earned some money and handled its expenditure. He may have some savings, or a head or two of livestock. He has been "outside," on shopping trips, hauling stock to market, or visits, perhaps on "work jobs." He is anxious to break away from his father's economic domination, a situation which is "all work and being bossed" without ever being consulted about "where should we plow today?" or "Which field should we plant to corn next year?" He "has no opportunity, working with his father."

He has "looked over the girl situation" and knows which girls he likes; he may be "in love" with one girl. His friends are "going away or getting married," and "there's getting to be nobody to have a good time with." He may "go away too" —likely to California. If he does, he may "look for somebody to marry out there;" if he stays away he may send home for a "home girl," or return home to marry one. If he marries a "stranger," he is almost certain to remain living away, because a girl from away "wouldn't be apt to like it here." The first once-over that Plainvillers give a bride from "outside," on her first visit to the community with her husband, is directed toward discovering whether she feels "above" or "persnickity" about the community's clothes, living arrangments, manners, and people. If he marries a home girl, his link with home is doubly strong. The chances are now about fifty-fifty that he will decide to live near Plainville; if so, he will almost certainly marry a girl from a neighborhood or community not far from his own. He would once have probably married within his own neighborhood, but is less likely to nowadays, because the car has widened the mobility and acquaintance-ship of youth. Some prestige is attached to "going with a girl" who lives at some distance, rather than with a neighborhood girl.

The only advance indications, generally, that the community receives of a marriage are these: the boy and girl "seem to be going together mighty steady"—they "seem to be getting serious." The boy may also be rumored to be "looking for a location" (a job or a farm to rent) or to be "saving his money." Most engagements are short (three or four months) and are nearly always kept secret until the actual marriage, which is a "surprise" to all except usually the adult members of both families ("children would tell") and perhaps a young confidant or two of each spouse. This seems to be the one secret few confidants will reveal. The reasons for secrecy are obscure, but a couple is gratified at "putting their surprise over on people." They are also pleased at foiling, for as long as they can, "shivaree" plans. Another reason given for the secrecy is that engaged girls would be "embarrased to walk up and down the street and have men look at them" if the men knew of the coming marriage.

The marriage is generally performed by a preacher, at the preacher's house, with a minimum of witnesses. When the school superintendent married one of his teachers, he bought the license at Discovery and the couple drove directly to Reverend B's farm. The preacher came in from a field, performed the ceremony "without being allowed time to change his clothes," and returned to his field work. The couple then drove out of the community for a short honeymoon, which in their case was a car trip lasting a week or two. They stopped several nights in tourist cabins, visited kinfolks for two or three days, and ended their trip by spending several days with the groom's mother on a farm thirty miles south of Plainville. Better-class people and all religious people like to be married by a preacher, but there is no "disgrace" to marriage by a justice of the peace. Church weddings are rare and are considered ostentatious.

The "honeymoon" of most "newlyweds" is a night or two spent at the house of one of their parents. Few take a longer honeymoon, and work is seldom interrupted for longer than a day or two, if at all.

The next step in life is to set up a home. This is usually done as soon as the couple's plans for a livelihood have been formulated (if these have been postponed until marriage). A house or a farm must be rented, and furniture and equipment bought or otherwise "wrastled together." A farm couple often "winters" with one of the parents, since the rental occupancy of farms is standardized to begin on March 1. Meanwhile the groom works at a job or "helps out" with whatever is to be done on the farm where he is living.

As soon as they are fully settled into a home of their own, the young couple begin to be considered full adults. They are supposed to quit "running around and spending money"—from now on. What few dollars they acquire should go into added equipment for the house or farm, a start in livestock, or interest and principal on debts. They should "want to start raising a family" and should "start thinking about owning a home of their own." They should "save" toward these ends.

The woman's talk should begin to center on housekeeping. She should begin to ask older women for recipes and "ask how to save." The man should start talking of "business and politics"—a farmer's business is stock, crops, and "how to manage." If they have not been attending church regularly, it is well if they now begin to do so.

Both members of the partnership must learn through enquiries from parents and other married people, and through "experience," all the things regarding the responsibilities of married adults which they have not already learned through observation and the participations of childhood and youth.

What the life of a young couple now getting married and settling down in Plainville will be or what the lives of their children will be it is not possible to forecast. The lives of present-day married people, during the twenty or thirty years when they are full adult working members of the society, bringing up and marrying off their children, can be implied from the present chapter on the life cycle—by shifting the emphasis from children to adults—as well as from all the rest of this book.

Each couple beyond their productive years will have to grow old and finally die—it may be said that people also have to "learn" to do both these things. The word "old" means different things to Plainvillers of different ages, but in the eyes of people in the prime of life, rearing families and participating actively in the community's social and economic institutions, a married couple begins to be considered "old" when one of the pair can no longer do his or her work. People who cannot work are quickly considered as belonging "on the shelf." A decline in full status and "respect" begins somewhat earlier, however: when children begin to marry off, parents have no further reason to maintain full participation in school, church, Sunday school, etc., and their diminishing importance as heads of functioning families is quickly reflected in the respect which they themselves, their activities, and their opinions enjoy in the eyes of neighbors. Increased activity by some elderly people through the lodges, church memberships and deaconships, and so forth seems to indicate that one function of such formal organizations is to serve as devices for maintaining status and partial respect in the community in the face of declining "real role" and "real respect."

Old people are not now greatly respected except by other old people, but they are respected more if they have saved enough to live on than if they have to accept Old Age Assistance. They retain relatively more respect also if they have "worked hard," "been honest," "lived clean moral lives," and "raised up their children right." They get no special credit for any prowess remembered from their younger days; they are laughed at and condemned if they boast of earlier physical strength, tasks accomplished, or leadership. Old people are liked best who "don't meddle or advise younger people," "don't complain of their ailments," and "don't criticize the younger generation too much." Old people have little contact with younger people, except their close kin.

At death people are embalmed, coffined, and buried in one of several cemeteries near Plainville. Many people come to the funeral, which is held either in church or in the home (older style). A deceased wealthy grocer, farmer, and pillar of the Methodist church was buried in 1939. His metal casket cost $300, and the flowers, imported from florists at Largetown, must have cost nearly as much. Not all of the crowd which gathered could get into the church. After the sermon those who had waited outside were allowed to file through the church aisles and view the corpse before the crowd inside walked by the casket. Not many except kin usually follow the hearse to the cemetery for the real "burying." There is usually a great demonstration of grief at funerals. Sometimes people without any ties whatever to the deceased sob hysterically. The wife of Reverend B, who preached the home-funeral of an aged "lower-element" neighbor (the father-in-law of their neighbor Billings), commented that the old man's children and grandchildren "took on (that is, mourned noisily) just like Christians." A whole complex of modern funeral traits, including embalming, flower girls, bought flowers, and expensive coffins was imported into the community about fifteen years ago by the present undertaker, an excellent businessman. People are very proud of present-day funerals. Embalming was the single element in the trait complex to meet resistance; it is still sometimes rejected. In the older days neighbors washed and dressed the corpse, and watched by it at night before burial. All close kin are notified of an expected death. Children, no matter where they are, who do not return home for a parent's funeral, are condemned. It is considered especially desirable for them to arrive in time to be present at the moment of death.

It is the wish of nearly all Plainvillers to have after death a suitable tombstone set up at their grave (costing anywhere from sixty to several hundred dollars). People take great pride in "putting away their dead" properly, and "children" who fail to set up a monument for their parents are criticized severely. The cult of large tombstones preceded modern undertaking techniques in the community by several generations. Some graves are unmarked, save for a mound or its sunken outline; some are wholly forgotten. Some bear only a wooden marker, or a flowering bush, or shrubs; or some table crockery laid over the grave to keep warm the memory of one once alive and loved. The tombstones erected for children are usually small. All others are generally of a size to recall what the people who bought them could afford. An ironical native, riding past a graveyard with me one day, waved his hand toward it and said, "If you want to know who robbed the people most, just read the names on the biggest gravestones."

6 Conclusion: Plainville and the Future

CHANGES in the region about Plainville have been very rapid and numerous throughout the hundred years during which a white farming population has been living from its mediocre resources. The rate of change has accelerated since the government undertook to reform local farming practices. The recommended agricultural changes are viewed by individual Plainvillers with every conceivable variation of understanding and misunderstanding, and with every conceivable combination of acceptance and rejection. The implied accompanying social reorganization is understood even less, but it is dreaded more.

A brief summary of what life has been like in turn for each successive group which has lived here may shed some light on possibilities for the future. Although the word "generation" has almost no significance when applied to groups larger than individual families, it will be convenient for discussion to divide the successive occupants of the community into five loose generations, as follows:

1) The first settlers (about 1830–60)
2) The second generation and the "second settlers" (about 1860–90)
3) The third generation (about 1890–1920)
4) The fourth generation (about 1920–37)
5) The fifth generation (1937–   )

The first settlers (from about 1830), as frontiersmen and prospective farmers, found ample timbered and bottom land for their needs, never far from "sweet" springs. With the simplest of "civilized" tools they were able to clear fields or patches, build permanent homes, and live a life of almost completely "pure subsistence" from wild game, wild fruits, and whatever they wanted to raise or could raise. The timbered hillsides and the prairies lay about them as free range for whoever wanted to develop livestock herds. Markets were at first very far, but not too far for those who wanted money or outside products to reach once or twice a year with surplus livestock, hides, homespun cloth woven by women, and tubs of salted butter. Merchants soon came, and towns were established. The merchants for a time profited well as the main economic intermediaries between Woodlanders and the distant outside world. Only they "knew the market." They were able for a long time to buy farm products at very low prices [1] and to sell merchandise very dear. Churches and a few schools were built, but the children of early Woodland County people learned a good deal less about reading and writing than their parents knew. With the formation of settled communities, many of the first settlers moved on to new frontiers, for the same reasons they had sought this one.

The children of those who stayed had opportunities very similar to those of their parents. Many of them were already grown when they came, or were at least large enough to drive wagons, ride horses, and herd cows along the rude trails by which their families arrived from Kentucky, Tennessee, and further east. For the older children there was still free or practically free land near natural water, for those who wanted it. Those who preferred still newer country could travel on westward, as their fathers and grandfathers had done before them—either into neighboring states as new lands were "opened" or by dangerous routes across the Great Plains to the Rockies and the Pacific coast. The spike which completed the first transcontinental railroad was not driven at Promontory Point, in Utah, until May 10, 1869, but the first settlers in Woodland County had by that time already contributed

[1] The livestock buying techniques of one (Methodist) merchant only thirty years ago are significant. When cattle or hogs were worth say $10 per cwt. on the Metropolis market and he wanted to buy up a rail carload to ship via Stanton, he would first hire a man to ride over the country to "explain the poor markets" to farmers and offer them $4-5 per cwt. for their animals. When his agent "had 'em all scared, then Ol' Squier he'd get on his *own* horse and ride out and offer 'em a cent or two more a pound. Then, they'd all sell, of course, and *he* was a good feller." (Told by the retired Methodist preacher, and in essence by several others.) Farmers now know market conditions from the radio. They even tend to overvalue "scrub stuff" with "prime" quotations.

numerous children to the development of "the real West."
The first settlers, with their older sons, completed the oc-
cupation of all the good bottom and hill land in Woodland
County.

The opportunities of the second generation—composed of
people attaining adulthood after about 1860—were to inherit
the first farms, spread out onto the prairie, or go West. Families were large in those days: ten or fifteen children born from
the same mother were not uncommon. Obviously only two to
four in each family, at most, could actually inherit the parental land (in the sense of replacing parents as occupants) except
by subdivisions which would quickly have reduced farms to
small patches. Most of the first farms were passed down pa-
ternal lines without much subdivision to sons who "bought
out" the shares of their brothers and sisters.

Other sons (and their wives) joined with a second wave of
settlement from outside the county and helped to homestead
the prairie. These "second settlers" were prairie-seekers, who
brought with them the steel-beamed plow (the "plow that
broke the plains"), a need for sawn lumber, and the knowledge
that men and livestock could live on the prairie, apart from
springs, if wells twenty to forty feet deep were dug. The bull-
tongued plow, with its affiliated traits of frame houses, wells,
and prairie farming, can be taken as a symbol of the first
social revolution in the county. In its wake came corn planters,
steel cultivators, mowing machines, binders, threshers, and
(more recently) tractors and combines—in short the whole
evolution of prairie technology and "manners," by which hill
life and frontier traits have been devaluated to the point of
being considered "comic," and the present class system has
been established.

The prairie was all homesteaded between about 1865 and
1890. Plainville was "surveyed and laid off into a town, with
streets, alleys, and a public square," in 1869. It had four business houses and a "steam flouring mill" in 1870, a "plain comfortable school building" in 1871, a church in 1888, and ap-
proximately its present population by 1890. Between 1869 and

1889, six separate newspapers had in turn made brief and unsuccessful appearances in the town.

Yet hills and prairie together probably did not absorb over half of this second generation, even though this was the period of enormous growth in the local population. The "Californy fever" which struck all America after the opening of the transcontinental railroad swept hundreds of youths westward from Woodland County communities, not only to California itself, but to Oklahoma, Texas, New Mexico, Arizona, Nebraska, the Dakotas, Colorado, Utah, Wyoming, Montana, Idaho, Oregon, and Washington. There was plenty of excellent free land everywhere, and frontier life for all who retained the ambivalent frontiersman's dislike of "settled ways." Plainville talk is full of names of those who became western cowboys or prospectors and then "disappeared and were never heard of again," as well as of those who became ranchers in every state in the West. Warm kin bonds still reach from Plainville to each state.

The third generation—maturing between about 1890 and 1920—saw great changes in opportunities between the early and the later years of this period. During the whole thirty years, of course, the established farms in the community offered homes to a fraction of young adults, as their parents grew old, and "retired" or died. The great changes were in migrational opportunities. In 1890 Western homesteads were still plentiful; by 1920 the land frontier was essentially ended, in reality if not in American dream. Between these two dates occurred the greatest development of western and midwestern American cities, railroads, mines, factories. The complex arrangement of modern industrialism which moved westward after the pioneers was now "completed" for the entire nation. Of surplus Plainville youth maturing during this generation, a large portion continued to occupy western land; other large numbers found jobs on western ranches, in Midwestern and Western cities, in mines, or on railroads. The proportion occupying new land was at first large, later small; the proportion securing jobs connected with industry was at first small, later

large. As always before and after in Plainville history, the jobs
that Plainvillers got were generally at hard, unskilled labor.
Several reasons explain this fact. In the first place, "city wages"
and "Western wages" of $3–$5 a day sounded fabulously large
to young men accustomed to thinking of "a dollar a day" as
the standard value of work and unaccustomed to placing much
money value on housing and food. Second, their training at
home and in school equipped them with no skills, economic
insights, or social "manners" adequate for any other approach
to industrial or urban life. Third, their personal contacts for
job seeking abroad were with kinsmen and friends who had
preceded them, and they often joined little colonies of Woodlanders where much of their home situation was duplicated
and sentiments for home were maintained. Some Plainvillers
were of course "glad to shake the dirt of Woodland County off
their feet," but some in the large Sacramento Valley "colony"
still lament that their children fail to "love the old home
(which they have never seen) as they should." Full acculturation to life in new regions is seldom accomplished except by
the children of migrants.

Few youths of this generation (or any other) entered professional life beyond rural school teaching, though this was
the last Plainville group for whom school teaching was a
reasonably convenient (and sanctioned) avenue for entering a
profession. The few Plainvillers who are now pointed out as
"successes" in the urban world all left home during the years
under discussion, however, or shortly afterwards, and nearly
all of them "got their start and their education" through school
teaching. The Oklahoma oil millionaire (already mentioned)
and several of his brothers, one a Tulsa lawyer, are exam-
ples. Others are: two or three civil service employees in Washington, D.C., a teacher in a Massachusetts business college, a
teacher in a small Maryland college, and a well-known scientist. One of the civil service employees is given special credit
because he was a "woods colt"; about the scientist a number
of myths have been created to discredit his childhood—genuine intellectual distinction, especially if it relates to "science,"

is apparently considered dangerous. A few other men also "made good outside." Two or three are merchants; two are physicians, the sons of the Plainville doctor and the Plainville hotelkeeper. No woman is ever mentioned as attaining distinction in the outside world, though some "married well-off."

The opportunities offered the fourth generation—from about 1920 to, say, 1937, when the first full-time county agent was employed in Woodland County—were equally changeful.

This was the period when Plainville and all similar communities began to receive the full impact of new inventions and ideas from the outside world so numerous and so important in implication as to rock the traditional community to its foundations. The best single symbol around which to collect for discussion all the changes which began to occur simultaneously is the automobile.

Plainville people began buying cars in numbers during the first World War. (People said of cars, "They won't work here!" People said, "They'll ruin the country.") This was the first time that Plainville had enjoyed a great inflow of money for its farm products. The car brought highways, and new highways brought more cars. The car brought greater mobility and range to all Plainvillers, virtually ending the community's geographical isolation. The car (together with the earlier telephones and RFD, and with radios later) brought increasing "knowledge" of the outside world. As a new "felt need" it became a great new source of expense, compelling people to think more in terms of "money" rather than "subsistence." Although cars are not "farm implements," their introduction altered many farming techniques. "The trouble with cars for a farmer is they don't have colts and they don't make manure." The car changed the old social structure greatly, disturbing neighborhood and community solidarity, weakening family bonds, and transforming innumerable social values.

The car also brought new economic opportunities: filling-station and repair-garage jobs and ownership; jobs as truck-drivers and bus drivers; factory jobs in Metropolis and other large cities, in automobile assembly plants or in steel mills which were feeder plants to the automobile industry. Other jobs, on ranches, in transportation services, at mining, and at various industrial occupations, were also plentiful for all who wished to migrate, until 1930, when the great depression began. As always, however, what the Plainviller "knew how to do," at any rate when he first left home, was unskilled labor; no new system of instruction had entered homes, schools, or churches to prepare him, or encourage him to prepare himself, to do anything else.

Yet at the very beginning of this period the Plainville consolidated school was established, and the high school course was soon increased from two years to four. Syllabus changes were also initiated, in imitation of outside fashions. In high school, Latin was dropped; mathematics was practically dropped; the formal study of history (as "facts and dates") and of English (as "correct grammar" and a few "classics") slackened almost to extinction. Vague "social studies" and games (here basketball, practiced indoors in a sunless gymnasium) were substituted. Very late in the period, vocational agriculture, "business subjects," and home economics were added. It is significant that the first vocational agriculture teacher (hired in 1933) solved the problem of hostility to book-farming by becoming a community-wide "good fellow" and by stressing "shopwork" more than "good farming." ("It was *safe* to teach the boys how to braid rope and make five-cent funnels.") It is also significant that the typing and bookkeeping teacher learned both subjects at normal school during the summer before he began teaching them, and that the "cooking teacher" is a "home girl" without special training. She is paid $700 annually out of local funds, although state and federal government would each contribute one-third of the salary (up to $2,400) for a vocational home economics teacher.

While most of the older subjects were of questionable value and interest to Plainville pupils, it is doubtful if they learn anything more stimulating or useful from the new. Syllabus-makers are generally too far removed from an understanding of rural life and rural high school teachers are separated by too many stages (including provincial normal schools) from the centers of modern educational theory for "social studies" to turn into anything much more than a conversational rehash of "the last game" of basketball. Typing and bookkeeping (business bookkeeping, not farm bookkeeping) were considered very "practical," when introduced, though for what it would be hard to say, since these skills are valued little locally and it would be "dangerous" for their teacher, even if he wanted to, to teach them as stepping stones toward assimilation into urban life.

As the depression intensified, the Plainville population, for whom on some basis or other the safety valve of migration had always before worked, began to increase. Youths growing up stayed at home and others who had gone forth to "see the world" or find work began to return home in failure. People did not return in great numbers because coming back meant only moving from one "poverty" into another, but enough came home to cause noticeable increase in the pressure for local land and housing.

Plainville people who met the depression with least inconvenience were (1) those upper-class farmers (or business-men) who owned their land or other property without any debt burden and who could therefore easily retreat from money economy back into nearly complete self-subsistence, (2) farmers who had "always" lived mainly by subsistence farming or "out of the streams and timber," [2] and (3) people who "did not mind" or "soon learned not to mind" applying for direct relief or WPA work when these became available. Most people of the second two groups were of the lower class. Heavily mortgaged farms were foreclosed and a number of

---

[2] These suffered almost no inconvenience. ("They didn't even know there *was* a depression".) It is curious that a way still persists in many sections of rural America whereby people, in exchange for knowing little and wanting little, can keep immune from all disasters caused by their fellow men except wars and epidemics.

business houses went under—for the second time within fifteen years. In the early 1920's the deflation of first World War land prices "broke up" many mortgaged farmers, closed all the banks in the county except one, and with other factors (including the car), ruined old-style small-town merchandising, which had been particularly profitable and exploitive. The depression of the 1920's, however, only briefly interrupted opportunities for jobs outside.

The group called in this book the fifth generation is the youth of the community today: those who began reaching maturity in 1937, a year selected as distinctive because it was the year when the first full-time county agent came to Woodland County.

In 1939–40, when this study was made, this generation faced a slight upturn in number though not in kinds of opportunity for livelihood outside, as compared with its immediate predecessors. In 1943, it faces many new things, which lie beyond the province of the present discussion.

The young people of this period were to inherit land [3] one half depleted by careless cultivation from its original mediocrity. Their minds were saturated, as were no previous minds in the community, with the material and social values of the outside world, which reached them daily through talk, trips, movies, radio, newspapers, weekly picture magazines, "comic books," and so forth. "They know all the advertising slogans." Due more to the car and the radio than to all other influences combined, the fifth generation had many new wants and needs, and a growing discontent with the community's poverty in money, resources, opportunity, and entertainment. Like all "Protestants" everywhere, they were inclined to rebellion

[3] One interesting aspect of the inheritance of rural land relates to the way in which farming communities, through migration of children, contribute inherited wealth to cities: children generally inherit equally, whether they remain at home or migrate, and a great number of rural children migrate to cities. Let us consider a hypothetical case: Of four children of a farm owner, two settle at home and two migrate. When the farm is sold, one half its value passes outside the community in cash or mortgage principal. Thus the cash value of many farms has been repeatedly passed outside rural communities, as successive owners died. The flow countryward of city tax money for schools, highways, etc., is not entirely one-sided.

against parental authority and "wisdom"—less so than youngsters in less "traditional" communities, where intellectual
growth and freedom are at least tacitly sanctioned, but more
so than any of their predecessors. ("Kids here don't *hang their
heads* as much as they used to.") They had no better formal
educational opportunities than earlier youth, with these exceptions: (1) Vocational agriculture was now well taught in
Plainville as a "functional" subject despite jealousy of other
teachers and the constant efforts of most of them to discredit
the subject and to undermine the teacher and his family in
the community. By an accident, music, but no other subject,
was also well taught. (2) A large new consolidated school
which any community might be proud of was being built with
WPA funds.

Vocational agriculture and the new WPA school building
are both very important as symptoms, because the salient fact
about the fifth generation was that it stood face to face with
the reformers. In 1940 there were vocational agriculture
teachers in two other Woodland County towns besides Plainville. ("They can't rest till they get what we get.") At Discovery there was an AAA office, headed by the county agent,
an FSA office, and a Social Security office, which handled com-
modity distribution, direct relief in cash, and certification
for WPA, CCC, and NYA, and administered cases receiving
ADC and OAA. A home economics demonstrator was later
added to the AAA office to assist the county agent in his work
among women. A WPA library, established in Plainville in
1940, was quickly followed by WPA libraries in other towns;
Stanton's library had actual seniority, but no one imitated
Stanton. A District Health office [4] forty miles away served five
counties including Woodland.

All this reform comes to such communities as Plainville
from "outside," though each county (or community) must, of
course, "ask for it before they get it," just as local people had

---

[4] The District Health Office has "just barely scratched the surface" in the
county. The visiting nurse said, "We know there's a lot of rickets and t.b., but
we don't know how much t.b., and we don't know yet whether there's any
trachoma."

actually to *want* steel cultivators, binders, cars, and tractors badly enough to be willing to pay money for them before outsiders could introduce them. The "outside" nature of reform is best indicated by the fact that the government allows only outsiders to hold key positions in county offices of the program. The theory behind this regulation apparently is that native administrators might practice favoritism in dispensing money and would be too deeply imbued with all aspects of the local value system for much reform to result from their work.

For all the achievements of the reformers to date several important criticisms can be made of the whole reform program. The first criticism is commonplace. Part of the program was designed to provide "relief" during an emergency, without constructive rehabilitation. Local people state this criticism by saying, "That Social Security stuff is just handouts." The principle of "cash without work" shocked rural people deeply, in Plainville and elsewhere. Plainvillers were little troubled by the distribution of actual commodities where needed. This resembled earlier charity gifts of food (without "cash value") by neighbors. They were shocked deeply, however, by the fact that money distributions (especially for relief and OAA) disregarded local opinions of the morals and past performances of the recipients—the only aspect of the program that shocked them more was "that time the triple-A killed all them little pigs." "WPA-ers" were criticized because "worthless men" (in native eyes) were hired, and because much of the work was "made work." The CCC got little criticism no matter from what class the enrollees were recruited, because it "built boys up" (physically) and "learnt 'em things."

Actually, rehabilitation programs would have been cheaper than relief, and they would have conflicted less with the traditional ideals of the people. The best local example of rehabilitation was the work of the Farm Security Administration, which in 1940, in Woodland County alone and at negligible cost, had restored over eighty families to self-support. The FSA loans averaged under $500 per family, and less than 10 percent of them were delinquent. Objections were offered, of course, to some of the families selected for rehabilitation, and the word "rehabilitation" was disliked, but the techniques of the FSA worked.

A second criticism is that the main agency for reform, namely, the AAA office, does not reach very far down into the community. County agents are instructed to propagandize through outstanding local "leaders," not through the "poorer" or more "backward" farmers who need instruction most, and whose children more than any other children need the fruits of such instruction. Those who instruct and direct county agents apparently do not know that "poor" and "backward" farmers also have "leaders"—a fact which local politicians forget in no other circumstances. As a result, the poorest farmers (and some of the most conservative of the wealthier farmers) do not cooperate with the AAA office at all, or cooperate only "to get the payments." Most lower-class men and women would feel uncomfortable in the presence of their "betters" who attend AAA meetings and form Home Economics clubs.

The situation regarding vocational agriculture is somewhat similar. Unlike the county agent, the vocational agriculture teacher does not receive frequent instructional sheets from "headquarters," advising him what to do next and how to do it (through getting the leaders behind it), but the fact that he teaches in high school limits his area of major activity. Most of those who "need to know something most" still don't send their children to high school. Some boys who go are forbidden to study agriculture. Others report at home what they learn in class only to hear such "book nonsense" and its teacher laughed at and condemned. Very few parents, except the county agent's leaders in the Plainville community, wholly sanction this instruction—many boys have to "conceal" their new scientific lore from parents as if it were a new type of rebellious "meanness" in the same category with the "outlaw traits of boys." The vocational agriculture teacher has no "bribe," like the county agent's crop reduction payments, to hold parents in line. Yet with those boys whom he teaches for four years, mainly upper-class lads, but some hillbilly lads too, he does a more thorough theoretical job than the county agent is able to do with their seniors, because he "catches them younger" and spends more time with each individual. How much influence this will actually have on their own later farming practices it is too early to tell.

Scientific agriculture may well prove to be the third in the series of great trait-complexes which, introduced from outside, have "revolutionized" the local society. The first was the plow that broke the prairie. The second was the car. With each came many associated traits. The agricultural reform program faces squarely the community's primary problem of rebuilding depleted soil and lifting local living standards. The experts believe that great improvement is really possible. One evening in 1940 the county agent and the vocational agriculture teacher agreed without argument to the following proposition: "If these people would just believe what we tell them about farming, and practice it, the scale of living for the whole county would double within five years."

Perhaps more would "believe," and believe sooner, if sociological techniques were devised to disseminate the new knowledge through local leadership other than that of a few relatively "rational" farmers. In propagandizing a "rational" program, the agricultural reformers view "tradition" as only a hurdle to leap or bypass, and they fail to understand the interdependence of all local institutions. The county agent, aside from ignoring the lower class and its leaders, makes little or no effort to win the influence of merchants, lodge members, or ordinary school teachers. No effort is made to exploit the traditional power and leadership of the churches and the preachers. All resident experts go to church, to avoid personal criticism, but the county agent "wouldn't touch churches with a ten-foot pole" as propaganda aids. The churches and preachers either ignore or throw their power subtly against scientific agriculture, yet if preachers became interested in better crops, housing, diet, and health, the churchly sanction would immediately influence hundreds of people now influenced, only grudgingly, by the "payments." The retired Methodist preacher asked, "Why don't they sell the preachers first? The preachers are *looking* for a way to be useful, because they know they're not doing anything useful now!"

The final and most important criticism of the whole reform program is that the eyes of its employees are focused too narrowly upon the county and its communities. The reform program neither does anything nor directly suggests anything to be done about Plainville's second most pressing problem. The problem is: how can surplus youth, natively as intelligent and potentially as able as youth anywhere, be introduced, at less social and educational disadvantage than they now suffer, to the situations, mainly urban, which they must face when they migrate?

Neither reformers nor schools, nor parents, handle realistically the fact (though the reformers understand it well enough) that the community produces more children than it can accommodate permanently. Everybody realizes that many children must leave, or "will want to leave," yet each parent hopes that his own children will not be among the "ones to go." No effort is made to prepare any children for life beyond Plainville in any capacity except as day laborers, since school teachers do not dare to encroach on territory regarding which parents have such strong feelings, and reformers concern themselves only with alleviating or improving local conditions. When families were much larger, and land claims were free in the West, parents were apparently better adjusted to the migration of children.[5] Children were then only repeating a pattern familiar to all farm parents, but children who migrate to cities are frequently considered "lost" in more ways than one. The hostility to "new ideas" and to "higher education" and the stressing in churches of the "sins of cities" are devices

[5] For a discussion of a French-Canadian rural community with a similar ideal of a limitless land frontier to which surplus youth could migrate, see Horace Miner, *St. Denis,* University of Chicago Press, 1939.

by which, whatever their other functions, parents strive to keep their children in Plainville, and effectually restrict their success when they leave.

Few youths are permitted to leave Plainville for life in the outside world without the guilty feeling that they are "deserting their family" added to all the other disadvantages under which they go forth. The special discouragements to young people starting out in life at home are (1) poor financial backing, (2) their own present day recognition that "this is poor land and poor country at best," and (3) the widespread hostility to "new ways."

The main conflicts in the community today are variously phrased, as: the "old fogies" vs. young people, the old ways vs. the new ways, "country ways" vs. "sinful city ways," religion vs. modernity, the "old-time religion" vs. "cold religion" or "no religion," "morality" vs. "car-riding," the Bible vs. "science," "field-farming" vs. "book-farming," practical knowledge vs. book-learning, country schools vs. high schools, "running things the way we want to" vs. "running things the way they tell you to," "a free country" vs. the New Deal, "honest work" vs. "these here gub'ment handouts." However fierce, mistaken, or tangential to the main issue the phrasing, the real situation represents a partial breakdown, through soil depletion and newly felt wants and needs arising from too rapid impact with the outside world, of a "traditional" social, religious, and technological system.

The deep roots of the tradition penetrate downward in time through Plainville's recent geographical isolation and the days when 90 percent of Americans, instead of 35 percent, were farmers, into the frontier and frontier life. Many "sources" of the tradition are of course still more ancient than that, but Plainville "memory" cherishes nothing earlier than the frontier. In sociological language, one climax of social integration for Plainville was reached about the time of the first World War when the prairie-hills social and technological systems (on an old-crop basis for both areas) must have been operating in a community-wide equilibrium relatively "isolated" from the outside world. Outside contacts were numerous even then, but they were not daily contacts, by cars, or hourly and momentary ones, won at a flick of the radio dial.

With the car came knowledge, and comparisons. In its wake came other new and expensive "machinery" and still more rapid and intimate forms of communication. More "money" was needed, just when the soil was beginning to show great depletion from the old crops. Conflicts between "old ways" (here) and "new ways" (here and outside) intensified. Conflict between "old age" and "youth" intensified. Ridicule and contempt for "the hillbillies" intensified, and the class structure became rigid. The leadership of old-style merchants failed, and lodges ceased functioning importantly. Neighborhoods and extended families lost much of their solidarity. Only the churches remained as strong as before, out of all the old forms of social organization; they became in some ways even stronger, because the car lessened the number of churches while increasing each congregation. The power of the churches was cast in no direction, or "backward," toward restoration of the old days. The community was "disintegrating."

What kind of new "integration" will occur is anybody's guess. One fact, however, is very clear: though many Plainville citizens would gladly "go back to the old days," there is no way to go back, because Plainville is no longer isolated. The roots of her tradition are still in the frontier, but the leaves and branches of that tradition have already begun to touch and chafe against the boughs of all other American "traditions," rural and urban.

The agricultural movement in 1939 and 1940 was toward (1) bringing more farm families and their land into the government program; (2) shifting land from soil-depleting crops to leguminous pasture or hay, and simultaneously shifting cash incomes from crop sales to sales of livestock and poultry and their products; (3) "educating" housewives, through Home Economics clubs, to better knowledge of poultry-raising, child-rearing, gardening, diet, canning, and sewing;

(4) attempting to organize self-governing committees and clubs of farmers, their wives, and their children. The apparent hope was that such movement, once started, might develop a social mechanism whereby farmers might solve their own problems democratically.

Progress toward this kind of an integration seems slow, but it is really very fast. It seems slow because resistance to it is loud spoken, and because progress itself is for the most part indirect. Few farmers will accept a direct recommendation from an "expert," a fact well understood by the experts. But farmers will "follow the leader." If Mahlon James does it, then it must be all right, because "he sure don't aim to lose no money." Better wait a couple of years, though, and see how it works. In two years, Mahlon is imitated by several. If anyone ever heard that Mahlon's new crop, or new farming or breeding method, was originally recommended by the expert, that fact has been conveniently forgotten—the expert's next recommendation is again just one more item of "book-farming." People said ten years ago of Korean lespedeza, "It won't grow here. Anyhow, it don't grow big enough to cut." In 1934, less than 100 acres were in lespedeza. In 1939, 10,500 acres, or 12.5 percent of the county's plowable cropland and pasture land were given over to lespedeza. It has become the favorite pasture and hay crop, and it is soil building because it is a legume. Lespedeza is the legume of lowest grade in a series which rises through sweet clover, white clover, and red clover to alfalfa; the soil will not yet grow any legume of higher grade. People now argue pleasantly about "who started growin' that lespedeza around here." No one "blames the gub'ment" for introducing it.

Yet the tactful expert gains "total converts," too, just as the preachers do. Scattered farmers throughout the county have made of their farms local demonstration stations for contour farming, terracing, crop rotations, fertilizing, liming, vaccination of horses against sleeping sickness, pure-bred herds, and scores of other reforms.

For all the hard things people say about his miserliness and money-mindedness, Mahlon is the most influential of such converts. People say, "They do what Mahlon says do because they owe him money and have to," but they also do what Mahlon says, and imitate what Mahlon does, because he is the outstanding successful farmer in the community; starting with nothing, he "got there the hard way." His farm, with its outbuildings, crops, pastures, and livestock, is a model. His wife's poultry flock is a model. Nothing in Mahlon's talk or dress and not much in his house or its contents distinguish Mahlon ostensibly in daily life from his better-class neighbors, except that people can see that his corn ordinarily grows a foot taller than corn separated from it by only a line fence; and people can count his wife's egg crates as he delivers them to the Produce House. It need hardly be mentioned, regarding Plainville, that many people either do not "notice" even these such eloquent testimonials to "book farming," or else explain them away by irrelevant rationalizations ("Mahlon always had the *luck* . . . Whatever *he* touches just nach'ly turns into dollars . . . Mahlon works harder'n any *white* man ought to.") But Mahlon and the rest of the converts, both as "leaders" and "first doers" are gradually accustoming their neighbors to new farming habits.

For the average farmer a new habit or trait must "get into the tradition" through acceptance by neighbors before he ceases resenting it enough to try it. Separate traits often gain acceptance with remarkable rapidity. In 1938, one conservative farmer who observed a neighbor haul a wagonload of "government lime" past his farm said, "I'd prosecute a man that put lime on my land. Joe's place will never grow another crop." In 1940, both men bought lime. Lespedeza is already a universally accepted part of the tradition, though its acceptance has already altered the whole older farming tradition. A man would be proud to be able to establish priority for himself as "the first man to raise lespedeza around here," just as pride is now taken by men whose fathers "owned the first corn-planter," the first double-shoveled cultivator, the first mowing machine, the first telephone, the first car, and the first radio.

Adult converts to scientific farming, both men and women, are "saved"—to resume the church metaphor—through the office of the county agent. Youths are converted by the vocational education teachers. When the parents of boys studying agriculture happen also to be interested in the county agent's work, really excellent results are attained. While certainly not everybody coming even directly under the influence of the agricultural experts either accepts or understands the entire import of what the experts teach, the full converts can be said to have accepted a "whole new tradition"—the tradition of scientific farming. They have become farming rationalists. They put no credence whatever in the waning "moon lore" or in "holler tail," or in any methods of soil care, crop raising, or animal breeding merely because "that's the way it's always been done." They sanction the work of agriculture experiment stations and credit the findings of such experiments as are transmitted to them orally and in print. They "trust the experts."

By most farmers, however, scientific farming practices are only accepted one by one, as they trickle down into the ancient tradition.

Satellites of the county agent are accused of cooperating with him to get "big AAA payments" and to get the jobs of signing up their neighbors for the program. Their payments are, of course, like anybody else's, though they do often get the jobs. Their recommendations and their own actions begin to be followed because they are successful farmers. The main value of Plainville society can hardly be said to be "wealth," but even people who put salvation above rubies want to make a better living.

It might even turn out in the course of years that many farmers, instead of just a few, will learn to add two and two and begin trusting the experts as formal advisers and counselors. If they do so, then the reformers will have won their battle. They have already won the first skirmish. Yet if congressmen in the national capitol, many hundreds of miles away, should fail to appropriate funds for the Department of Agriculture, this movement would be reversed or at least arrested. So tightly is Plainville's fate locked today with the fate of every other American community.

The first local problem is how to make a better living out of poor land, but this is not Plainville's only problem, or even the most important problem. If "everybody listened" to the experts and local incomes were doubled, Plainville would still be a "submarginal" community according to conventional money standards. Better diet and sanitation would result from increased income from the land, because the agricultural program stresses these things. More money would of course bring greater consumption of city-produced goods and further imitation of city ways. Not all of these gains would be beneficial, because the new goods would be mainly the cheapest and most uniform of city-made goods, and the new "ways" would be mainly the most stereotyped and uniform of city ways. What Plainvillers would get—for all their disbelief in "news and advertising"—are things that are "sold." Reform brings many hazards.

The greater problem for all "backward" and "poor" communities like Plainville is one which doubled or even tripled income will not solve. For better or for worse, they are doomed as "traditional" communities. As their ancient value systems crumble under the blows of a new "tradition" imposed from outside, their problem is to learn to participate more fully in the cultural rewards of the greater society. Plainville children who must migrate need training for entry into urban life. Those who will inherit the community and spend their lives there need "education" and the fruits of education as greatly as those who leave. This is no place to discuss what that education should be. On the formal side it should certainly be something more than "courses of study" designed by city educators for city children. Informally, it should be something more than the rivers of influence which stream in daily from newspaper offices and radio stations. The "decent" urban knowledge upon which our industrial and "money-conscious" civilization depends is beyond reach of the majority who are born and die in cities. Plainvillers have virtually no contact with it. Since there are millions of "Plainvillers" in America, the problem of Plainville is the problem of America.

Index

Index

Deal, 30; woman's place in, 47, 50; during depression, 213
Sunday church-going, 148, 162
Swedish settlers, 5

T

Taboos, moral, 122; see Morals
Teaching, as occupation, 20, 27, 28, 210; salaries, 27, 212; training, 78, 212
Technology, agricultural, 8-11, 120, 208; household, 9, 10, 32, 46; a criterion of class status, 120
Telephones, 10, 14, 17, 32n, 71
Temperatures, 7
Tenant farmers, 49, 51
Thievery, 93, 132
Threshing, 73
Thumb-sucking, 174
Timber, 7
Tombstones, 205
Tools and implements, see Technology
Topography and location, 1 f.
Towns and cities near Plainville, 2-4, 12
Tractors, 10
Trading, and traders, 20 f.; when superseded by cash sales, 47
Tradition, attitude of reformers toward, 218; deep penetration of: a cause of main conflicts in the community, 220 f.; communities doomed as traditional, 225
Trapping and hunting, 200
Travel, extent and nature of, 4, 18; earliest: changes in mode of, 11-13
Trucks, 13
Tuberculosis, 46, 215n

U

Uncles and aunts, 63
Undertaking techniques, 204, 205
Urban community study, 116n, 136n

V

Vegetables, 45
Veterans' pensions, 29
Visiting, 69n, 71, 72
Vital statistics, 165

Vocational agriculture, well taught, 79, 189, 215; the only course appropriate functionally to need: community's reaction, 79
Vocational agriculture teacher, xi, 26, 84, 102n, 212, 215, 224; quoted, 80, 218; considered a "reformer," 163; conditions limiting work of, 217; probable influence, 218
Voters, bribed, 86; forced, 89; independent, 90

W

Wages, boys', 200; rural and "outside," 210
Warner, W. Lloyd, and Paul S. Lunt, 116n, 136n
Water supply, 33
Wealth and poverty both exist, 42; as criterions of class, 121
Weaning, age for: routine, 172 ff.
Weaving of rugs and carpets, 35n
Wesley, John, 161
Whipping as disciplinary measure, 178, 188
Widows, number of, 105
Wife-husband obligations, 60; see also Men: Women
Women, innovations in domain of, 9, 10; vanishing techniques, 10; difference between home domains of men and, 34; clothing, 38, 39; contrasted with men: in cleanliness, 36; in appearance: more progressive, 40; rural division of labor, 46, 186; of economic transactions, 47, 50; grandmothers, 58, 59, 63; family obligations, 60 f., 170; social life, 69n, 72; neighboring, 71, 72, 73; clubs, 82, 84, 134, 221; attitude toward politics, 85, 91; gossip groups and their influence, 103-5; exclusive cliques, 106, 133; in the outside world, 211; class lines sharper than for men, 128; agricultural education program, 221
Woodmen, 82, 134
Work, see Labor
WPA, xii; occupational survey, 19; employment by, 26, 29, 30, 86, 89, 213; attempt at social organization, 83; library founded, 84, 215, **social**